Especially for

_____

From

_____

Date

_____

Daily Devotions
for Women

Jewell Johnson

BARBOUR
PUBLISHING

Published by Barbour Publishing, Inc., P.O. Box 719, Uhrichsville, Ohio 44683
www.barbourbooks.com

Our mission is to publish and distribute inspirational products offering exceptional value and biblical encouragement to the masses.

Member of the
Evangelical Christian
Publishers Association

Printed in China.

Special Thanks

To my husband, LeRoy, for his unfailing support in all my writing endeavors. To Donna Goodrich, Rosemarie Malroy, Ann Velia, and Sylvia Burke, who gave of their time to read this text and give wise advice. Thanks, too, to the Fountain Hills Christian Writers' Group for reading my manuscripts at every meeting and for their insightful suggestions.

Introduction

As a child I enjoyed reading history books. When I became an adult, I found biographies fascinating. Contemplating Christian women of the past, I saw myself in their experiences. As with mine, the pieces of their lives didn't always fit together. Like me, they became frustrated with child-rearing problems. They had health problems. They faced the deaths of loved ones. At times they struggled to live the Christian life—just like I did. But they survived!

This is the common bond of the women I write about in *Daily Devotions for Women*. In fact, these women did more than just survive—they kept trusting God in the face of their struggles and helped others along the way. Their stories are completely human and powerfully inspiring.

Over the course of a year, you'll read brief biographical sketches of more than two hundred women. They lived in different times and places and came from many backgrounds. Some of their viewpoints and actions were controversial in their age—and could still be today. But each one offers some lesson for us now.

Listen to their voices on the following pages. Feel their doubts. Cry for them and sympathize with them. Above all, learn from them. With so great a cloud of witnesses looking down on us and cheering us on, we, too, will make it to the finish line!

Gladys Aylward

Missionary
1902–1970

> Our help is in the name of the LORD,
> the Maker of heaven and earth.
> PSALM 124:8 NIV

"Your qualifications are too slight, your education limited. The Chinese language would be far too difficult for you to learn," the mission board director told young Gladys Aylward in 1932 when she applied for a missionary appointment to China.

Convinced God had called her, Gladys determined that if the mission board wouldn't send her, she would send herself. Using money she earned as a parlor maid, she paid her own fare to travel overland by rail to China.

Without support, money was scarce as Gladys began her work. But when the Central Government decreed that the binding of women's feet must cease, the mandarin (governor) of the province needed a foot inspector. "You are the only woman in the province with big feet," he told Gladys. "You must take the job."

Gladys traveled from one remote village to another. During the day she inspected feet, but at night, at first in halting Chinese, she told the people about Jesus. The woman who was told she could not learn the Chinese language ended up mastering six Chinese dialects.

What difficult task are you called to do? Like Gladys Aylward, God may be asking you to learn a skill that seems beyond your ability. The One who made heaven and earth is your Helper. With Him, you will accomplish the impossible.

Lillian Trasher
Missionary
1887–1961

But Jesus said, "Let the children come to me. Don't stop them!
For the Kingdom of Heaven belongs to those who are like these children."
And he placed his hands on their heads and blessed them."
MATTHEW 19:14–15 NLT

As a young girl, Lillian Trasher moved with her family to Georgia. There a Christian neighbor told Lillian, who was not a believer, she could know Jesus and be a friend of God. Lillian believed the neighbor and prayed, "Lord, I want to be Your little girl. If ever I can do anything for You, let me know and I'll do it."

Later, when God led Lillian, now a young woman, to work in a faith-owned orphanage, she said, "Yes." When she heard God's call to be a missionary, in spite of no financial support, she again answered, "Yes." And when God told her to begin an orphanage for Egypt's neglected children, Lillian did it without pledged support.

At her death, Lillian's orphanage had cared for over eight thousand children, and she had earned the title "Mother of the Nile." This all started when one little girl said, "God, let me know if I can do anything for You."

As children show an interest in God, His church, or the Bible, bless them, support them, and encourage them. You cannot imagine the marvelous feats God will do through the dedication of even one child.

Harriet Beecher Stowe

Author, Hymn Writer

1811–1896

> Nothing can ever separate us from God's love. Neither death nor life. . . . Our fears for today nor our worries about tomorrow. . . nothing in all creation will ever be able to separate us from the love of God that is revealed in Christ Jesus our Lord.
>
> ROMANS 8:38–39 NLT

Harriet Beecher Stowe, author of *Uncle Tom's Cabin*, was raised in a religious home. Her father was an outstanding Puritan preacher in New England. As a child she had memorized over twenty-five hymns and long passages from the Bible.

For all her religious heritage, as an adult Harriet began to have conflicts of faith. Her doubts increased when her child died of cholera in 1849. Then her husband, suffering with depression, was taken to a sanitarium, and Harriet was left to make a living for their large family.

Under these conditions, it is easy to understand why Harriet had a lapse of faith. However, she did renew her trust as seen in this hymn she wrote.

> *Still, still with Thee, when purple morning breaketh,*
> *When the bird waketh, and the shadows flee;*
> *Fairer than morning, lovelier than the daylight*
> *Dawns the sweet consciousness, I am with Thee!*

It is no shame if you, like Harriet, are tempted at times to doubt God's ways. Most Christians deal with confusing doubts now and then. However, Jesus does not leave you in these times, nor do your doubts separate you from God. Even when you don't sense His presence, Jesus' hand remains firm in yours.

Hannah Whitall Smith

Author
1832–1911

For our present troubles are small and won't last very long.
Yet they produce for us a glory that vastly outweighs them and will last
forever! So we don't look at the troubles we can see now; rather,
we fix our gaze on things that cannot be seen.

2 CORINTHIANS 4:17–18 NLT

It was a drastic move when Hannah and Robert Smith decided to leave the Quaker faith they had been raised in. Hannah's parents, usually good-natured, declared their daughter a renegade and said, "Thou shalt leave this house!"

Hannah wrote of that time: ". . .like an outcast from my earthly father's house. But not from my heavenly Father's house."

No one can decide who was right in this situation. However, the move may have been necessary for Hannah, who in 1875 wrote of her struggles in *The Christian's Secret of a Happy Life* and other books. For decades these writings, translated into several languages, have helped troubled, confused believers.

Metal is heated, beaten, and plunged into cold water as part of the process to make a strong piece of steel. In the same way, trials are necessary to develop a strong Christian.

Do you feel beaten by testing? Allow these trials to drive you to Christ. Though not pleasant now, in years to come you will see these as necessary to build your Christian character.

Ida Scudder
Medical Missionary
1870–1960

"Father, if you are willing, take this cup from me;
yet not my will, but yours be done."
Luke 22:42 NIV

"I know one thing I will not do," young Ida Scudder said. "I will not be a missionary in India like my parents and fifteen other Scudders have been. I'm going to do something exciting."

Later in 1890, Ida returned to India to care for her ill mother. During her stay, a Brahman man came to the Scudder home asking for help for his fourteen-year-old wife, who was having a difficult time in childbirth. Because his religion prohibited men from attending women, the man begged Ida to help. The same night two other men came with the same request. With no medical training, Ida was unable to help the women. In the morning the tom-toms tolled the death for all three women.

That day Ida told her parents, "I'm going to America to study to be a doctor so I can help the women of India."

Dr. Ida Scudder returned to India in 1899, and over the next sixty years, she founded a hospital, established roadside clinics, branch hospitals, and eye camps. This happened when one woman said, "Your will be done."

Like Ida, you may have your future mapped out. Have you talked to God about it? He could have other ideas. When you say "Not my will," you will be led away from good plans to better ones—plans that help others and give you a more fulfilled life.

Mary Slessor

Missionary
1848–1915

"The rich man also died and was buried. In Hades, where he was in torment, he looked up and saw Abraham far away, with Lazarus by his side."
LUKE 16:22–23 NIV

While growing up in the slums of Dundee, Scotland, Mary Slessor described herself as a "wild lassie." An old widow used to watch the children running wild on the streets and, in her anxiety for their souls, one cold day she invited the children to sit by her fire.

Suddenly the woman pointed to the flames. "Do you see that?" she said to them. "If ye dinna repent and believe on the Lord Jesus, your soul will burn in the lowin bleezin' fire for ever and ever!"

The words struck terror in Mary's young heart. Images of hellfire kept her awake at night. Tormenting fears drove her to repent of her sin and move into Christ's forgiveness.

Jesus told the story of the rich man and Lazarus to help us understand the worlds beyond. Hell is a place of torment reserved for the devil, his angels, and those who follow him. Heaven, on the other hand, is a place of happiness beyond imagination, the dwelling place of God and those who have accepted His Son. Jesus put heaven's welcome mat out for all peoples when He said, "Come to me, all of you who are weary" (Matthew 11:28 NLT).

Like Mary Slessor and multitudes of others have done, choose Jesus, His love—and heaven.

Grace Livingstone Hill

Author

1865–1947

God has chosen to make known among the Gentiles the glorious riches of
this mystery, which is Christ in you, the hope of glory.

COLOSSIANS 1:27 NIV

"Take the gospel out of your books," an editor advised Grace Livingstone Hill when she submitted her novel for publication. She refused, and instead dedicated her writings to communicate the unshakable fundamentals of Christian living.

When Grace's husband died in 1899, leaving her the sole support of their two daughters, she assessed her talents and decided to be a writer. There was no question what kind of novels she would write. She said, "I am not writing to be writing. I am attempting to convey a message." Her books are romance novels with the underlying message of hope in Christ.

During World War II, Grace wrote of a soldier's struggle to regain lost hope, and letters poured into her desk from men who saw themselves in Grace's story. People evidently needed the message, because her one hundred novels have sold more than four million copies.

Jesus opened the way for every human being to have hope. Place your trust in Him for your day-to-day existence and heaven after death. Either way, Christ in you is the sure hope of your soul.

Pandita Ramabai

Educator, Author
1858–1922

> The woman said, "I know the Messiah is coming—
> the one who is called Christ. When he comes, he will explain
> everything to us." Then Jesus told her, "I Am the Messiah!"
> JOHN 4:25–26 NLT

"After reading the fourth chapter of St. John's Gospel, that Christ was truly the Divine Savior, my heart was drawn to the religion of Christ," said Pandita Ramabai.

Raised in the Hindu religion in India, Pandita married a man of a lower caste. A missionary gave her husband a Bengali Gospel of Luke, and the couple eventually came to faith in Christ. As a Christian, Pandita dedicated herself to alleviating the oppression of women, especially the widows.

When Pandita's own husband died after only eighteen months of marriage, she refused to accept the fate of widows who were expected to disappear from society for the remainder of their lives. Rather, she traveled throughout India, rescuing temple prostitutes. Later she established a community especially for women in need.

But Pandita also experienced doubts. Eight years after she was baptized in water, she truthfully wrote, "I have the Christian religion. . . but I had not found Christ, Who is the Life of the religion." Thus, she began her quest to discover the Christ of the Bible.

Perhaps you, too, have accepted a Christian lifestyle, but you can't say you know the person of Jesus. You can know Him. Christ is revealed in the pages of the Bible and by heartfelt communion with Him in prayer.

Elizabeth Payson Prentiss
Hymn Writer, Author
1818–1878

Even when we are weighed down with troubles, it is for your comfort and
salvation! For when we ourselves are comforted, we will certainly comfort you.
2 CORINTHIANS 1:6 NLT

Sorrow! Pain! Loss! Elizabeth Prentiss and her husband experienced
all these emotions and more when they lost their oldest child. Their
grief intensified further when another child died. One day when the
parents came home after placing flowers on the children's graves,
Elizabeth cried, "I don't think I can stand living for another moment,
much less a lifetime."

In her anguish, Elizabeth turned to her hymnbook. After
reading Sarah Adams's hymn, "Nearer My God to Thee," Elizabeth
felt a measure of peace return. As she prayed, the words came to her,
"More love to Thee, O Christ, more love to Thee."

Elizabeth was helped by Mrs. Adams's hymn, and God gave
her poem to share with other hurting people. Thirteen years later,
Elizabeth printed the verses in a leaflet, and eventually the words
were set to music.

More love to Thee, O Christ! More love to Thee!
Hear Thou the prayer I make, on bended knee;
This is my earnest plea, more love, O Christ to Thee,
More love to Thee! More love to Thee!

As you have been comforted, pass on the comfort you have
received. Whether you write a hymn, send a card, or speak a kind
word, it's all part of God's plan for alleviating pain in a world
overwrought with grief.

Hannah Marshman
Missionary
1767–1847

As it is written in the book of the words of Isaiah the prophet:
"A voice of one calling in the wilderness, 'Prepare the way for the Lord,
make straight paths for him.' "
Luke 3:4 NIV

A young English couple, Hannah and Joshua Marshman, read about William Carey's missionary work in India and offered to work in the Serampore mission. Hannah adapted well to the new situation as the missionaries lived as a community, took meals together, and shared household duties.

A pioneer in every sense of the word, Hannah, who arrived at the mission with her husband in 1799, was one of the first women to leave England for missionary work in India. She helped produce the first editions of the New Testament in thirty Oriental languages and dialects. She was one of the first missionaries to insist that India's caste system be excluded from the church. She also helped establish and teach in the first school for India's children.

Hannah walked where no one had previously walked. She made a way where there was no way. John Marshman later said that his mother was "a woman of feeling, piety and good sense, of strong mind. . .nothing was ever known to have ruffled her temper."

Someone has to be first, to trample down the bushes and make a way so others can walk a smooth path. By the way you conduct your life, by your speech, you make "straight paths" for others to follow Jesus.

Mrs. Meredith
First Sunday School Teacher
18th Century

> All they asked was that we should continue to
> remember the poor, the very thing I had been eager to do.
> GALATIANS 2:10 NIV

"I can't handle these ragamuffins anymore," Mrs. Meredith told Gloucester's newspaper editor, Robert Raikes, in 1780. "They're dirty and ill-behaved. They shout profanities and muddy my floors."

Gloucester's poor boys and girls worked twelve hours a day, six days a week, in a pin factory. Sunday, their day off, they ran wild in the streets. Robert Raikes believed the conduct of the children could be improved by Christian education. That's where Mrs. Meredith came in: raikes hired her to teach them in her kitchen.

The first Sunday, ninety boys came at Mr. Raikes's invitation. The class met for six hours and was instructed in reading, the catechism, and Isaac Watts's hymns. After a few weeks Mrs. Meredith saw that the job was too much for her. Yet to her goes the honor of teaching the first Sunday school class.

Mr. Raikes was not easily discouraged, and he hired May Critchley to instruct the classes. Girls soon joined in, and, from that simple beginning, Sunday school has evolved until today it embraces both children and adults, the rich and poor.

Helping a poor child, the homeless family, or a frail aged person is not a suggestion in the Bible, but a command Christ's followers take seriously. The command carries with it a promise: God's blessing rests upon that person (Psalm 41:1–3).

Helen Barrett Montgomery
Church Leader, Author, Translator
1861–1934

> "If you cling to your life, you will lose it;
> but if you give up your life for me, you will find it."
> MATTHEW 10:39 NLT

"The only way to keep money, or land, or talent, or happiness is to give it away," Helen Barrett Montgomery wrote to her sister. "If only everyone had studied the divine arithmetic, what a world it would be."

Helen had money, talent, and happiness, and she shared it with the world. After a happy childhood, she married successful businessman William A. Montgomery. Together they dedicated themselves to God's work. Helen taught a Sunday school class in the same church for forty-four years. She received a license to preach and traveled in the cause of missions. At age forty-nine she became the president of the Northern Baptist Convention, the first woman to hold such a post.

However, Helen's most lasting contribution to the world was her translation of the Greek New Testament into modern English. She is the only woman to publish such a work. The Centenary Translation, issued in 1924, gave people a translation in the language of everyday life.

Opening your hand, letting go of what you have, putting others before yourself, seems a strange recipe for happiness. Yet, if you follow this "divine arithmetic," it leads to something greater than happiness; it brings "inexpressible and glorious joy" (1 Peter 1:8).

Hannah More

Author
1745–1833

> "Write down the revelation and make it plain
> on tablets so that a herald may run with it."
> HABAKKUK 2:2 NIV

In 1774 Hannah More began to write dramas for the theater. Eventually she realized this was not the place for her talents. She renounced the stage and left London.

Disturbed because of corrupt social issues, she wrote a series of papers in which she did battle with those that promoted atheism and radical political views. With these inexpensive religious leaflets, called tracts, Hannah awakened readers to the truth. She said, "It is vain to write what people will not read. . . . I propose printing striking conversions, Holy Lives, Happy Deaths, Providential Deliverances." Beginning in 1795 she published and distributed three tracts a month. The leaflets reached a circulation of nearly two million and became the foundation for the Religious Tract Society.

How can people change if they don't know the truth? And how will they come to know truth unless someone shares it with them? If you have been especially helped by a religious book, magazine, or tract, share it with another person. God will use it, as He did Hannah's tracts, to awaken others to their need of the truth as found in the Bible.

Joy Ridderhof
Founder of Gospel Recordings
1903–1984

"For I know the plans I have for you," says the LORD. "They are plans for good and not for disaster, to give you a future and a hope."
JEREMIAH 29:11 NLT

"If only I could have left my voice behind," Joy Ridderhof said, when she returned after six years of missionary work in a remote village in Honduras. She was weak from malaria with no prospects of returning to the land of her calling. As she lay in her parents' attic bedroom in Los Angeles, she thought of the gramophone records that had blared out popular Spanish tunes in the villages she had left. If only she could make a record with Christian songs and a gospel message in Spanish and send it to Honduras. And Joy did!

On that day in 1939, Joy thought of reaching only one tribe, but God had greater plans. From the first three-and-a-half-minute recording she made to send to her tribal people, Joy's dream grew into an international organization. By the time of her death, Joy had recorded the good news in over four thousand languages and dialects and sent them around the world.

Has God given you a vision? Nourish it with prayer. Write a plan of advance. Share your thoughts with wise counselors. Start small, but dream big. As Joy's vision eventually encompassed the globe, yours also has that potential.

Helen Duff Baugh

Christian Organizer
1903–1996

> "You did not choose me, but I chose you and appointed
> you so that you might go and bear fruit—fruit that will last."
> JOHN 15:16 NIV

In 1912, Helen Duff's father made plans to emigrate from Ireland to America with the intent to preach in the new land. Mr. Duff went ahead of his family, scheduling his wife and children to come later on the maiden voyage of the *Titanic*. The time dragged on for Mrs. Duff and, eager to be with her husband in America, she made arrangements to sail two weeks earlier than planned. The mother and children docked in Boston the day the *Titanic*'s tragic sinking was announced.

From the beginning of Helen's life, it was evident God had His hand on her. Later, when her husband died tragically, she knelt with her children at his coffin and gave herself to do whatever God had planned for her. She began women's prayer groups in San Jose, California, which eventually led her to organize Christian Business and Professional Women's groups. Six years after her husband's death, Helen had established twenty-six councils of women.

God chose Helen Baugh to do a specific work for Him. He also has plans for you. As you read your Bible and pray, listen to His voice. Dedicate yourself to do His will. Then watch opportunities open for you to bear fruit—a bumper crop that will last!

Coretta Scott King
Wife of Civil Rights Leader Martin Luther King Jr.
1927–2006

> Do not be overcome by evil, but overcome evil with good.
> ROMANS 12:21 NIV

Coretta Scott met Martin Luther King Jr. while she was studying music in Boston. To her surprise, he told her on their first date that she was everything he wanted in a wife. They married in 1953, and the next year Martin became a pastor in Montgomery, Alabama.

Coretta and Martin were disturbed by the treatment of blacks in the South, but what could they do to change the segregation laws so long observed? They decided the only acceptable and Christian way to change the plight of black people was by nonviolent means. As the Kings became involved in peaceful protests, they felt the animosity of those who opposed their efforts.

Hate mail arrived daily at the parsonage, and Martin was repeatedly jailed. One day Coretta heard a thud on the porch. She grabbed their baby and ran to the rear of the house as sticks of dynamite exploded.

President John F. Kennedy was assassinated in 1963, and Coretta's heart lurched when Martin told her, "This is going to happen to me." And it did—in 1968. Instead of seeking revenge for her husband's murder, Coretta continued to use peaceful means to work for equality for all people.

You also may have felt the sting of racial hatred, and your natural reaction is to retaliate. Instead, pray as Jesus did for His enemies, "Father, forgive them." Hatred is conquered only by love.

Mary Bunyan
Wife, Mother
17th Century

The seeds of good deeds become a tree of life;
a wise person wins friends.
PROVERBS 11:30 NLT

Nothing is known of Mary Bunyan's childhood, and the record of her marriage in the late 1640s has been lost. We do know she had no dowry when she married rowdy John Bunyan—who later described himself as having few equals in cursing, lying, and blaspheming the name of God. Instead, she brought two books to their marriage: *The Plain Man's Pathway to Heaven* and *The Practice of Piety*. Bunyan said, "I should sometimes read with her, wherein I also found some things that were somewhat pleasing to me."

Mary's books were pleasing enough to cause John to think about making changes in his life. For a start, he began attending church with her and after a long, painful struggle, he became a Christian. Later he was imprisoned for preaching—illegal for those not ordained by the Church of England. Because he wouldn't stop preaching, John was often in jail where he wrote books destined to be classic religious works. His most famous writing was *The Pilgrim's Progress*, an allegory of the Christian life. Yet, it all began when a young woman wisely wielded influence on her husband.

As you pray for opportunities to influence people for God, you may be guided to say kind words to a friend or give a carefully chosen book to a family member. God doesn't need much; one wise act can have positive effects for generations.

A. Wetherell Johnson
Missionary, Bible Study Organizer
1907–1984

Because of the LORD's great love we are not consumed, for his compassions never fail. They are new every morning; great is your faithfulness.
LAMENTATIONS 3:22–23 NIV

"I was forty years old when I came from the mission field in China to America," Wetherell said, who was raised in England. "I was entering a country where I was not known. Besides, there was the burden on my heart for Chinese Christians." In her confusion, God whispered to her troubled heart, "I am faithful."

While she was living in California, five women came to Wetherell and asked her to teach them the Bible. "There's plenty of churches in America where they can study God's Word," she said. "But I promised to pray about it."

Wetherell agreed to teach the five, and they soon brought their friends. She wrote questions for the studies, and the group soon outgrew the house where they met. Wetherell experienced more of God's faithfulness when she organized the Bible Study Fellowship. In the next twenty years, more than one hundred thousand people took her five-year Bible study course.

Like Wetherell, you may be bewildered by unplanned twists of circumstances. Hold on to God. As year after year the seasons come on schedule, so is His faithfulness to you. Confusion must give way to peace as you trust the faithful Creator.

> Oh, how I love your law! I meditate on it all day long.
> Your commands. . .make me wiser than my enemies.
> PSALM 119:97–98 NIV

Mrs. Mumford was selective in what she allowed her daughter to read. While other young girls of the day were devouring cheap romance novels, she restricted her daughter Catherine's reading to the Bible, *The Pilgrim's Progress*, and other religious works.

After a spiritual struggle, seventeen-year-old Catherine called out to God and received assurance of salvation. A year later she became ill, and the doctor ordered her to rest for the entire winter. During this time she continued a diligent study of the scriptures.

Catherine's knowledge of God's Word served her well when she founded the Salvation Army with her husband, William. The philosophy of the new organization became, "Conquer the World with the Gospel."

As Catherine began preaching evangelistic services, she wrote of the Bible, "I love this Word and regard it as the Standard of all faith, and practice, and our guide to live by." After hearing her speak, an attendee said, "She brought me into the personal presence of Jesus Christ."

Daily reading the Bible, meditating on its words, and memorizing scripture verses has a domino effect. The more truth you assimilate, the more the Word will influence your daily decisions. As a result, you will enjoy a depth of happiness and purpose possible only through knowing God's precepts.

Elizabeth Freeman
Missionary Martyr
19th Century

> Christ will be exalted in my body, whether by life or by death.
> For to me, to live is Christ and to die is gain.
> PHILIPPIANS 1:20–21 NIV

In 1851, five weeks after their wedding, Elizabeth and John Freeman sailed for India to begin missionary work. Elizabeth plunged into her new life with fervor. On board ship, she studied the language and upon their arrival she began a ministry to children and women. Adjustments for the new missionary were difficult, however. She wrote to her niece, "Unless you should come with your heart filled with love to God and these poor perishing heathen, you would be sadly disappointed."

Elizabeth soon needed a heart full of God's love and courage when, in 1858, the mission received word of threats being made upon English people in the region. The missionaries assessed their situation and realized they were in grave danger with no possible escape.

After a week of terror, at seven o'clock in the morning, Elizabeth, her husband, and three other missionary couples were marched to the parade ground and killed.

We don't understand why good people die prematurely, yet the Bible speaks of a Christian's death in comforting terms. "Precious in the sight of the LORD is the death of his faithful servants" (Psalm 116:15 NIV). It is reassuring to know that no matter how or when death occurs, for those who love God, dying is gain.

Dale Evans Rogers
Actress, Author
1912–2001

And he [Jesus] took a child, and set him in the midst of them:
and when he had taken him in his arms, he said unto them,
Whosoever shall receive one of such children in my name, receiveth me.
MARK 9:36–37 KJV

When singer and actress Dale Evans married cowboy actor Roy Rogers, both brought children into the new home. Dale hoped Roy's three children would readily accept her, but barriers arose. She also had the worry of Hollywood divorce statistics. Could the marriage endure the stresses of their lifestyle? Dale's child, Tom, came up with the answer by suggesting his mother take the children to Sunday school and church.

Dale had accepted Christ at age ten, but following a teenage marriage and divorce, as a single parent trying to build a singing and acting career, she had left her faith. Now she made peace with God, returned to church, and took the family with her. Dale also introduced table-grace, family devotions, and scripture memorization as part of the family's schedule. It started with a simple suggestion from a child.

Often when Jesus wanted to teach a spiritual lesson, He used a child. Children's minds, uncluttered by unimportant issues, seem to see to the core of matters. Observe children, listen to them. They live within earshot of God's voice and often come up with brilliant solutions.

Eliza Davis George
Missionary
1879–1979

> They [the righteous] will still bear fruit in old age, they will
> stay fresh and green, proclaiming, "The LORD is upright;
> he is my Rock, and there is no wickedness in him."
> PSALM 92:14–15 NIV

At a chapel service at Central Texas Christian in 1911, Eliza Davis heard God call her to Africa. She answered "yes" and in 1913, when she was thirty-two, she sailed for Liberia, the first black woman from Texas to go as a missionary to that continent.

In 1945, after thirty-two years of service, the mission board called sixty-five-year-old Eliza home to retire. Yet her heart beat with love for the people of Africa, and she raised her own support and returned to Liberia. In the next twenty-five years she established a mission society and remained in leadership until she was in her nineties. When Eliza died at one hundred years old, she had spent more than half of her life in Africa, birthed eight schools, and established more than one hundred churches.

Eliza Davis George's life is proof that usefulness in God's work has no age limit. Regardless of your years, there is a work to be done. A senior woman grows violets to give to shut-ins. A woman in a nursing home has an extensive prayer ministry. As you make yourself available to God, doors will swing open to pray, feed the homeless, give, encourage the downhearted, and visit the sick. Even in advancing years you will proclaim to the world, "He is my Rock!"

> "Study this Book of Instruction continually. Meditate on it day
> and night so you will be sure to obey everything written in it.
> Only then will you prosper and succeed."
>
> JOSHUA 1:8 NLT

"We had such long hours and hard work, but we surely did read the Bible and pray," said Morrow Graham, mother of evangelist Billy Graham.

Frank and Morrow Graham were dairy farmers. The family rose at 2:30 in the morning and milked as many as seventy-five cows. Sandwiched between work was the Word of God. Morrow said, "At breakfast I read a verse from a scripture calendar. Before we ate, my husband asked God's blessing on the food. As I packed lunches, I could hear him helping the children memorize Bible verses.

"In the evening we gathered in the family room for a time of Bible reading and prayer," she said. "It was the most important thing in our life."

Bible reading and prayer—Christian disciplines—how important to the development of vibrant believers! If you are tempted to neglect these with the excuse that you don't have time, remember Morrow Graham. In the midst of life's rush, she and her husband gave priority to these basic disciplines, and it paid big dividends for them, their offspring, and the entire world.

Elvina M. Hall
Hymn Writer
1820–1889

Who will free me from this life that is dominated by sin and death?
Thank God! The answer is in Jesus Christ our Lord.
ROMANS 7:24–25 NLT

Elvina Hall squirmed in her seat in the choir loft of the Methodist Church in Baltimore, Maryland. The pastor had begun the morning prayer, and he prayed on and on until Elvina thought he'd never stop. As the prayer continued, she took a hymnbook and began scribbling in the flyleaf. The prayer lengthened, and Elvina's doodling turned to words. In fact, she wrote an entire poem during that prayer. Later she showed the words to the church organist, John T. Grape, who wrote music for the verses.

Because of a lengthy prayer, a hymn was written. Whether Elvina was justified in using the time allotted to prayer to write her hymn, no one can judge, but the words she wrote are inspiring.

I hear The Savior say: "Thy strength indeed is small,
Child of weakness, watch and pray. Find in Me thine all in all."
Jesus paid it all, all to Him I owe;
Sin had left a crimson stain.
He washed it white as snow.

Elvina's hymn teaches a powerful truth: no one can earn God's salvation. It is obtained only by accepting Christ's work on the cross. When you invite Him into your life, you stand justified before God, your heart white as snow. Jesus' cross is enough!

Jennie Evelyn Hussey
Hymn Writer
1874–1958

Then Jesus said to his disciples, "Whoever wants to be my disciple must deny themselves and take up their cross and follow me. For whoever wants to save their life will lose it, but whoever loses their life for me will find it."

MATTHEW 16:24–25 NIV

Most of her adult life Jennie Hussey cared for her invalid sister. She lovingly prepared meals, changed bedding, and administered medicine, doing what she could to alleviate her sibling's suffering. The work continued year after year. To escape the drudgery of the work, Jennie wrote poetry.

Reading the last stanza of her hymn, "Lead Me to Calvary," gives insight into how she viewed her life and in what spirit she cared for her sister. When her poem was put to music, a great hymn was born.

> *May I be willing, Lord, to bear daily my cross for Thee;*
> *Even Thy cup of grief to share, Thou hast borne all for me.*
> *Lest I forget Gethsemane; lest I forget Thine agony;*
> *Lest I forget Thy love for me, lead me to Calvary.*

Discipleship involves a cost. It means doing the right thing when other people are doing as they please. It means being loyal when you'd rather avoid responsibility. To be a disciple means your wants no longer matter. In the light of Calvary, is it too much to ask that you willingly lose your life for others?

Dorothy Carey
Missionary Wife
1755–1807

Mine enemies would daily swallow me up: for they be many that fight against me, O thou most High. What time I am afraid, I will trust in thee.
PSALM 56:2–3 KJV

Dorothy Carey initially refused to accompany her husband, William, when he prepared to go as a missionary to India in 1793—and for good reason. She had recently lost a two-year-old, she was three weeks away from delivering a child, and she had three older sons to raise.

William wanted to at least take the Careys' oldest son with him. But when the ship's departure was delayed, Dorothy had a change of heart; she agreed to accompany William provided her sister also go with the party.

Missionary work for the Careys in India is difficult to imagine. Compared to England's climate, the heat was oppressive. Poisonous snakes and fierce animals were a constant threat. Sadly Dorothy watched her husband labor for seven years before making a convert. But perhaps the hardest trial was when another son died, and the Careys were forced to bury him themselves with only the remaining children at their side.

Saints of all times have faced fearful situations—some more severe than others. The cure for fear is trust in God. As you confront life's inevitable fears, declare with believers of all ages, "My trust remains secure in the most High God."

Charlotte Elliott
Hymn Writer
1789–1871

As Jesus walked beside the Sea of Galilee, he saw Simon and his brother
Andrew casting a net into the lake, for they were fishermen. "Come,
follow me," Jesus said, "and I will send you out to fish for people."
MARK 1:16–17 NIV

Charlotte Elliott faced severe illness most of her life, but those who
knew her said she never lacked for joy. After she finally became
bedridden at age thirty-two, she claimed the Bible as her church and
Jesus her High Priest who waited to receive her prayers.

After her death, letters poured in expressing gratitude for her
hymn, "Just As I Am." Her brother, a prominent English minister,
said he had some results from his ministry, but Charlotte's one hymn
saw more fruit than all his sermons.

Just as I am, without one plea,
But that Thy blood was shed for me,
And that Thou bidd'st me come to Thee,
O Lamb of God, I come! I come!

Many people over time have found God's forgiveness as this
song was played. Evangelist Billy Graham was said to have walked to
the altar to receive Christ as Charlotte's hymn was being sung, and
later he used it in his crusades.

God uses people. It matters not our situation or occupation.
Charlotte Elliott was crippled. Peter and Andrew were simple
fishermen. As Jesus' followers, we know He wants to use us to bless
others. Pray for a sick friend or make a phone call to a housebound
neighbor. Make yourself available, and join the ranks of Christ's
"fishers of men."

Mary McLeod Bethune
Christian Educator
1875–1955

> When they came to the border of Mysia, they tried to enter Bithynia,
> but the Spirit of Jesus would not allow them to.
> ACTS 16:7 NIV

"But I'm called to be a missionary to Africa," Mary McLeod said when the mission board rejected her application to go to that continent. She applied again, and her request was rejected the second time.

Mary was born in South Carolina, one of seventeen children of former slaves. After her conversion, Mary felt a strong call to be a missionary and prepared by attending Moody Bible Institute.

Though disappointed by the mission board's decision, Mary accepted the rejections as from God and believed He had another plan for her. She began teaching African-American children, and in 1904 she founded the Daytona Normal and Industrial School for Girls.

Through Christian education, Mary sought to restore the dignity of black women. In 1936 Franklin Roosevelt appointed her director of Negro Affairs of the National Youth Administration—the first African-American woman to act as a presidential advisor.

Don't take rejections and closed doors too seriously. Crumbling dreams don't mean the end of God's plans for you; they may mean He is steering you in another direction. Paul, the apostle, attempted to enter Bithynia, but the door was closed. However, God directed him to Macedonia. When a door slams shut, keep your heart open to the One who holds all the keys. Be assured—God will have the last word.

Amy Carmichael
Missionary, Author
1867–1951

> Fire will reveal what kind of work each builder has done. The fire will
> show if a person's work has any value. If the work survives,
> that builder will receive a reward.
>
> 1 Corinthians 3:13–14 NLT

As young Amy Carmichael and her brother walked home from church on a cold Sunday, they noticed a bedraggled woman shuffling along the side of the road. She staggered under the burden of a heavy bundle, and Amy knew this was one of Dublin's outcasts. Leaving their usual path, she and her brother rushed to the woman's aid.

"It was a horrible moment," Amy said. "We plodded on, a wet wind blowing us and the rags of the poor woman." As the three passed a stone fountain, a Voice said to Amy, "Gold, silver, precious stones, wood, hay, stubble. . .fire shall try every man's work of what sort it is."

She turned to see who had spoken, but no one was there. With that incident, Amy discovered her destiny: she was to turn from hay, wood, and stubble—temporary things—to minister Christ's love to the world's outcasts. Later, she spent fifty years in India, rescuing girls from prostitution.

What kind of materials are you building your life upon? If you seek only money, fame, and success, these will be burned on the day of judgment. On the other hand, if you build with materials such as generosity, sacrifice, kindness, humility, patience, and love—these works will stand the fire, and you'll receive rewards.

Annie Johnson Flint

Poet
1866–1932

So let us come boldly to the throne of our gracious God. There we will receive his mercy, and we will find grace to help us when we need it.
HEBREWS 4:16 NLT

After finishing a year of teachers' training, Annie Johnson signed a three-year contract to teach school. In her second year, she began to experience symptoms of arthritis. The pain increased and soon she struggled to walk. Adding to her stress at that time was the death of her parents, which left Annie and her frail sister penniless.

Annie had written her first poem when she was nine. Now an invalid, she turned to writing to make a living and as a distraction from pain. With bent fingers and swollen hands, she wrote poems of strength and hope. While her joints throbbed with pain, she told of God's undying love. In spite of a crippling disease, from deep within, Annie found a spring of life and conveyed hope to others through her writing.

When Annie submitted the poems for publication, letters arrived telling how people were blessed by her work. Later, her readers discovered she was an invalid and donated to her care.

You may also be held captive by pain or weakness. Keep trusting Jesus. Through prayer, you will overcome and say with Annie Johnson Flint:

> *He giveth more grace when the burdens grow greater,*
> *He sendeth more strength when the labors increase;*
> *To added affliction He addeth His mercy,*
> *To multiplied trials, His multiplied peace.*

Fanny Crosby
Hymn Writer
1820–1915

I have learned the secret of being content in any and every situation. . .
I can do all this through him who gives me strength.
PHILIPPIANS 4:12–13 NIV

"If you could have just one wish granted, what would it be?" evangelist D. L. Moody asked Fanny Crosby, the blind hymn writer, thinking she would ask to have her sight restored.

"I'd wish that I might continue blind the rest of my life," Fanny Crosby said.

Early in life, Fanny had made a decision: she would be content with blindness. She said, "Soon I learned what other children possessed, but I made up my mind to store away a little jewel in my heart which I called content."

When Fanny Crosby was six months old, she contracted an eye condition. The treatment resulted in total blindness for the infant. The same year, her father died and her mother was forced to take a job outside the home.

With her grandmother's help, the little girl memorized entire books of the Bible. The knowledge would serve her well when she began writing hymns. This blind woman who seemed destined for obscurity became acquainted with four United States presidents, addressed the US Congress, appeared in Carnegie Hall at age ninety-two, and wrote more than seven thousand hymns.

Perhaps you, too, are battling a physical or mental problem. Instead of thinking of what you lack, do as Fanny Crosby did; take the jewel of contentment and move on to the greater things God has planned for you.

Ann Hasseltine Judson

Missionary, Author, Teacher
1789–1826

I consider everything a loss because of the surpassing worth of knowing
Christ Jesus my Lord, for whose sake I have lost all things.
I consider them garbage, that I may gain Christ.
PHILIPPIANS 3:8 NIV

"We have endeavored to count the cost and be prepared for the many severe trials resulting from this change of sentiment," Ann Judson wrote after she and her husband changed their church affiliation on their way to the mission field in 1812. This was only the beginning of the price Ann would have to pay to "go into all the world."

Fun-loving Ann Hasseltine married Adoniram Judson, and two weeks later they sailed for Calcutta. From there they transferred to Burma, where Ann learned the language, helped with translation work, wrote a catechism, and produced scripture portions in the Burmese language.

When a war broke out, Adoniram was imprisoned and tortured for two years. Ann remained near him and delivered a child during this time. However, the ordeal took a toll on her health, and shortly after her husband's release, Ann died at age thirty-six.

Suffering the loss of all things—was it worth it? Ann would no doubt answer, "Yes," for her short life inspired countless others to accept the challenges of difficult mission fields.

Are you willing to lose to gain Christ? Perhaps you need to lose a prideful attitude, the desire for popularity, or wanting to have your own way. This "loss" will seem as nothing when you bow before Him in heaven.

Frances Ridley Havergal

Hymn Writer
1836–1879

But God forbid that I should glory, save in the cross of our Lord Jesus Christ,
by whom the world is crucified unto me, and I unto the world.

GALATIANS 6:14 KJV

While studying in Germany, eighteen-year-old Frances Ridley Havergal saw a painting of Christ's crucifixion and read the words engraved beneath: "This I have done for thee; what hast thou done for me?" Deeply moved by the message, she reached for a pen and wrote the poem, "I Gave My Life for Thee."

Later she read the verses, and in disgust said, "This falls short of what I want to say." She crumpled the paper and threw it in the fire, but the paper leaped from the flames and fell to the floor. Frances then showed the words to her father, who wrote a melody for the poem.

I gave My life for thee, My precious blood I shed,
That thou might'st ransomed be, And quickened from the dead;
I gave, I gave my life for thee, What has thou giv'n for zzzMe?

"Repulsive, cruel," some people say when confronted by the crucifixion. For others, the death of a person who lived hundreds of years ago is meaningless. And there are those, like Frances, who sense they owe a debt to the One who died. What is your response to the cross? May you, like the apostle Paul, ponder the meaning of Jesus' sacrifice and respond, "I will glory in it!"

Catherine Marshall

Author
1914–1983

> Though you have not seen him, you love him; and even though
> you do not see him now, you believe in him and are
> filled with an inexpressible and glorious joy.
> 1 PETER 1:8 NIV

As a young woman, Catherine enjoyed a storybook romance that culminated in marriage to the successful pastor Peter Marshall. A few years later she knew the joy of motherhood. Then, three years into their marriage, Catherine became ill with a serious lung disease and spent the next years as an invalid.

During her illness, Catherine sought God for healing, but her health did not improve. She struggled to make her faith effective, yet peace escaped her. In her unrest, she began to read Hannah Whitall Smith's book, *The Christian's Secret to a Happy Life*. Catherine discovered happiness is not dependent on outward circumstances; rather, it is an inward fountain flowing from Christ. She said, "The Christian life must be lived in the will, not the emotions." Finally peace came to her and, eventually, healing.

Is it possible to be a Christian, have your sins forgiven, be on your way to heaven and be unhappy? Yes, if your happiness depends upon circumstances. If your joy comes from Christ within, no tragedy, no sickness, will snuff out the joy of God. He is enough!

Mary Lee Bright

Mother, Housewife
1890–1983

"You are the light of the world. A town built on a hill cannot be hidden.
Neither do people light a lamp and put it under a bowl. Instead they
put it on its stand, and it gives light to everyone in the house."
MATTHEW 5:14–15 NIV

"Is that you, Bill?" Mary Lee Bright called in the darkness.

"Yes, it is, Mom," he answered, and in the distance Bill could see
the faint glow of the light his mother carried.

When the Bright children stayed after school to participate in
extracurricular activities, often it was evening when they arrived
home. Concerned for their well-being, their mother would meet
them on the dark road and guide them safely home with her lantern.

Mary Lee Bright, mother of seven, held a light out for her family
in more than one way. Her son, Bill Bright, founder of Campus
Crusade for Christ International, said of her, "The greatest influence
in my life has been my mother's life and prayers. She was the most
godly person I have ever known."

The world is a dark place; there is a need for light. You can be
that light. Reflect godly attributes and a prayerful attitude, and
people will be drawn to Christ. Even one faint glow in the blackness
of night makes a difference.

Cecil Frances Alexander

Hymn Writer, Poet
1818–1895

> O LORD, what a variety of things you have made! In wisdom
> you have made them all. The earth is full of your creatures.
> PSALM 104:24 NLT

At age nine, Cecil Frances Alexander began to write poetry. Afraid her father would not approve, she hid her poems under her bedroom rug. When her father discovered the poems, he kindly gave her a box to store them in. As an adult, Cecil wrote over four hundred hymns and poems, all of them intended to help children better understand the scriptures.

Cecil married a pastor, and in the early years of their marriage they ministered in an impoverished, rural area of Ireland where they daily encountered sickness and poverty. She chose not to dwell on the harsh world around her, but saw beauty in what God had created. This frame of mind is reflected in the hymn, "All Things Bright and Beautiful."

All things bright and beautiful,
All creatures great and small,
All things wise and wonderful,
The Lord God made them all.

We live in a world where ugliness abounds due to disease and evil. Rather than dwell on these depressing circumstances, look up and beyond. See God in the sky, a cloud, or a child's smile. As you look for beauty, you will find it all around.

Edith Moules
Missionary
1900–1949

> Praise be to the God and Father of our Lord Jesus Christ!
> In his great mercy he has given us new birth into a living hope
> through the resurrection of Jesus Christ from the dead.
> 1 PETER 1:3 NIV

As the congregation sang "There Is a Fountain Filled with Blood," tears ran down Edith's face. "Do you believe that Jesus died for you?" the minister asked the twelve-year-old. She quickly replied, "Yes!"

In spite of saying she was a Christian, Edith later confessed that the experience had not touched her heart. Her attempts to read the Bible were discouraging. The plan of salvation confused her. She tried to do what was right but failed.

One day Edith asked Ethel, a Christian friend, why the two of them seemed so different. "It's because Jesus doesn't live inside you," Ethel answered honestly. The Holy Spirit used those words to spark a desire in Edith for the "real thing." Using the Bible, Ethel explained the plan of salvation to Edith, who finally accepted Christ in her heart. "What a change!" she said.

In a missionary service at age eighteen, Edith heard the Lord say, "Come follow me." That call led her to Africa. Decades of fruitful missionary service resulted because years earlier a young girl had invited Jesus into her heart.

Miracle of miracles! Christ can live in the human heart through the new birth. If Jesus is not present in your heart, invite Him in. Rejoice in this marvelous hope—God, in the person of His Son, lives in you!

Mary Ann Paton
Missionary
1840–1859

> Martha answered, "I know he will rise
> again in the resurrection at the last day."
> JOHN 11:24 NIV

In 1859, nineteen-year-old Mary Ann Paton sailed with her husband, John, for missionary work in the New Hebrides. What the couple found on the island of Tanna shocked them. The natives were steeped in superstition, vicious, void of natural affection, and constantly at war among themselves. After killing their enemies, they feasted on them.

Shortly after their arrival, John wrote that his wife was "in excellent health and full of all tender and holy hopes." Mary Ann immediately gathered a class of eight women that met regularly for Christian teaching.

She had a son in February. At first she and the child prospered, but Mary Ann contracted a fever that led to serious problems. In March she died, and her son died shortly after. Before her death the young missionary said, "I did not regret leaving home and friends, though at the time I felt it keenly."

After Mary Ann died, a resolution was passed by missionaries on the island that read, "Her earnest Christian character, her devoted missionary spirit, her excellent education. . .excited expectations of great future usefulness."

What could have been, if only. . . Are you also trying to make sense out of a loss? Just now, think about another time, another place where "he will swallow up death forever" (Isaiah 25:8).

Helen Purviance
Salvation Army "Doughnut Girl"
1889–1984

> God is not unjust; he will not forget your work and the love you have shown him as you have helped his people and continue to help them.
> HEBREWS 6:10 NIV

When the United States entered the war in France in 1917, Evangeline Booth, general of the United States Salvation Army, offered the services of her organization to President Wilson. Officer Helen Purviance went with the first contingent of workers assigned to the American 1st Division. The workers held religious services and provided food, beverages, books, and writing supplies for the soldiers.

One rainy day in a tent near the front line, Helen mixed dough, cut it into strips, and shaped and fried crullers over a potbellied stove, becoming the first "doughnut girl." She said, "I was literally on my knees when the first doughnuts fried, seven at a time. . . . Also a prayer in my heart that somehow this home touch would do more for those who ate the doughnuts than satisfy a physical hunger."

The pleasant aroma drew the battle-worn soldiers, and soon long lines of men stood in the mud and rain day after day, waiting to get the doughnuts. From the crude tent, Helen's operation improved until, with others, she fried up to nine thousand doughnuts a day.

What a morale booster the homemade doughnuts were to homesick soldiers! It's not always some huge deed you do that touches a heart. The recipient of your kindness won't forget even the smallest act done in love. God remembers them, too.

Mary Reed
Missionary
1854–1943

All these people earned a good reputation because of their faith, yet none of them received all that God had promised. For God had something better in mind for us, so that they would not reach perfection without us.
HEBREWS 11:39–40 NLT

Mary Reed received an appointment as a missionary to the zenana women in India, but soon after her arrival on the field in 1885, her health failed. When she retreated to the Himalayas to recover, she visited a leper colony. Mary was deeply moved by the poor conditions under which the lepers lived.

When her health broke a second time, she returned to America, where she was diagnosed with leprosy. Rather than give up her calling, she went back to India and became superintendent of the Leper Homes in Chandag, the place she had visited earlier. Without help from other missionaries, Mary built a church, chapel, and homes. Under her leadership the colony became self-supporting, and through Mary's preaching and witnessing, many lepers received Christ. All this she accomplished while living with an incurable disease.

The Bible teaches that some believers won't be delivered from their trials, because God has something else in mind for them and others. If you remain in a valley of sickness, trial, or trouble, take heart. Remember, for you, God has a better plan; with His strength, you will go through.

Florence Nightingale
Nurse, Social Reformer
1820–1910

> Then I heard the voice of the Lord saying, "Whom shall I send?
> And who will go for us?" And I said, "Here am I. Send me!"
> ISAIAH 6:8 NIV

"God spoke to me and called me to his service," Florence Nightingale wrote in her diary at age seventeen. When she announced to her family she was called to be a nurse, her parents—members of the English aristocracy—were horrified.

Nursing at that time, in England and much of the world, was a despicable job, reserved for prostitutes and drunkards. To be admitted to a hospital in that era was a death sentence.

Florence stood firm in her calling and, after a bitter struggle, when she was thirty-two, her parents reluctantly allowed her to train at the Institute of Protestant Deaconesses at Kaiserswerth. In 1854, she heard of the sad conditions of the soldiers in the Crimea during England's war with Russia. Forty-one percent of the men died from wounds and diseases. Florence volunteered to take thirty-eight nurses to the war zone. Through their untiring efforts, the death rate was reduced to two per cent. This happened when one woman said "yes" to God.

God's callings are as varied as the people He calls. When you hear Him speak your name, make yourself available as Florence did. From a sincere heart pray, "Lord, here am I!"

Louisa M. R. Stead
Hymn Writer, Missionary
1850–1917

> Trust in the LORD with all your heart; do not depend on
> your own understanding. Seek his will in all you do,
> and he will show you which path to take.
> PROVERBS 3:5–6 NLT

It started as a happy family outing. Louisa Stead packed a picnic lunch, and she, her husband, and daughter planned to spend an afternoon at Long Island Sound Beach.

As the family relaxed on the sand, they heard a cry for help from the surf. In a moment Mr. Stead rushed into the water to rescue a young boy. Louisa and her daughter watched as her husband and the boy were pulled under the water and drowned.

Returning home that day, Louisa poured out her grief in prayer and asked God, "Why?" The answer came: she was to *trust* her plight to Jesus. Later she translated her thoughts into a poem. When the verses were set to music, a song of hope and trust was born.

'Tis so sweet to trust in Jesus,
Just to take Him at His word;
Just to rest upon His promise;
Just to know, "Thus saith the LORD."

You, too, may have felt a thud as you hit bottom after experiencing a death, divorce, or financial loss. Lean on Jesus. When you don't understand, trust Him. When you can't see what the outcome will be, trust Him. Trust Him with *all* your heart. Who is more trustworthy?

Sarah Johnston Lincoln

Stepmother of Abraham Lincoln
1788–1869

> Every wise woman buildeth her house.
> PROVERBS 14:1 KJV

Sarah Johnston was a widow with three small children when Tom Lincoln appeared at her cabin in Kentucky in 1819. A year earlier, Tom had lost his wife, leaving him with two youngsters. He asked Sarah to marry him, and she accepted.

What Sarah found at the Lincoln cabin in Indiana, however, saddened her. The floor was dirt. The children barely had clothes on their backs. Soon after Sarah's arrival, wooden planks covered the dirt floor, and the Lincoln children had new clothes.

Sarah, a kind, cheerful person, knew how to manage children. From her, young Abe Lincoln learned about fairness as he saw Sarah treat the stepchildren and her own children the same.

She sensed great potential in Abe, and although she could not read or write, she encouraged him to educate himself. There were few books in the one-room cabin, but they had a Bible, and he read it until he knew much of it by heart. Years later, Abe's speeches and writings were enriched by quotations from the Bible.

Abraham Lincoln said of his stepmother, "God bless my mother; all that I am or ever hope to be I owe to her."

Good homes don't just happen: they are built. Live by biblical principles and teach them to your children and they, like "honest Abe," will be a strong force for good in a fallen world.

Harriet Beecher Stowe

Author, Hymn Writer
1811–1896

> "Be strong and courageous. Do not be afraid or terrified because of them,
> for the LORD your God goes with you."
> DEUTERONOMY 31:6 NIV

"If I could use a pen as you can, Harriet, I'd write something that would make this whole nation feel what an accursed thing slavery is," Isabella Beecher wrote to her sister-in-law.

Slavery was tearing the United States apart. The Fugitive Slave Law, enacted in 1850, enabled slave hunters to travel north, capture runaway slaves, and send them south in chains.

As Harriet sat in her parlor reading Isabella's letter, her six children played nearby, and a new baby slept in his cradle. Suddenly Harriet rose from her chair. "I will write something," she said. "I will—if I live."

Soon after, while she sat in church, images began to form in Harriet's mind. She went home and scribbled the vision. The novel *Uncle Tom's Cabin* was the result. The book was so effective in uncovering the injustices of slavery that when Harriet met President Lincoln, he said, "So you're the little woman who wrote the book that made this great war."

Harriet Beecher Stowe risked her life to expose a great evil, and it was enough to help turn an entire nation from slavery. Perhaps you also need courage to stand for what is right, but you don't think the little you can do will make a difference. God doesn't need much to turn a bad situation around: only your willingness and availability.

Helen Steiner Rice
Poet, Writer
1900–1981

> "You can ask for anything in my name, and I will do it,
> so that the Son can bring glory to the Father.
> Yes, ask me for anything in my name, and I will do it!"
> JOHN 14:13–14 NLT

As a young woman, Helen Steiner was asked to speak at a convention. Although she came prepared, when she got to the platform, she panicked. "I didn't know where to start, or what to say," she said. "Then a thought came to my mind: your Father knows." Right there she asked the heavenly Father for help, and words came to her. Depending on God, and asking for His help, became the hallmark of this soon-to-be greeting card writer.

During the 1930s depression, Helen's husband, a successful banker, lost everything and subsequently took his life. Again Helen asked God for help to make a living for her family, and she was directed to write greeting cards for the Gibson Art Company.

Helen learned early in life that nothing of eternal worth can be accomplished without God's help. What do you need help to do? Ask, seek, knock until the answer comes. No prayer goes unanswered when you come to your Father who threw open the door of heaven when He said, "Ask."

A portion of Helen's poem, "On Wings of Prayer," reads:

Just close your eyes and open your heart
And feel your worries and cares depart
Just yield yourself to the Father above
And let Him hold you secure in His love.

Corrie ten Boom
Author, Evangelist
1892–1983

Why, my soul, are you downcast? Why so disturbed within me?
Put your hope in God, for I will yet praise him, my Savior and my God.
PSALM 42:5–6 NIV

Corrie ten Boom and her family were part of an underground movement to protect Jews in Holland during the Nazi occupation. For this, the ten Boom family was arrested in 1943. As they were taken from their home, Corrie managed to place a small Bible in a cloth bag and tie it around her neck. "As we stumbled up a hill I felt the little Bible bumping on my back," she said. "As long as I had that, we could face hell itself." Corrie and Betsie, her sister, were soon to face hell in Ravensbruck concentration camp.

As guards searched the women, Corrie asked God to shield the Bible. "The woman ahead of me was searched," she said. "Behind me Betsie was searched. They did not even look at me."

In barracks 28, the words of that Bible were shared with other women until their building became known as "the crazy place, where they have hope."

Is your hope running low? Pick up a Bible. Read it. God wrote the scriptures with you in mind. As you meditate on His Word, you will soon find what you are looking for—unshakable hope in God for the future.

Susanna Wesley
Christian Wife and Mother
1669–1742

> [Our fathers] disciplined us for a little while as they thought best;
> but God disciplines us for our good,
> in order that we may share in his holiness.
> HEBREWS 12:10 NIV

Susanna Wesley gave birth to nineteen children, nine of whom lived to adulthood. She taught the surviving children six days a week for twenty years in basic subjects, the Bible, and Christian conduct.

When her family was grown, her son John, founder of the Methodist movement, asked her to write down the principles that had guided her in the family's rearing. The list included strict rules of discipline, but Susanna also showed great respect and fairness. One principle on her list states, "No girl is to be taught to work till she can read very well."

Discipline and correction are also necessary in the family of God. Our heavenly Father often uses the Word of God to correct us. We respond, make necessary changes in our lives, and the discipline ends. Other times when we don't readily respond, God, like any loving father, may increase the chastisement.

If you are feeling the correcting hand of God on your life, ask Him what He's trying to teach you. When God disciplines, it is always for your betterment; to make you more like His Son Jesus. The Lord corrects His own children.

Anna Bartlett Warner
Hymn Writer, Author
1827–1915

> God demonstrates his own love for us in this:
> While we were still sinners, Christ died for us.
> ROMANS 5:8 NIV

After theologian Karl Barth had given a lengthy dissertation, a reporter asked him to summarize what he had just said. Barth thought a moment, then said, "Jesus loves me, this I know. For the Bible tells me so."

This is also the title of one of the world's best-loved hymns, a song that has been translated into languages wherever the gospel is preached. When China was closed under communism, little was heard of Chinese Christians. In 1972 a letter came through with this sentence, "The 'this I know' people are well." The message passed through censors, but Christians understood the meaning.

The writer of this hymn, Anna Warner, and her sister lived on the Hudson River near the military academy of West Point. For more than fifty years, the sisters regularly conducted Bible classes for cadets in their home. When Anna died at ninety-five, she was given military honors at West Point.

Missionaries have often used Anna's song to explain the gospel. Once in the Canadian wilderness, a man heard strains of the tune sung in French. He asked the Eskimo where he had learned the song. "At the mission," came the reply.

If the scriptures are hard for you to understand or you're confused by doctrine, forget the arguments and repeat the simple words, "Jesus loves me! This I know, for the Bible tells me so." That's all you need to know.

> "Keep on asking, and you will receive what you ask for. Keep on seeking,
> and you will find. Keep on knocking, and the door will be opened to you.
> For everyone who asks, receives."
>
> MATTHEW 7:7–8 NLT

One day Fanny Crosby, the blind hymn writer, needed a specific amount of money and she asked God to supply the need. As she rose from her knees, the doorbell rang and Fanny opened the door to greet a stranger. The two visited. When the person turned to leave, they shook hands and Fanny felt a bill slip into her hand. Later she discovered it was the exact amount of money she had prayed for. As she meditated on God's faithfulness, words formed in her mind. The lines were eventually put to music and became the hymn, "All the Way My Savior Leads Me."

All the way my Savior leads me; What have I to ask beside?
Can I doubt His tender mercy, Who through life has been my Guide?
Heavenly peace, divinest comfort, Here by faith in Him to dwell!
For I know, whate'er befall me, Jesus doeth all things well.

God knows exactly what you need, but He invites you to ask. Coming to God shows your dependence upon Him and is pleasing to your heavenly Father. Mothers may tire of hearing their child's continual requests, but not so with God. He hears every prayer and promises to answer them.

Annie S. Hawks

Hymn Writer

1835–1918

> He is my mighty rock, my refuge. Trust in him at all times,
> you people; pour out your hearts to him, for God is our refuge.
> PSALM 62:7–8 NIV

"I don't know what I'd do without the Lord." These words are often spoken by Christians when they pass through difficult times. God helps and comforts us in our trials, and many hymns have been written as a result of heart-wrenching situations.

But this was not true of the inspiration for Annie Hawks's hymn, "I Need Thee Ev'ry Hour." She said, "I remember well the morning when in the midst of the daily cares, I was so filled with the sense of the nearness of my Master that, wondering how anyone could live without Him, these words, 'I need Thee every hour,' flashed into my mind."

Annie took a pencil and wrote:

I need Thee ev'ry hour, most gracious Lord;
No tender voice like Thine can peace afford.
I need Thee; O, I need Thee; Every hour I need Thee!
O bless me now, my Savior, I come to Thee.

Trusting God is not just for difficult times; we need Him in the good times as well. Today, enjoy His friendship. Pray and trust Him for help in simple, everyday tasks and you are storing up strength for the days ahead whether these are troublesome or pleasant.

Elizabeth Ka'ahumanu

Christian Hawaiian Queen
Late 18th–Early 19th Century

"I am the LORD your God, who brought you out of Egypt,
out of the land of slavery. You shall have no other gods before me."
EXODUS 20:2–3 NIV

A powerful woman in size, Ka'ahumanu stood six feet tall and weighed over three hundred pounds. She also wielded powerful influence over the people of the Hawaiian Islands during her reign as queen. Through the efforts of missionaries, she came under the teachings of Christ, and, after struggling with the message of Christianity for four years, she accepted Jesus and became a powerful witness for the Savior.

Before Ka'ahumanu was baptized in water in 1824, she instituted new laws for her subjects based on the Ten Commandments. She ordered the pagan idols to be removed and destroyed the sugar cane fields to stop rum production. She became a friend and protector of Protestant missionaries and, in her later years, she was noted for her religious zeal. A critic of Protestant missionaries said of Ka'ahumanu, "She died a Christian. . .she really believed in and practiced the principles of the Christian religion."

No one intends to make money, pleasure, or work their idol, yet when you put these ahead of God, they become gods. The Ten Commandments, like white lines on the highway, are given for your protection and guidance. Check your priorities in light of these ancient but relevant laws. Like Ka'ahumanu, institute God's ten rules for happiness in your life.

Arabella Catherine Hankey

Hymn Writer
1834–1911

But they that wait upon the LORD shall renew their strength;
they shall mount up with wings as eagles; they shall run,
and not be weary; and they shall walk, and not faint.
ISAIAH 40:31 KJV

In her twenties, Catherine Hankey spent part of every week teaching a Bible class for London's factory girls. Then in her thirties, Catherine became ill. During her long recovery, she missed her friends, and she felt isolated. How she wished someone would come to encourage her!

If no one will help me, I'll help myself, Catherine thought. During the lonely hours, she read the Bible and wrote poetry. Her writing efforts resulted in a fifty-verse poem of the life of Jesus from which two hymns were written: "Tell Me the Old, Old Story" and "I Love to Tell the Story."

No doubt meditation on God and His Word played a large part in Catherine's return to health. Catherine recovered and traveled to South Africa in the interest of missions. In her last years, she spent time visiting patients in London hospitals.

Are you suffering mentally, physically, or emotionally? Meditate on Jesus. Read the Bible regularly. Use devotional books and religious magazines for inspiration. Not all medicine is in a bottle; you will find some in the Book—the Bible.

I love to tell the story, of unseen things above,
Of Jesus and His glory, of Jesus and His love.
I love to tell the story because I know 'tis true;
It satisfies my longings as nothing else can do.

Frances Ridley Havergal
Hymn Writer
1836–1879

> In him [Jesus] we have redemption through his blood, the forgiveness
> of sins, in accordance with the riches of God's grace that he lavished on us.
> With all wisdom and understanding.
> EPHESIANS 1:7–8 NIV

Frances Ridley Havergal was forty-two years old when she was told she didn't have long to live. "That's too good to be true," she said. Her sister, Maria, remained at her sister's side when she died. She said in Frances's last moments, she began to sing, "Golden Harps Are Sounding," a song she had written.

"There was a radiance on her face as she passed," Maria said. "It was as though she had already seen the Lord."

Death was not Frances's enemy, and it need not be for you. Fear of dying comes because of sin. God provided a covering for your sin; you triumph over death by accepting Jesus' blood as your covering.

If you have placed your sins under His blood, rejoice. If not, make preparation by sincerely praying these lines written by Frances Havergal:

> *Take my life, and let it be*
> *Consecrated, Lord, to Thee;*
> *Take my hands, and let them move*
> *At the impulse of Thy love,*
> *At the impulse of Thy love.*

Narcissa Whitman
Missionary
1808–1847

> We were crushed and overwhelmed beyond our ability to endure,
> and we thought we would never live through it. . . But as a result,
> we stopped relying on ourselves and learned to rely only on God.
> 2 CORINTHIANS 1:8–9 NLT

When word came East requesting volunteers to bring the "Book of Life" to the Nez Perce Indians, Narcissa Prentiss felt called to go. Marcus Whitman, a physician, also was drawn to the mission field and wanted a wife to accompany him. He proposed to Narcissa, and together the zealous couple crossed the Rocky Mountains in 1836 to begin a mission in Oregon Territory.

For Narcissa, the romance of the missionary field quickly vanished as she found herself feeding and housing travelers who stopped at the mission. Cold winters, cramped quarters, and the drowning of her two-year-old daughter also took a toll on her zeal. One observer recorded, "Mrs. W. [Narcissa] in a sad mood all day, did not present herself at the breakfast table. Went outdoors, down by the river to cry."

Tragically, Narcissa's dream of a fruitful ministry ended when Cayuse Indians attacked the mission in 1847 and killed her, Marcus, and twelve others.

It is not difficult to understand why the allure of Narcissa's calling quickly faded. Perhaps you, too, are faced with challenging circumstances. A job, a ministry, marriage, or motherhood appeared so glamorous at the onset, but the excitement has paled as you face the day-to-day chores. Only one thing will sustain you in trying times—God. Rely on Him. He is faithful.

> "The harvest is plentiful, but the workers are few. Ask the Lord of the harvest, therefore, to send out workers into his harvest field."
>
> LUKE 10:2 NIV

When Minnie Abrams arrived in Bombay, India, in 1887, she was overwhelmed by the thousands of people on the streets. *How can all these be reached by the gospel?* she wondered. She was further stirred when she visited an opium den where she saw enslaved addicts. *Darkness all around and so few to tell them of Christ*, Minnie thought. For two years, she diligently studied the language and prayed that the Lord would send more workers.

Pandita Ramabai, who operated the Mukti center for abandoned child-widows, had prayed for a person to teach the Bible to the women. Minnie became that teacher.

When Minnie heard of a revival in Wales and Australia, she challenged the girls at Mukti to pray for a similar movement to arise in India. Seventy girls volunteered to pray. Soon four hundred girls offered to go to villages to tell of Jesus. Minnie went to America to enlist workers to accompany the girls, and six young women answered the call. They, along with the national women, pushed into the unreached northern areas of India.

"The Lord led me into the work of Pandita Ramabai," Minnie said, "because He wanted me to have a little part in answering my own prayers."

As you pray for workers to bring in lost souls, don't be surprised if God also asks you to be one of the harvesters.

Bertha Munro
College Dean
1887–1983

> Christ will be exalted in my body, whether by life or by death.
> For to me, to live is Christ and to die is gain.
> PHILIPPIANS 1:20–21 NIV

It is helpful to have a creed to live by, a statement that defines your purpose for being. Bertha Munro lived by what she called the "Munro doctrine," which stated: Truth cannot contradict truth, God will not waste a consecrated life, persons are more important than things, and not somehow but triumphantly.

One day as Bertha traveled from Washington DC to Boston, the train derailed and she was trapped in the wreckage. The accident left her with a crippled hand and a weak back. But the accident also made her think seriously about her life, and she made a commitment to do a lasting work for God.

Bertha became a college professor, and when Eastern Nazarene College opened, she was appointed dean. But disappointments were never far away. After working two years writing her thesis for an advanced degree, Bertha discovered her subject had been duplicated and she had to choose another topic.

Because Bertha had established a basic set of principles for her life, she kept moving ahead over distressing circumstances and a handicapped condition.

The apostle Paul summed up his life's creed with the words, "For to me, to live is Christ." Choose a simple, biblically based creed for your life. It will help you keep a godly perspective on every event of life—good or bad.

Emma Moody

Wife of Evangelist D. L. Moody
1842–1903

Her husband has full confidence in her and lacks nothing of value.
She brings him good, not harm, all the days of her life.
PROVERBS 31:11–12 NIV

Emma Revell met Dwight Moody at a Chicago mission where she taught a class. When Moody began his own Sunday school and needed teachers, she volunteered. They were married in 1862, and Moody said, "I never cease to wonder. . .the miracle of having won the love of a woman who is so completely my superior." Their admiration of each other was mutual, for Emma wrote Moody's mother, "Your son is a gem of a husband."

Yet it was a marriage of opposites. She was educated, refined, and of a quiet disposition. On the other hand, her husband had not had the advantages of a good education; he was impulsive, outspoken, and had poor manners.

Emma traveled with her husband in evangelistic meetings in the United States and England and was sometimes criticized for not appearing on the platform with him. However, she supported her husband in other ways, preferring a behind-the-scenes role, often working with individual people seeking salvation and taking care of Moody's correspondence.

Not all wives are as retiring as Emma, but every woman can strive to develop the character and integrity she possessed. Like her, you can support and respect your husband—doing him good all the days of your life.

Henrietta Soltau
Christian Worker
1843–1934

It is because of him that you are in Christ Jesus, who has become for us wisdom from God—that is, our righteousness, holiness and redemption.
1 Corinthians 1:30 NIV

When Henrietta Soltau heard missionary J. Hudson Taylor speak of the need for missionaries to go to China, she answered "yes." However, she was unable to go because of an illness. Henrietta did not sit idly by, but organized a women's Bible class that eventually reached an attendance of two hundred women. Later Henrietta established a home for missionary children in England.

Henrietta's greatest challenge came in 1889 when Taylor asked her to take charge of a program designed to screen and prepare prospective women missionaries to go to the foreign field. Henrietta wavered. How could she possibly prepare women to go where she had never been herself?

In spite of misgivings, Henrietta stepped into the new role. Using God-given wisdom and knowledge gleaned from preaching, street evangelism, and caring for children, she served at her post for twenty-six years. She instructed, counseled, and loved the missionary candidates. One woman said, "Had it not been for Miss Soltau. . .no Mission Board would have entertained the thought of accepting me for foreign service."

Because the future is uncertain and unknown, we need divine wisdom. God is our source, united with His Son. Christ becomes all we need for redemption, holiness, righteousness—and even wisdom for everyday decisions.

Hannah Whitall Smith

Author
1832–1911

> It is expedient for you that I go away: for if I go not away, the Comforter will not come unto you; but if I depart, I will send him unto you.
> JOHN 16:7 KJV

When Hannah Whitall Smith's five-year-old daughter died from a bronchial infection in 1857, Hannah was inconsolable. She wept and questioned God. No amount of talking or comforting by family and friends relieved her grief.

That summer the family spent their vacation at a beach, and Hannah took only one book with her to read during the holiday—the Bible. While the water lapped on the sand and gulls called overhead, Hannah read on and on, day after day, looking for the elusive, needed comfort.

Then it happened: one day as she read, the healing, comforting peace of God touched her entire being. She rose from the beach chair and shouted, "I believe, Oh, Lord, I believe!" Later, she shared the experience in her book, *The God of All Comfort*.

Perhaps you, too, have been touched by tragedy until your heart feels like one gaping wound. You question whether the struggle of living is worth the effort. Jesus made a special provision for your grief; He sent His Holy Spirit, the Comforter. Allow the third person of the Trinity to clean the sorrow from your heart and gently push together your wounded spirit until only God's peace remains.

Sarah Flower Adams

Hymn Writer

1805–1848

> Let us draw near to God with a sincere heart and with the full assurance that faith brings, having our hearts sprinkled to cleanse us from a guilty conscience and having our bodies washed with pure water.
>
> HEBREWS 10:22 NIV

Her dream was to become an actress, but illness kept Sarah Flower from reaching that goal. Instead she channeled her creative abilities into writing.

While daily dealing with weakness, Sarah's faith sometimes wavered, but in those times she drew near to God. The strength and faith He gave to her is reflected in her writings. Her most popular hymn says:

Nearer, my God to Thee, nearer to Thee!
E'en though it be a cross that raiseth me;
Still all my song shall be, nearer, my God, to Thee,
Nearer, my God to Thee, nearer to Thee!

When the song appeared in hymnbooks, it became a favorite and was sung in churches across America and Great Britain. As President William McKinley lay dying from an assassin's bullet, he was said to have whispered the first line of Sarah's hymn and told the doctor, "This has been my constant prayer."

If you feel estranged from God for any reason, call Jesus' name in prayer, read God's Word, attend a Bible study, or sing this hymn. Take the first step, and He'll be there to quiet your anxious spirit, cheer your drooping emotions, and speak peace to your troubled mind.

Marie Monson
Missionary
Early 20th Century

He [Jesus] went up on a mountainside by himself to pray.
Later that night, he was there alone.
MATTHEW 14:23 NIV

When God spoke to young Marie Monson about missionary service in China, she answered, "Yes." After completing a year of nursing training, she prepared to leave, but her sailing date was delayed. God used the delay to teach Marie a lesson—one she would need for ministry in China.

During this time Marie observed the devotional life of a friend. Each day without fail, the friend spent time studying the Bible and praying. Such a simple discipline, but Marie had missed it. Now she adopted the practice. It would make a huge difference in her spiritual growth and in the lives of those she helped in China.

Think of Jesus. The Son of God found it beneficial to daily talk to His Father. Alone with God, you'll hear His voice. Alone with God, you'll see yourself as He sees you. Time alone with Him will reveal Jesus as the altogether sufficient One. Tend to the basics— Bible reading and prayer—and you open the door for a joy-filled relationship with Jesus. Time with God is never wasted; it provides you with strength and joy for the journey.

Susanna Wesley
Mother, Author, Teacher
1669–1742

Her children arise and call her blessed; her husband also, and he praises her: "Many women do noble things, but you surpass them all."
PROVERBS 31:28–29 NIV

When Susanna Wesley's young son was miraculously saved from a house fire, she said, "I do intend to be more particularly careful of the soul of this child." She kept this promise, and the child, John Wesley, went on to became the force in a great spiritual awakening, and the founder of Methodism.

Well-educated, Susanna taught her nine children six hours daily for twenty years. The curriculum included Latin, Greek, French, logic, and religion. She also wrote three textbooks.

Samuel, her husband, also a learned person, was poor with money, so Susanna managed the household affairs. When Samuel spent a year in jail for not paying a debt, she sent him her only jewelry, a wedding ring, to be sure he had something to barter for food.

While Samuel was away from home, Susanna gathered the family around her on Sunday evenings to sing psalms and listen to the reading of sermons. It was not long before her kitchen was filled with neighbors who wanted to be included in the meetings.

Most women today can't possibly hope to accomplish all that Susanna Wesley did. However, it is important to strive to possess the character, integrity, and dedication of this woman. Your superb Christian lifestyle will also become known in your community, and serve as a model for your family, friends, and future generations.

Eliza Agnew
Missionary
1807–1883

> "More are the children of the desolate woman
> than of her who has a husband."
> ISAIAH 54:1 NIV

Eliza Agnew didn't have children of her own, yet her obituary read, "She was well called 'the mother of one thousand daughters.' All claimed her as their mother."

As a young woman, Eliza went to Ceylon in 1840 to teach in a mission boarding school. There were only a few converts, boys, in Ceylon and India at that time, but because of Miss Agnew's prayers, example, influence, and Christian teaching, more than six hundred girls became Christians. It was said of her, "She probably led more brides to the marriage altar than any other person living."

Miss Agnew served as principal of the school until she retired. After retirement, she stayed at the school, visited her former students in their homes, and lived to see her pupils' children walking with the Lord into the third generation. Never once in her forty-four years on the mission field did she take a furlough.

If you, like Eliza Agnew, are childless, you can be a spiritual mother. Wherever children congregate—clubs, Sunday schools, nurseries—make yourself available. Young people need the example, friendship, and prayers of a Christian woman like you.

Emily H. Tubman

Philanthropist, Emancipator

1794–1885

> "The Spirit of the Lord is on me, because. . .He has sent me to proclaim
> freedom for the prisoners and recovery of sight for the blind,
> to set the oppressed free."
>
> LUKE 4:18 NIV

After her husband died in 1836, wealthy plantation owner Emily Tubman called her slaves together and, although it was against Georgia law, declared them free. Then she gave the former slaves a choice: they could stay in America or she would establish them in Liberia, West Africa.

When seventy freed slaves chose to leave America, Emily chartered a ship and provided homes for them in Africa. The remaining former slaves stayed in America, where Emily gave them land, homes, food, and clothing.

Twenty-five years before the United States enacted the Emancipation Proclamation, Emily Tubman declared freedom for 145 people. Emily, reported to be a "true student of the Bible," acted in accordance with biblical truth, although it was against the culture of her day. She is a picture of Jesus, who, the psalmist declared, "led a crowd of captives" (Psalm 68:18). The scripture is talking about the captivity of sin, which Christ defeated. When you acknowledge your sin and accept the covering of His blood, Christ liberates you from its bondage.

Every "slave" set free from sin's chains can shout, "Thanks be to God for His gift of freedom—Jesus!"

Wilhelmina
Queen of the Netherlands
1880–1962

> "Yet you have a few people in Sardis who have not soiled their clothes.
> They will walk with me, dressed in white. . . .
> The one who is victorious will, like them, be dressed in white."
>
> REVELATION 3:4–5 NIV

It was an unusual funeral when the mourners at Queen Wilhelmina's burial did not wear the customary black, but white garments as she had requested before her death. The music, too, was different for a state funeral when the rousing gospel hymn, "There Is Sunshine in My Soul Today," was sung.

In 1940, the Germans invaded the Netherlands and attempted to capture Queen Wilhelmina. She was able to escape to London, where she directed her armed forces in Germany and Japan. When the war ended, her people joyfully welcomed her home, and she ruled the Dutch people until her death.

To be "dressed in white," speaks of the purity of one who has washed his garments in the blood of the Lamb. It also depicts the faith of the wearer; in face of grave danger that person remained faithful. This was true of Queen Wilhelmina. When her dying requests were honored, the watching world knew she had died a Christian.

You may not have to say a word to your friends and family about your faith in Christ. Simply wear your "white garments"—a clean life—and they will know you walk with the Holy Son of God.

Maggie Van Cott
Evangelist
1830–1905

"The LORD bless you and keep you; the LORD make his face shine on you and
be gracious to you; the LORD turn his face toward you and give you peace."
NUMBERS 6:24–26 NIV

Maggie Van Cott began her ministry leading prayer meetings and
distributing tracts. But eventually word spread of her preaching
ability. Although reluctant to enter a field dominated by men, she
applied for an Exhorter's License in 1868 and became the first
woman licensed in the United States Methodist Episcopal Church.
Later when a critic questioned her right to preach, Maggie said,
"God allows it. I received my commission from Him, brother."

When Maggie conducted meetings at a women's college in
Evanston, Illinois, Frances Willard, the college president, described
how, at one point in the services, Maggie placed her hands upon each
girl and asked the Lord's blessing upon her life. This simple act of
faith resulted in a remarkable move of God upon the students.

In 1873, Maggie reported to church officials that in a five-
week meeting four hundred souls were saved. She remained on the
"sawdust trail" for thirty years, blessing her hearers with the preached
Word. On her seventy-fifth birthday, she announced she would soon
begin revival meetings in Iowa.

Maggie Van Cott recognized the power of the blessing. When
you ask God to bless people, His favor, protection, and peace flows
in their direction. To enrich the lives of your family and friends, use
His divine blessing often.

Irene Webster-Smith

Missionary
20th Century

> If we confess our sins, he is faithful and just and will forgive
> us our sins and purify us from all unrighteousness.
> 1 John 1:9 niv

Before Japanese war criminals were to be executed following World War II, the wife of one of the prisoners was converted to Christ and begged missionary Irene Webster-Smith to visit her doomed husband. Irene received clearance and met with Nishizawa San.

"I've committed terrible sins," he said. "How do I get forgiveness?"

Irene quoted Bible verses, prayed with Nishizawa San, and he accepted Christ's forgiveness. Then she told him, "I want you to find one person in prison and tell him what the Lord has done for you." In spite of being in solitary confinement, he managed to share his testimony with another prisoner.

A week later, Irene received a call from general headquarters. A prisoner named Shibano requested a visit from her. One by one prisoners accepted Jesus and passed the word on. In all, Irene helped fourteen war criminals receive Christ's forgiveness.

She received a report of two of the men's deaths: "Their Testaments clasped in their manacled hand, they were singing, 'Nearer, My God, to Thee.'"

How do you deal with the sin in your life? Jesus' death on the cross paid the penalty for every sin you will ever commit. When you honestly admit your sins to Him, He forgives them and wipes your slate clean.

Florence Young
Missionary, Teacher
Late 19th Century

> "Who knows but that you have come to
> your royal position for such a time as this?"
> ESTHER 4:14 NIV

Blackbirding! What is it? In search of easy money, unscrupulous men came to the Pacific Islands in the late 1800s and bribed native men and boys to work on sugar cane plantations. What the innocent were not told was that they would work ten to twelve hours a day in the scorching sun, receive cruel treatment, and probably not survive to see their native island again.

When Florence Young visited her brothers' sugar cane plantation in Queensland, she became aware of this form of slavery. A Christian and a Bible student, she determined to take the gospel to the enslaved workers.

With ten pupils, Florence held her first class in 1882. Soon she had eighty attendees. Even after working long hours in the blazing sun, the men came to her Sunday and evening classes.

She branched out to other plantations and enlisted help from men missionary teachers. By the end of the century, Florence had found her destiny in bringing Christ to the forsaken sugar cane workers, and thousands of them found the Savior through her Bible classes.

Do you see a situation that needs changing? Kindly, gently, like Florence Young, do what you can to find a remedy. God may have raised you up for just this task.

Amanda Smith
Preacher, Revivalist, Musician
1837–1915

Everyone who wants to live a godly life in
Christ Jesus will be persecuted.
2 TIMOTHY 3:12 NIV

Amanda Smith was born to slave parents. Her only leisure activity growing up was attending "red hot" revival meetings. She was greatly influenced by a godly mother and grandmother. In spite of the drudgery of slave life, both women enjoyed an exuberant faith, and shared it with the people in the "big house."

As an adult, Amanda felt a strong call to preach the gospel. She traveled north and south in post-Civil War America, preaching to all races. She also spent fourteen years in England, India, and Africa conducting revival meetings.

But opposition was a constant issue for this black woman preacher. In her church, officials kept their distance, fearing Amanda would seek to be an ordained minister. Unconcerned, she said, "I received my ordination from Him." Often when people realized she was a former slave with only three and a half months of education, they wouldn't listen to her.

While she was in England, religious groups put articles in the newspapers defaming women preachers. Amanda wisely avoided arguments.

It will happen: because of your circumspect living, you'll become the object of criticism, rude remarks, and threats. However, don't worry; you are in good company. Many great Christians throughout the centuries have been misunderstood and persecuted—even our Lord.

Laura Ingalls Wilder

Author
1867–1957

All Scripture is given by inspiration of God, and is profitable for doctrine, for reproof, for correction, for instruction in righteousness, that the man of God may be complete, thoroughly equipped for every good work.
2 TIMOTHY 3:16–17 NKJV

As a child, Laura Ingalls memorized more than one hundred Bible verses to win a competition in church. These and other scriptures became the stabilizing force in her life for the years ahead.

To supplement her family's scant income, Laura, at age twelve, took a job caring for a sick neighbor. Away from home for the first time, Laura became homesick. Encouraged by scripture to bring every need to God, she prayed and felt "a hovering Presence, a Power comforting and sustaining me."

Laura also needed comfort from God's Word when her sister Mary lost her eyesight. She leaned on Bible promises when her family moved seven times in ten years. She required divine wisdom when she took her first teaching job at age fifteen. Later came the loss of a child and a home destroyed by fire. In 1911, at age forty-four, she leaned on God's Word as she began writing for publication. The scripture verses learned as a child profited Laura her entire life.

God never intended for you to face the unknown future without help. He has given the Bible for your profit. It is not too late to begin hiding scripture verses in your heart. In the years ahead, you, too, will need the comfort and help God's Word offers.

Sojourner Truth
Evangelist
Late 18th–Late 19th Century

> "These commandments that I give you today are to be on your hearts. Impress them on your children. Talk about them when you sit at home and when you walk along the road, when you lie down and when you get up."
>
> DEUTERONOMY 6:6–7 NIV

Mau Mau Bett, an illiterate slave, worked long and hard, yet she found time to teach her children about God. Isabella, her young daughter, often slipped away to an alcove of willow branches where she called out to God. Little did Mau Mau know how important her teachings would be to the girl in the future.

When only a child, Isabella was sold on the auction block several times. One owner promised to free her, but later he refused to honor his word, and she had to work another two years for her freedom.

In 1843, Isabella, now free, received a command from God to preach. She changed her name to Sojourner Truth and, in spite of not being able to read, she fearlessly preached a message of love and tolerance. Later, she worked to abolish slavery, and after the Civil War she helped ex-slaves find jobs and homes. It began when a slave mother taught her child simple truths about God.

Do you want your children to make God-honoring decisions? This will happen when you teach them basic Bible truths, take them to a house of worship, and live the Christian life before them. God's promise stands; this child will not depart from faith in Christ.

Harriet Tubman
Emancipator
Early 19th–Early 20th Century

Christ redeemed us from the curse of the law by becoming a curse for us,
for it is written: "Cursed is everyone who is hung on a pole."
GALATIANS 3:13 NIV

Around 1849, Harriet Tubman, a slave in Maryland, heard rumors that she might be wrenched from her family and sold at auction. Rather than suffer this fate, she escaped to Philadelphia and freedom. Not content to be free herself, in the next ten years she made approximately nineteen trips south to lead slaves to freedom through the Underground Railroad. She evaded bloodhounds, endured beatings, and outsmarted slave catchers, and despite a forty-thousand-dollar reward offered for her capture, she managed to free three hundred slaves, including her aged parents.

There is a bondage worse than slavery: sin. The consequence of this enslavement is eternal separation from God. However, there's no need for anyone to remain under this yoke. So we wouldn't have to bear our own punishment, Jesus took the curse of sin upon Himself on the cross.

Harriet Tubman escaped slavery. You can escape sin's bondage. Accept God's rescue plan—Jesus' death on the cross—and you'll indeed be free!

Hannah Whitall Smith

Author
1832–1911

A person is not justified by the work of the law, but by faith in Jesus Christ.
So we, too, have put our faith in Christ Jesus that
we may be justified by faith in Christ.
GALATIANS 2:16 NIV

One day Hannah Whitall Smith, a young Quaker woman, made an astounding discovery while she studied the scriptures: Christ was her salvation! He bore her sins on the cross. Wearing dreary clothes did not declare her right before God. She was not in better standing with God because she did not wear jewelry. Nor did struggling to improve her conduct justify her. The redemption of her soul was a free gift from God. For Hannah, the discovery was similar to stepping from a shadow into brilliant sunlight.

In the fall of 1858, any person who happened to come to her door met a zealous Hannah, eager to share her newfound faith. Neither could she get enough of Bible reading as each page glowed with golden truth.

No good deed, no church, no ritual will justify you before God. Jesus' life given on the cross is God's provision for your sinful nature. Have you, with Hannah, made this freeing discovery?

Catherine Booth
Cofounder of the Salvation Army, Author
1829–1890

> We have been made a spectacle to the whole universe,
> to angels as well as to human beings. We are fools for Christ.
> 1 CORINTHIANS 4:9–10 NIV

Catherine Booth rose from her seat in London's crowded Bethesda Chapel on Pentecost Sunday in 1860 and walked to the pulpit where her husband stood. "William," she said, to her husband's surprise, "I want to say a word."

Catherine, a small, gentle woman, continued, "I have never been willing to be a fool for Christ. Now I will be one." She confessed that although she had proclaimed a woman's right to preach, she had not been willing to be a preacher of the gospel. In Victorian England, where women rarely raised their voices in public, much less preached in church, Catherine soon changed that tradition. Her fame and popularity as an evangelist endured for thirty years and forever altered women's roles in ministry—all because she was willing to obey Christ, regardless how foolish it seemed to her or others.

Being a fool for Christ means you will be honest when others at your workplace dilute truth. It may mean you stand alone on social issues, and when others belittle evil, you will speak against it. Like Catherine Booth, commit to being Christ's "fool."

Betsie ten Boom

Watchmaker
1884–1944

> Listen! It's the voice of someone shouting, "Clear the way through
> the wilderness for the LORD! Make a straight highway
> through the wasteland for our God!"
>
> ISAIAH 40:3 NLT

"Corrie, we are in hell," Betsie ten Boom whispered to her sister when they arrived in the Nazi prison at Ravensbruck in 1944.

Betsie and Corrie, together with their father, had been committed to helping the Jews, victims of Hitler's annihilation plan during World War II. The sisters were arrested and placed in prison. Their aged father died soon after his imprisonment.

Malnourished and weak from disease, Betsie died before she and her sister were liberated. However, before her passing, she told Corrie, "We must tell them that there is no pit so deep that He is not deeper still. They will listen to us, Corrie, because we have been here."

All women Corrie's age were scheduled to be exterminated, but through a clerical error, she was liberated. When she returned to her home in the Netherlands, Betsie's words to "tell them" gave direction to Corrie and prepared her for what lay ahead. Later, doors opened for her to travel to sixty-one countries with the news of the all-sufficient Christ.

As Betsie inspired Corrie to tell people of Jesus, so can you, with a few simple words, remove obstacles from people's paths and help them through a desert of suffering to do the greater, higher, and better things God has planned for them.

Lillian Trasher
Missionary
1887–1965

> Now all glory to God, who is able, through his mighty power at work within us, to accomplish infinitely more than we might ask or think.
> EPHESIANS 3:20 NLT

As a young woman growing up in Florida, Lillian Trasher dreamed of marrying and having children. The dream was about to come true when she became engaged to a minister. Two weeks before their wedding, Lillian attended a missions service and became convinced God wanted her to be a missionary instead. She broke her engagement and in two weeks' time—without financial help or the support of a mission board—she was on her way to Egypt.

One day shortly after Lillian arrived in Egypt, she brought an infant home. When fellow missionaries told her to take the child back, Lillian said she couldn't because the mother had died. Instead, she rented a house and began an orphanage.

Fifty years after dreaming of having her own family, Lillian could look out the orphanage window and see twelve hundred of her "children" being fed, clothed, and taught the Good News of Jesus.

You can dream big, but God's dreams for you are even bigger. Be open to the larger picture. Through your prayers and deeds, He wants to do things beyond your wildest dream; deeds that benefit multitudes of people and enlarge His kingdom.

Mary Unwin

Encourager
18th Century

> They sent Barnabas to Antioch. . .he was filled with joy,
> and he encouraged the believers to stay true to the Lord.
> ACTS 11:22–23 NLT

History books barely mention her. Men don't applaud her. She passed through life virtually unnoticed. Yet Mary Unwin's talent for encouraging others played an important role in the writing of several great hymns.

William Cowper, described as a shy, fragile man, suffered from depression. He spent time in a mental institution. At times he was suicidal. In an effort to help the young man, Mary invited him to stay with her and her family for two weeks. William's stay extended to twenty-two years.

To help him overcome depression, Mary urged William to write poetry. He admitted that writing helped him be "merry." William became merry enough to write hymns such as "There Is a Fountain Filled with Blood" and "Oh, for a Closer Walk with God."

In all, William blessed the church with sixty-eight hymns. It never would have happened without the encouragement he received from Mary. William paid tribute to her when he wrote, "She is the chief of blessings I have met within my journey, since the Lord was pleased to call me."

Barnabas had the ability to encourage New Testament believers, and the early church used him when believers needed a spiritual lift. People in your home, church, and workplace also suffer varying degrees of discouragement. Cultivate this most important gift and use it to lift heavy hearts. Be a Barnabas or a Mary Unwin.

Anna Skau
Missionary Nurse
20th Century

> Because of my imprisonment, most of the believers here have gained confidence and boldly speak God's message without fear.
>
> PHILIPPIANS 1:14 NLT

Norwegian-born Anna Skau, a missionary nurse, went to China in 1938. When the Communists took over China in 1949, she didn't know if she should leave the country or stay. Chinese Christians said if she didn't stay, it would appear that she wasn't meant to be a witness for Christ. "So I stayed," Anna said. As a result, she was jailed for nine days on one occasion and for a week another time.

"The Lord gave me peace of heart," Anna said of her time in jail. "I'm not one to be calling out Hallelujah, but that first night I praised God the whole night through."

"What are you talking about in there?" a guard had asked.

"I am praising the Lord, my God," she said.

He replied, "He must be a poor God if He puts you in prison."

"No," Anna said. "I know He has put me here because He means me to do something, and I am happy."

Then the miracle happened: Christians heard Anna was in prison and risked their lives to help her. They started meeting for worship, and they, too, were arrested. Yet they kept gathering.

More important than what happens to you is how you react to the circumstances. While in prison, the apostle Paul remained thankful and optimistic. His attitude spoke volumes of sermons. Look at your troubles from God's perspective. No doubt He means to do something good in them through you.

Mary Slessor
Missionary
1848–1915

> I look up to the mountains—does my help come from there?
> My help comes from the LORD, who made heaven and earth.
> PSALM 121:1–2 NLT

Mary Slessor grew up in the slums of Dundee, Scotland. She was poorly educated, a mill girl working twelve hours a day in a factory. How could she ever hope to become a missionary? Yet this was her dream. She told no one her desire, but waited for the right time.

In 1874 news came of the death of famous missionary-explorer David Livingstone, and waves of missionary fervor swept over Great Britain. The call went out for workers.

Mary, at age twenty-seven, assessed her situation. She had been the sole support of her family. Now her sisters were older and independent. She applied for an appointment to Calabar in Africa, and in August 1876 said a tearful good-bye to family and friends. Her dream had become a reality.

What dream has God given you? His dreams are as varied as the people He has created. God's work, too, requires workers of different skills and temperaments. Not everyone is called to Calabar; people near you need support, teaching, and prayer. Reality sees the need, but faith sees Christ's great power available to help you to grasp hold of your dream.

Mary Custis Lee
Wife of General Robert E. Lee
1808–1873

> How do you know, wife, whether you will save your husband?
> Or, how do you know, husband, whether you will save your wife?
> 1 CORINTHIANS 7:16 NIV

Young Mary Custis, great-granddaughter of Martha Washington, read Latin and Greek. She could discuss politics intelligently with any man. Also an attractive woman, she was courted by eligible bachelors, but it was her distant cousin, Robert E. Lee, who won her heart. They were married in 1831.

Shortly before their wedding, Mary had placed her faith in Christ and said, "I was made to feel willing to give up all for God, even my life if God should require it." Concerned for her husband's spiritual condition, Mary prayed for Robert, and her prayers were answered one Sunday when he accepted Christ after hearing a sermon.

At the onset of the Civil War, Mary, confined to a wheelchair because of arthritis, saw her husband and two sons off to battle. On the couple's wedding anniversary, Robert, in the throes of war, wrote his wife, "Do you recollect what a happy day 33 years ago this was. . . ? I pray He may continue His mercies and blessings on us, and give us a little peace."

Mary Lee's prayers and consecrated life helped bring her husband to faith in Jesus. If your spouse is not a Christian, use these same powerful means to help move your unsaved husband toward Christ's great salvation.

Jemima Luke
Christian Worker, Hymn Writer
1813–1906

> Whatever your hand finds to do, do it with all your might,
> for in the realm of the dead, where you are going, there is neither
> working nor planning nor knowledge nor wisdom.
> ECCLESIASTES 9:10 NIV

Jemima Luke had a passion for missions and was accepted to go as a missionary to India. However, poor health hindered her from going. Rather than grieve over lost dreams, she followed her strong desire to serve God, which propelled her into other avenues of ministry.

Jemima taught a Sunday school class, helped provide housing for poor ministers, wrote books, and published a children's hymn, "I Think, When I Read That Sweet Story of Old." She taught the song to her Sunday school class. Later, it appeared in a religious magazine and from there it passed to the world. With this one song Jemima indeed become a missionary! Her zeal for missions is reflected in the last stanza of her hymn:

> *But thousands and thousands who wander and fall,*
> *Never heard of that heavenly home;*
> *I wish they could know there is room for them all,*
> *And that Jesus has bid them to come.*

You, too, may have aspired to do a great work for God, but the dream has not become reality. Open your eyes, look around. Sunday school classes need teachers, shut-ins need visits, sick people need prayer, the grieving need comfort. All opportunities aren't an ocean away. Jemima found open doors for missionary service in her own city, and so can you.

Gertrude Chambers
Wife, Writer
1883–1966

"God opposes the proud but favors the humble."
So humble yourselves before God.
JAMES 4:6–7 NLT

Gertrude Chambers became a widow at age thirty-four when her husband, the renowned author, preacher, and teacher, Oswald Chambers, died. Biddy, as her husband had called her, and her four-year-old daughter were left with no financial support.

However, she had the notes of her husband's sermons. In their seven years of marriage, Biddy had taken shorthand notes as Oswald preached. Would death forever silence his voice? Not if she could help it.

With her daughter, Biddy moved to England, where she operated a boardinghouse. In her spare time she transcribed Oswald's sermons and Bible studies. When a publisher expressed an interest in a collection of daily readings from Oswald's talks, she faced the momentous task of writing 365 devotionals, each with a single theme. In 1927, after three years of work, *My Utmost for His Highest* was published. Nowhere in the book does Biddy mention her part in producing the work. Only the initials "B. C." appear in the text.

Biddy Chambers is best described as a humble servant. Servanthood is the road of choice for every believer. As our example, Jesus washed disciples' feet, touched outcasts, and ate with despised tax collectors. When you choose to follow the carpenter from Nazareth you, too, are willing to serve without recognition so He alone receives the praise.

Mrs. Crosby
Fanny Crosby's Grandmother
Early 19th Century

I am reminded of your sincere faith, which first lived
in your grandmother Lois and in your mother Eunice and,
I am persuaded, now lives in you also.
2 TIMOTHY 1:5 NIV

"I will be her eyes," the grandmother said when she learned that Fanny, her six-month-old granddaughter, was permanently blind.

As Fanny grew, her grandmother patiently matched descriptions of songbirds to the calls of the blue jay, crow, robin, and starling. Lovingly the older woman explained the color of flowers, the beauty of a tree, and the sky at sunset. She taught the blind girl to sew and knit. Soon, because of her grandmother's patient teaching, Fanny could "see."

She also taught Fanny the Bible until she could repeat from memory the first five books, most of the poetic books, and the four Gospels. Later, Fanny said, "It was my grandmother who brought the Bible to me, and me to the Bible." She would draw on this knowledge when, as an adult, she wrote more than seven thousand hymns, making Fanny Crosby the most prolific hymn writer of all time.

Grandmothers wield a powerful influence in the lives of their grandchildren. If miles separate you and your grandchildren, keep in touch with them by sending cards and gifts. If they live nearby, give them the gift of your time. Whether near or far, by your example, let your grandchildren know you are a woman of faith.

Clarissa Danforth

Preacher

1792–1851

> Christ's love controls us. Since we believe that Christ died for all,
> we also believe that we have all died to our old life.
>
> 2 CORINTHIANS 5:14 NLT

Why would an early nineteenth-century woman choose to become a preacher, a field dominated by men and having little financial return? Yet women kept appearing in pulpits of that era.

Clarissa Danforth was described as "the sensation preacher of this decade." When she held meetings in Vermont in 1814, it was reported, "Every church was visited in mercy and large accessions were made."

She preached in Rhode Island and congregations packed churches to the rafters. After the meetings, the revival continued and several new churches began as a result. Clarissa also preached in Wethersfield, Vermont, her hometown, where more than one hundred people were reported converted.

No doubt Clarissa was called by God and gifted as a preacher. But it was more than that: The love of God in her heart propelled her to use her gift to reach out to the lost.

Not every woman has the talent to preach, but every Christian woman can express Jesus' love in new, exciting ways. Here are some suggestions: pray for the sick, teach children, be a patient mother, an understanding wife, or an uncomplaining employee. Can you think of other ways Jesus may want to show His love through you?

Charlotte Elliott

Hymn Writer
1789–1871

"Here I am! I stand at the door and knock. If anyone hears my voice and opens the door, I will come in and eat with that person, and they with me."
REVELATION 3:20 NIV

"Are you a Christian?" the minister asked Charlotte Elliott.

"I do not wish to discuss religion," she answered defiantly.

The minister explained that he asked only because she seemed so unhappy.

Charlotte could not get the minister's words out of her mind. She had been raised in a Christian home; her father and grandfather were preachers. But she had never been born again. Besides, she was depressed because of poor health.

One day, feeling better, Charlotte went to the minister. "I want to be saved," she said, "but I don't know how."

"Come to Him just as you are," he said. These words were enough, and Charlotte came to Jesus. Sadly, her health did not improve and, feeling she could do little to serve God with a burdened heart, she wrote:

Just as I am, without one plea,
But that Thy blood was shed for me,
And that Thou bidd'st me come to Thee,
O Lamb of God, I come, I come.

Perhaps you, like Charlotte, need Christ's redeeming power. No need to clean up your life. Come as you are. With one simple prayer, Jesus' blood will cleanse your heart, and He will take up residence within.

Angelina Grimke
Author
1805–1879

Sarah Moore Grimke
Author
1792–1873

> Don't just pretend to love others. Really love them.
> Hate what is wrong. Hold tightly to what is good.
> ROMANS 12:9 NLT

Angelina and Sarah were born into a wealthy South Carolina slaveholder's family. The sisters, devout Christians, accepted slavery as the norm, but in 1819 Sarah accompanied her father to Philadelphia and came in contact with the Quakers. For the first time, she heard someone speak against the slave system. When she returned home, she began a Sunday school class for slaves and, although it was against the law, she taught them to read.

Angelina wrote in her diary, "That system must be radically wrong which can only be supported by transgressing the laws of God." When the sisters took an open stand against slavery, they were ostracized by family and friends.

After their father's death, Sarah and Angelina's mother gave them their share of the family estate, and they immediately freed their slaves. When the sisters discovered their brother had fathered two sons by a slave, they took the boys into their home.

It took great courage for the Grimke sisters to stand against the evil of slavery. It will also take a lot of courage for you to stand for right when it is not popular to do so. You may be criticized and shunned. Stand for just causes, and justice will eventually prevail.

Elizabeth Clephane
Hymn Writer
1830–1869

"And if you give even a cup of cold water to one of the least of my followers, you will surely be rewarded."
MATTHEW 10:42 NLT

Elizabeth Clephane died at age thirty-nine. Five years later, one of her poems appeared in a Glasgow newspaper. Ira Sankey, song leader for evangelist D. L. Moody, saw the poem and tried to interest Moody in the verses, but the evangelist was busy that day. Sankey then tore the poem from the paper and thrust it into his pocket.

The next day, after preaching to a large crowd, evangelist Horatius Bonar asked Mr. Sankey to sing an appropriate hymn. An inner voice told him to sing the verses he had found in the newspaper.

Sankey pulled out the scrap of paper with Elizabeth Clephane's poem, "The Ninety and Nine," struck a key on the organ, and began to sing. Note by note, the music and words flowed together. To this day not one note of the song has been changed.

Elizabeth also wrote "Beneath the Cross of Jesus." She never lived to hear either of her hymns sung, yet her songs have blessed millions for years.

Is it possible a letter you wrote, a good word you said, or a kind deed you did will be recalled after your passing and help the recipient? The smallest kindness is never forgotten by God and will receive a reward.

Mary Livingstone
Missionary
1820–1862

"Be faithful, even to the point of death,
and I will give you life as your victor's crown."
REVELATION 2:10 NIV

Mary Moffat was twenty-three when she met famous missionary-explorer David Livingstone. This refined, proper young woman, in her Victorian-style dress, cared for him through an illness, and when Livingstone proposed marriage in 1845, Mary accepted.

Mary's life in Africa was like that of a pioneer woman. She faced sickness, constant work, perilous travel, death of her children, and threats from natives and wild animals. More than once she was left temporarily paralyzed, possibly from insect bites. On another occasion, when Mary, her husband, and their children set out in ox-drawn carts for remote parts of Africa, David wrote, "It is a venture to take wife and children into a country where African fever prevails . . .may He bless us and make us blessings even unto death."

Exhausted from the rigors of missionary life and frequent pregnancies, at one time Mary and her six children returned to England so she could regain her health. The family was said to have lived those four years in abject poverty. Though her husband showed love and concern for the family, he was seldom with them.

Mary Livingstone received few "crowns" in this life, but that will be remedied in heaven. If you or someone you know have been faithful, but received little in return, be encouraged: God keeps records. A crowning day is coming.

Marian Anderson
Musician
1902–1993

"Blessed are you when people insult you, persecute you
and falsely say all kinds of evil against you because of me."
MATTHEW 5:11 NIV

Marian Anderson was said to have a singing voice that occurs once in a century, yet she had much to overcome to use her talent. Her parents were unable to afford voice lessons, so Marian's Philadelphia church raised money for her training. When she applied for entrance to music school, she was refused because of her race. Later, when she was chosen over three hundred vocalists in a competition to sing with the New York Philharmonic Orchestra, newspapers said, "She has a beautiful voice. Too bad she's a Negro."

In spite of negative comments and situations, Marian never abandoned the Christian principles she'd been taught. Her mother once told her, "When a door closes, God will work something out." And He did. Though restricted from performing in some of America's largest music halls because of her race, Marian never complained. "The Lord isn't prejudiced," she said. "He gave this gift to a Negro."

When she appeared before Joseph Stalin in the USSR, she was told not to sing anything religious. Nevertheless, when she sang about heaven and "crossing Jordan," the crowd responded with thunderous applause.

In the face of injustice, we're tempted to retaliate. However, that is not God's way. If you are experiencing offenses, conquer injustice the way Christ did: "Jesus remained silent" (Matthew 27:12 NLT). Then turn around and do a kind deed for your offender.

Amy Semple McPherson
Evangelist, Missionary, Author
1890–1944

> But what does it matter? The important thing is that in every way. . .
> Christ is preached. And because of this I rejoice.
> PHILIPPIANS 1:18 NIV

The music was upbeat, her illustrated sermons dramatic, when young Amy McPherson preached to the crowds that thronged Angelus Temple in Los Angeles, California.

A few years earlier, Amy and Robert Semple had gone to China as missionaries. Soon after arriving on the field they became ill, and in 1910 Robert died. Amy and her infant daughter returned to the United States and, with her mother, Amy began traveling across the country in her "gospel car"—a vehicle decorated with scripture verses and religious slogans—conducting revival meetings.

In 1922 Amy moved to Los Angeles and began preaching. Soon the crowds numbered in the thousands. Her message: Christ is Savior, healer, baptizer in the Holy Spirit, and soon-coming King. She was also the first woman to broadcast sermons on the radio.

Unlike most preachers of that era, Amy's ministry was sensational and often the subject of controversy. Yet, she was a humble, willing servant of God. She said, "It isn't how important you are and what great knowledge you have—it's a willingness to do it. To let God fill your life."

Amy's unique ministry is proof that God can use a variety of talents and methods to convey the gospel. The apostle Paul reminds us, "What does it matter as long as Christ is proclaimed?"

Mary Smith Moffat

Missionary

1795–1870

> Greet Priscilla and Aquila, my co-workers in Christ Jesus.
> They risked their lives for me. Not only I but all the churches
> of the Gentiles are grateful to them.
> ROMANS 16:3–4 NIV

An excited young lady, Mary Smith, sailed for South Africa in 1819 to marry missionary Robert Moffat. For fifty years the two worked together to establish a successful mission.

Mary taught school, washed clothes in a river, and gave birth to ten children in the most primitive conditions. When three native children were to be buried alive with their dead mother, Mary rescued the children and adopted them.

There were discouraging times. Mary wrote, "Could we but see the smallest fruit, we could rejoice midst the privations and toils we bear. But as it is, our hands do often hang down."

To her credit, Mary was able to maintain a stable home in an unstable situation. Five of her children went on to serve as missionaries in Africa.

Shortly after the Moffats retired to England in 1870, Mary died. Her husband paid tribute to her when he said, "For fifty-three years I have had her to pray for me."

Romans 16 lists the names of thirty-eight people who helped Paul in his missionary work. He expresses appreciation for their commitment to the job. Mary Moffat's name could be added to the record. As you are faithful, your name, too, will appear on the list of those who committed to God's work and stuck with it to the end.

Anne Bradstreet
Poet
1612–1672

> Then he [Jesus] said to Thomas, "Put your finger here; see my hands.
> Reach out your hand and put it into my side. Stop doubting and believe."
> Thomas said to him, "My Lord and my God!"
> JOHN 20:27–28 NIV

Imagine living in a castle surrounded with manicured gardens, having access to a vast library, then being thrust into a harsh country devoid of these luxuries. That is what happened to Anne Bradstreet when her Puritan father, a business manager for an English nobleman, sought religious freedom in the New World.

In Massachusetts Bay Colony, Anne gave birth to eight children, faced death and illness, and struggled to survive. But perhaps worse were the doubts she experienced. *Is the Bible true?* she wondered. *Did the miracles of scripture really happen? Are the Puritans Christ's true believers?* These questions occupied Anne's mind, and she expressed her thoughts in poetry. When her brother-in-law returned to England, he took her writings with him and, to Anne's surprise, had them published in a book, making her the first American woman to publish a volume of poetry.

Under the circumstances, no one can fault Anne Bradstreet for having doubts. Nor does God condemn anyone struggling with faith issues. If your trust in God wavers at times, share your feelings with Christ. But don't stop there. Let your questions lead you to greater heights of faith.

Evelyne Brand

Missionary
1879–1974

> Be strong in the Lord and in his mighty power.
> EPHESIANS 6:10 NIV

Young Evelyne Harris had strength of character—enough to persuade her wealthy, overprotective father to allow her to go to India as a missionary. In Madras she met missionary Jesse Brand and fell in love with him. However, Jesse was engaged. A brokenhearted Evelyne plunged into language study in an effort to forget him. Later he wrote Evelyne that his engagement was called off. Would she marry him?

As the couple worked in the mountains of India, Hindu priests openly opposed them and, after seven years of labor, the couple had only one convert. A break came when a Hindu priest died and left his children in Evelyne's care. She eventually became mother to several abandoned Indian children.

Most missionaries of that time sent their young children out of the country to be educated. Evelyne, who had strength for most challenges on the mission field, found herself devastated when she waved good-bye to her two children, knowing they would be separated for years. "As I stood watching them," she said, "something just died in me." It was the hardest test she had ever faced.

Perhaps your strength, too, is being stretched to the breaking point. Although we don't seek perplexing situations, this is one way our faith grows. Rather than being a victim of your struggles, plant your feet firmly on a promise of God and stand. Supernatural, divine strength is available for all situations—even those that break your heart.

Helen Duff Baugh
Christian Organizer
1903–1996

They all joined together constantly in prayer, along with the women
and Mary the mother of Jesus, and with his brothers.
ACTS 1:14 NIV

One morning in the 1930s, a young housewife in San Jose, California,
opened her Bible and read the above verse. She thought, "What am I
doing praying alone? I should get others to pray with me."

Helen Baugh called the wife of the city manager, who agreed to
join her. When other women heard of the prayer meeting they, too,
wanted to participate. Soon twenty-four groups met each week for
prayer in the city. From these small prayer groups, big things began
to happen under Helen's leadership.

She invited Christian speakers to address the women, and they
organized as Christian Business and Professional Women's Council.
She also became burdened for people in rural areas and began Village
Missions. Then came Stonecroft Bible Studies and Friendship Bible
Coffees as a means for people to study God's Word. It all began when
two women came together to pray.

You may not be called to begin a worldwide ministry, but
perhaps you need wisdom to deal with a rebellious teen or help for a
troubled marriage. Ask a friend, your spouse, or a child to pray with
you. God promises to move on people and situations when believers
join hands and hearts in prayer.

Amy Carmichael
Missionary, Author
1867–1951

> "Whoever welcomes this little child in my name welcomes me;
> and whoever welcomes me welcomes the one who sent me.
> For it is the one who is least among you all who is the greatest."
> LUKE 9:48 NIV

Amy Carmichael made a horrifying discovery when she went as a missionary to India in 1896. Young Indian girls were being taken into pagan temples, married to the gods, and made available for evil practices.

When a girl named Preena fled from a temple, her hands branded because of previous escapes, she came to the missionary. From then on, the rescue of children from prostitution became Amy's life work.

Not everyone was happy with her rescue efforts. Amy was dragged into court, charged with kidnapping, and her life threatened. She persevered until, twelve years after taking in Preena, her mission sheltered 130 girls.

Children are often the target of men's wicked schemes. Follow Amy's example: pray for children, support ministries that reach out to them, volunteer to help in your church's nursery, or be a classroom helper. Give attention to a child and you welcome Jesus. That makes you the greatest in His kingdom!

Katherine Lee Bates

Hymn Writer

1859–1929

> In the beginning God created the heaven and the earth. . . And God said,
> Let there be light: and there was light. And God saw the light, that it was good.
> GENESIS 1:1, 3–4 KJV

After watching the sun rise on Pikes Peak during a vacation in
Colorado in 1893, Katherine Bates and her friends spent the evening
talking about the beauty of the American landscape. That night
Katherine couldn't sleep. Instead, she felt compelled to write words
describing what she had seen on the mountain.

> *O beautiful for spacious skies, for amber waves of grain,*
> *For purple mountain majesties above the fruited plain!*
> *America! America! God shed His grace on Thee,*
> *And crown thy good with brotherhood from sea to shining sea!*

Katherine put the poem in a notebook, where it stayed for two
years. In 1895 she sent it to a Boston publisher. When "America, the
Beautiful" was published, it immediately captured public attention.
Later, Samuel Ward wrote a melody for the verses.

Katherine saw the goodness of God in His creation. His goodness
can also be seen in the plan of salvation He has made available in
Christ. And His goodness doesn't stop there; He also has a good plan
for every person's life. Sin may have thwarted the plan, but through
Jesus you can rediscover God's goodness. Declare with the psalmist,
"Surely goodness and mercy shall follow me all the days of my life"
(Psalm 23:6 KJV).

Bertha Smith
Missionary
1888–1988

God is our refuge and strength, an ever-present help in trouble.
Therefore we will not fear, though the earth give way
and the mountains fall into the heart of the sea.
PSALM 46:1–2 NIV

It was a hectic time for missionary Bertha Smith when the Japanese invaded China in 1938, and people flocked inside the Tsinging mission for safety.

Planes roared overhead, falling bombs shook the earth, and the Japanese army closed in, but Bertha was not afraid. She said of that time, "Anything touching me would have to pass by God, the Father. Then it would have to get by Jesus Christ, the Son, before it could reach me and if it did, there would be the Lord inside me. There will be no problem."

After the raid, dust lay thick inside the mission, but no one was hurt, and God's supernatural strength sustained Bertha during the havoc.

What if I'm in an accident? What if I'm diagnosed with cancer? Does fear of what can happen sometimes overwhelm you? The psalmist, too, fancied the worst—mountains falling into the sea and the earth caving in. God doesn't want you to suffer from fear of disaster. Get a grip on your fears with God's promises. Say with Bertha Smith, "Nothing can touch me except it first pass through the Father, Son, and Holy Spirit." For real or imagined fear, God is your safe hiding place.

Mary C. Crowley
Christian Entrepreneur
1915–1986

> Yet in all these things we are more than
> conquerors through Him who loved us.
>
> ROMANS 8:37 NKJV

Mary Crowley, founder of Home Interiors and Gifts, said: "When I realized what it cost Him to redeem me, then I fully realized my worth." And there were reasons why she needed her self-worth restored.

Mary's mother died when she was eighteen months old. She was shuffled from her father's care to her grandparents' home. At age fifteen Mary learned about a personal God and committed her life to Him. Yet the road ahead was rocky. She married in her teens, then divorced and later weathered a bout with cancer. As a single parent with two children, she lost her job.

A discouraged adult with low self-esteem, Mary knew what to do; she consulted a pastor, took night classes, and eventually turned her life around.

"Out of disappointment came victory," Mary said. "You never gain by sitting around feeling sorry for yourself. Attitudes are more important than facts." She began Home Interiors and Gifts, Inc., a business to help women use their talents to succeed and develop self-esteem.

Perhaps you, like Mary Crowley, suffer from outward struggles and inner battles. Believers are not only promised victory in the future; we are *more* than conquerors now. In spite of various hardships, by faith, declare your victory in Christ today.

Carolina (Lina) Sandell Berg
Hymn Writer
1832–1903

The LORD is my rock, and my fortress, and my deliverer,
my God, my strength, in whom I will trust.
PSALM 18:2 KJV

When she was twelve, paralysis struck Lina Sandell, leaving her an invalid. One day while the family was at church, she asked God to help her. Slowly she managed to dress herself and, with great effort, took a few steps. From an overflowing heart, Lina expressed her gratitude to the Lord in poetry.

Ten years later Lina and her father were crossing a lake when the boat gave a sudden lurch. As she watched helplessly, her father fell overboard and drowned. In her grief, she learned to depend on the scriptures in a new way. From these experiences, hymns of comfort emerged. Following is a verse of Lina's hymn, "Day by Day."

Day by day and with each passing moment,
strength I find to meet my trials here;
Trusting in my Father's wise bestowment,
I've no cause for worry or for fear.
He whose heart is kind beyond all measure
gives unto each day what He deems best.
Lovingly, its part of pain and pleasure,
mingling toil with peace and rest.

You don't know what the next second will bring you on any given day. Commit your times into the Father's hands. As He gave Lina strength for dark days, He'll give you equal strength for an ordinary day or one that brings tragedy and pain.

Monica
Mother
331–387

> Then Jesus told his disciples a parable to show them
> that they should always pray and not give up.
> LUKE 18:1 NIV

All that is known about Monica is what her son Augustine recorded in his book, *Confessions*. He wrote, "Womanly in her dress but virile in her faith, mature in her serenity, motherly in her love, Christian in her piety."

Monica faithfully taught her young son about Christ and prayed for him. Yet Augustine remained far from God. When he became involved in heresy, Monica prayed on. One day Augustine heard a Voice say, "Take it, read it!" The words were repeated over and over. He took this to mean he should read the book of Romans. When he read Paul's admonition to make no provision for the flesh, Augustine believed, accepted Christ, and his life changed. He went on to become a leader in the early Christian church, and his writings profoundly influenced Protestant reformers.

Prayer is a powerful weapon in the hands of a Christian woman. Yet, the temptation is to give up when the answer isn't quickly realized. Jesus warns us against this pitfall. If you are on the verge of declaring some people or situations hopeless, take courage from Monica. She didn't give up, and God rewarded her persevering prayers with answers that changed not only her son, but through him, the entire world.

Edith Moules

Missionary
1900–1949

"Do not judge others, and you will not be judged. . . . The standard
you use in judging is the standard by which you will be judged."

MATTHEW 7:1–2 NLT

When Edith Moules began her first missionary term in Africa,
she spent two months with missionary C. T. Studd, absorbing his
philosophy of missions and learning more effective ways to reach the
millions on the dark continent.

Studd, a veteran missionary, had grown up in a mansion in
England, but in Africa he lived in a bamboo hut with only a few
books and the barest necessities. People sometimes found fault with
his harsh lifestyle.

When Edith saw the conditions under which Studd lived,
she, too, was tempted to criticize him and declare his dedication
to Christ extreme. One night while kneeling beside her cot, she
realized her focus on people was wrong. Edith made a commitment
to stop criticizing people or, on the other extreme, idolizing certain
personalities. She determined to keep her eyes upon Jesus only.

Edith was not the first woman tempted to have a critical attitude.
If you're not careful, you, too, will fall into the trap of judging
another person's lifestyle or appearance by your puny standards. The
Bible is clear: our role is to show love and compassion. In your home,
workplace, and church keep your eyes on Jesus alone.

Dale Evans Rogers

Actress, Author

1912–2001

I have been crucified with Christ and I no longer live,
but Christ lives in me. The life I now live in the body, I live by faith
in the Son of God, who loved me and gave himself for me.

GALATIANS 2:20 NIV

At the 1952 World Champion Rodeo in New York City, the committee tried to persuade Dale Evans and her husband, Roy Rogers, to drop the religious number at the end of their act. The Rogerses decided to do the closing number anyway, and Dale said, "We have prayed about this, and if we get booed out of the arena, then that will be that."

At the end of their performance that night, the lights were dimmed and a lighted cross shone as Roy counseled children in the audience to go to church and Sunday school. Then he sang, "Peace in the Valley," and Roy's horse, Trigger, knelt at the cross. After the act, the applause was deafening.

Years earlier when Dale Evans had committed her life to Jesus, she said, "My life revolves around a new hub—Christ."

Everyone's life has a focal point, a force that controls all one does. If your pivotal point is money, all your energies will turn on that axis. If it is to promote yourself or your career, you will gravitate in that direction. If family takes most of your time and energy, they will exhaust you. In the end, all of these can disappoint you. However, when the center of your life is Christ, you will never be disappointed.

Rachel Saint
Missionary, Bible Translator
1914–1994

"Love your enemies and pray for those who persecute you,
that you may be children of your Father in heaven."
MATTHEW 5:44–45 NIV

When Rachel Saint went to Peru to work as a Bible translator, her younger brother, Nate, was already a missionary pilot in Ecuador. Rachel felt called to work with tribes unreached by the gospel and transferred to work with the Huaorani Indians, a fierce tribe in Ecuador's jungle. With the help of Dayuma, a Huaorani woman who had left her people during a tribal dispute, Rachel studied the language.

Nate, with four other young missionaries, made contact with the Huaorani, but as a result, in 1956, the five men were killed by the tribal people. Two years later Rachel, with Elisabeth Elliot, whose husband was also killed, met peacefully with the Huaoranis and accepted an invitation to live with them and learn their language. Through their efforts many tribesmen turned to Christ and, nine years after the tragic deaths, the Gospel of Mark was printed in the tribe's language.

Christ's love in Rachel Saint's heart permitted her to bypass revenge, forgive her brother's murderers, and love them. Do you feel negative emotions toward people who have hurt you? Allow Jesus to flood your heart with this same love and you will also love to the uttermost.

Rebecca Lukens
American Industrialist
1794–1854

> Let us hold tightly without wavering to the hope we affirm,
> for God can be trusted to keep his promise.
> HEBREWS 10:23 NLT

It was an unprecedented occurrence in 1825 when a young Quaker woman, Rebecca Lukens, pregnant with her fifth child, became head of a major steel-making industry.

When Rebecca's husband, the owner of a Pennsylvania steel mill, lay dying, he made her promise she would manage the business after his death. Rebecca promised, but when she told the workers, they doubted a housewife with no training in the steel business could do the job. As the men began to look for work in other mills, Rebecca begged them to give her a chance. We can only imagine the struggles that ensued. She not only learned to manage the mill, but in nine years also paid off all debts. Rebecca's Christian faith, combined with prayer, helped her keep her promise.

Not all people are as faithful to keep their promises as Rebecca Lukens. However, One is always faithful; it is God. The Bible contains numerous promises He made to His people; promises to answer prayer, to be with them, to help them, and at the end of life, to receive them into heaven. Read the promises in God's Word. Claim these as your own, and soon your faith will rise to embrace life's greatest challenges—with the help of a promise-keeping God.

Hannah Marshman

Missionary
1767–1847

> We who are strong ought to bear with the failings of the weak and not to please ourselves. Each of us should please our neighbors for their good.
> ROMANS 15:1–2 NIV

India's exhausting climate, difficult living circumstances, and the death of her son took a toll on missionary Dorothy Carey until she became unable to care for herself or her family.

William, her husband, absorbed in translation and evangelistic work, had an easygoing nature that was an asset in the mission, but hindered him from being an effective parent. This is where Hannah Marshman's help became invaluable. She, with her husband, Joshua, joined Carey in 1799.

Hannah said of Carey's lack of firmness in disciplining his sons: "The good man saw and lamented the evil but was too mild to apply an effective remedy." Besides doing translation work, teaching Indian children, and caring for her own family, Hannah took upon herself the rearing of young Felix, William, and Jabez Carey.

If Hannah Marshman's only concern had been her family or ministry, she never would have acted as mother to the Carey children. However, the body of Christ functions for the common good. You may supply a meal for a sick mother, mow the lawn for a widow, or do grocery shopping for a crippled neighbor. When you reach out to supply another person's lack, the entire body of believers benefits.

Cecil Frances Alexander

Hymn Writer, Poet
1818–1895

> "I lay down my life—only to take it up again. No one takes it from me,
> but I lay it down of my own accord."
> JOHN 10:17–18 NIV

Where Cecil Alexander lived in Ireland with her pastor husband, the people were impoverished, education was costly, and most people remained illiterate.

Because Cecil loved children and they loved her, she determined to teach the gospel to poor Irish boys and girls through songs and poems. In five short verses her hymn, "There Is a Green Hill Far Away," successfully describes to a child the plan of salvation.

> *There is a green hill far away,*
> *Outside a city wall,*
> *Where the dear Lord was crucified,*
> *Who died to save us all.*
> *He died that we might be forgiven*
> *He died to make us good,*
> *That we might go at last to heaven,*
> *Saved by His precious blood.*

Because of its beauty and simplicity, this song has been described as a near perfect hymn. When it was sung for England's Queen Victoria, the monarch wept. Cecil wrote nearly four hundred hymns, many of which have been translated into other languages.

Redemption—the theme of Cecil's hymn—involves two elements, a redeemer and a ransom. Jesus willingly went to the cross and paid in full the price for your sins. The truth is so simple even a child can understand and accept it.

Civilla D. Martin
Hymn Writer
1866–1948

"Are not two sparrows sold for a penny? Yet not one of them will fall to the ground outside your Father's care."
MATTHEW 10:29 NIV

"How can you be so joyful?" Civilla Martin asked her friends, Mr. and Mrs. Doolittle. In spite of being confined to wheelchairs, the couple ran a successful business and overflowed with contagious joy and courage. "His eye is on the sparrow and He watches me," Mrs. Doolittle replied matter-of-factly.

Her friend's remark blessed Civilla, and she used it as the theme for the poem, "His Eye Is on the Sparrow." Charles H. Gabriel wrote music for the words, and later Ethel Waters made the song popular when she sang it in the Billy Graham Crusades.

Why should I feel discouraged, why should the shadows come,
Why should my heart be lonely and long for heav'n and home
When Jesus is my portion? My constant friend is He:
His eye is on the sparrow, and I know He watches me.

Sparrows abound and are worth only a few cents each. Yet, if even one falls from his perch, God knows about it. You are of much more value to God than any bird! Your mother and father may have cared little for you. You may be ignored by friends. Even if you *feel* insignificant, your friend Jesus cares and He's watching out for you!

Helen Keller
Advocate for the Disabled
1880–1968

> "Be strong and courageous! Do not be afraid or discouraged.
> For the LORD your God is with you wherever you go."
> JOSHUA 1:9 NLT

At nineteen months of age Helen Keller became ill with a fever that left her blind, deaf, and mute. In her dark, silent world, the child became unmanageable, kicking and clawing at people. Yet her parents knew Helen was a bright child because of the signals she used to communicate with them.

Annie Sullivan was hired to instruct the child. Later, Helen said of Annie's coming, "It was my soul's birthday." Using the girl's only remaining sense, the young teacher taught Helen by touching her palm.

As a result of Annie's efforts, others were also able to help Helen. Pastor Phillips Brooks was one who taught her about God. She remembers sitting on his knee as a little girl while he helped her understand that "God is Love and that His Love is the light of all men."

Helen received godly instruction and encouragement to live a productive life until she could say, "I thank God for my handicaps, for through them I have found myself, my work, and my God."

Like Helen, you may be confronting formidable challenges. Ask your friend Jesus for courage to conquer until you, too, can thank God for these testings. Because of them, not in spite of them, you will live a happy, productive life.

Ann Wilkins
Missionary
1806–1857

> "You have persevered and have endured hardships
> for my name, and have not grown weary."
> REVELATION 2:3 NIV

Despite the toll of lives, most mission boards of the early 1800s had no problem filling the ranks. At a camp meeting in New York, Dr. Nathan Bangs, the secretary of a Methodist mission, was handed a note that read, "A sister. . .is willing to give her life as a female teacher if she is wanted."

Ann Wilkins was wanted! She volunteered in spite of knowing upon his arrival in West Africa in 1833, the first Methodist missionary had died of African fever. Two couples and a single woman were appointed to fill the ranks. One couple died within three months. Broken in health, the other couple returned home. The single missionary endured more than twenty attacks of fever before she also left the field.

Ann, a young widow, described as a "born teacher," sailed for Liberia in 1837. She established a boarding school for girls and started a school for orphans that eventually became Millsburg Female Academy, the first American Methodist school for girls overseas. Twice Ann returned to the United States for health reasons. Despite attacks of malaria, she risked her life and stayed at her post for nineteen years.

The keys to surviving precarious situations are persistence and faith. And Ann Wilkins had plenty of both! Dire situations may also be part of your life, but as you persist, God will use these trials for His glory and the good of many.

Alexandrina Victoria
Queen of England
1819–1901

By me kings reign and rulers issue decrees that are just;
by me princes govern, and nobles—all who rule on earth.
PROVERBS 8:15–16 NIV

Before Victoria was crowned queen of England in 1837, she requested two hours of solitude while she prayed for wisdom and guidance to rule her people.

Was her request granted? During her sixty-four-year reign, England reached its height of power and enjoyed great industrial expansion at home and abroad. In Victoria's era, laws were passed to improve the sordid conditions endured by the laboring class. Education of children became compulsory. Also during her rule, missionary fervor flourished in Great Britain, and missionaries flowed from her shores to all nations. Great religious organizations such as the Salvation Army also came into being in England during this time.

Before Victoria's reign, English monarchs received little respect and were often self-indulgent. This changed with Victoria. Described as humble and honest, she brought dignity to the throne as she helped the poor and exercised her authority for good.

God uses people to govern the nations. Because their responsibility is great, the apostle Paul encourages Christians to pray for all in authority (1 Timothy 2:1–2). As we follow God's admonition, we will come nearer to His design for the nations: that we live quiet, peaceful lives in godliness and holiness.

Mary Kay Ash
Christian Businesswoman
1915–2001

"I have come that they may have life, and have it to the full."
JOHN 10:10 NIV

While growing up in Hot Wells, Texas, Mary Kay was often assured by her mother, "You can do it!" As a result, young Mary Kay developed a "can-do" attitude.

Her mother also taught the Golden Rule, "Do unto others as you would have them do unto you." Later, Mary Kay said of the business enterprise she began, "Every decision we make. . .is based on the Golden Rule."

In 1963 Mary Kay took her life savings of five thousand dollars and, with help from her son, established a cosmetics company. Her motivation for beginning the business was to offer women opportunities to improve their lives and those of their families. Her goal was achieved when *Fortune* magazine named her business one of the ten best companies for women.

But Mary Kay's goals weren't achieved without setbacks and disappointments. She said, "It took God a long time to prepare me for the job He had for me. . .by no stretch of the imagination has my life been an overnight success story."

Because of her Bible-based philosophy—God first, family second, and career third—Mary Kay's life brought her true fulfillment, and her business ventures helped others achieve success.

Assess your life goals. God never intended your life to revolve around only yourself. When God and others become the driving force, you will enjoy the abundant life.

Mary Slessor
Missionary
1848–1915

If any of you lack wisdom, let him ask of God, that giveth to all men liberally, and upbraideth not; and it shall be given him.
JAMES 1:5 KJV

Seated on the ground, her knitting needles clicking, Mary Slessor listened to the arguments of the natives and prayed for wisdom to judge fairly between them.

At Calabar Mission in Nigeria, Africa, where Mary Slessor served as a missionary, the people often asked her to help settle their disputes. This required wisdom, patience, and tact. According to native tradition, when a person died, another person was blamed for his death and required to eat a poison bean. If the person eating the bean lived, he was not guilty of murder. But if he died from the bean, he was guilty. This and other evil practices existed, and Mary attempted to arbitrate between tribes and individuals. Some of the meetings went on for several days. As a result of her wise judgments, many lives were spared.

You, too, need wisdom for life's decisions. The Bible speaks of three kinds of wisdom—human, worldly, and godly. Using human wisdom, your decisions will be based on what you think. If you operate in worldly wisdom, decisions will be influenced by the ideas of men. Godly wisdom comes from God and His Word.

Day by day, for big decisions or those with less serious consequences, ask God for His wisdom. He promises liberal amounts.

Kieko Yammamuro

Christian Worker
1874–1917

> The LORD would speak to Moses face to face,
> as one speaks to a friend.
> EXODUS 33:11 NIV

As she observed Japanese Salvation Army officers helping the poor, Kieko Yammamuro became interested in Christian work. After she joined the Salvation Army, she was made aware of young girls being kidnapped and forced to work as prostitutes.

Through the work of the army, the public was stirred by the need, the government intervened, and more than one thousand girls were rescued. Kieko established and directed Japan's first Salvation Army rescue home for fallen women.

She also felt compassion for victims of tuberculosis and longed to begin a sanatorium for them. Kieko wrote in her diary, "It seems too adventurous perhaps, but God is able. I have no one save the Holy Ghost to rely on. I must go forward. O Lord, fill me with the Holy Ghost!"

Excerpts from her diary like the one above reveal the source of Kieko's compassionate heart: an intimate friendship with Jesus. The Lord of the universe is your friend. There's nothing you can't talk to Him about. Jesus also speaks to you. The hymn writer said it this way, "Oh, what blessed sweet communion! Jesus is a Friend of mine."

Have you talked to your best friend today?

Florence Nightingale
Nurse, Social Reformer
1820–1910

See, the Sovereign LORD comes with power, and he rules with a mighty arm.
See, his reward is with him, and his recompense accompanies him.
ISAIAH 40:10 NIV

During the last forty years of her life, the famous lady of the Crimea, Florence Nightingale, made no public appearances. Yet she continued to command an influence over the progress of nursing, hospital administration, and world health. Her efforts to improve care for the sick, begun when she was a young woman, continued to produce throughout her lifetime. Even now the effects of her work are seen when you step into a clean, well-run hospital.

When you do good works with the right motive, when you give money to godly causes sincerely wanting to help, you are depositing treasure in heaven's bank.

Perhaps sometime during your life you taught a Sunday school class, visited the sick, or gave to the poor. You did it without recognition or hope of reward. Your influence lives on in the lives of those you helped, and your works are not forgotten by God. These deeds are delightful treasures, safely stored in heaven, waiting for you to enjoy.

Isabella Thoburn
Missionary Educator
1840–1901

> "The harvest is great, but the workers are few. So pray to the Lord who is in charge of the harvest; ask him to send more workers into his fields."
> MATTHEW 9:37–38 NLT

When Isabella Thoburn's brother returned after ten years of missionary work, he spoke of the need for women missionaries to teach the women of India. "I do not know of one Indian woman who can read or write," he said. "Yet Hindu men oppose education for their wives and daughters."

This news was enough for Isabella, a devout Christian, to answer "yes" to the plea. She sailed for India in 1869 and opened a school for girls in Lucknow. Beginning with six girls and a man with a club outside the door to protect them from those who opposed the school, Isabella's school grew to twenty-five pupils. She also engaged in evangelism, zenana work, and Bible studies.

When Isabella first talked of opening a women's college, other missionaries said it would not succeed. Yet, in 1887, she opened the first Christian women's college in all of Asia. One graduate said, "I shall never forget her Sunday afternoon prayer meetings with us. How clearly she explained the laws of the spiritual kingdom."

Over one hundred years ago Isabella answered God's call to go to India's women. The church continues to need laborers. Someone came to you with the Good News. Now pray for workers like Isabella to gather in the lost.

Ida Scudder
Medical Missionary
1870–1960

> And my God will meet all your needs
> according to the riches of his glory in Christ Jesus.
> PHILIPPIANS 4:19 NIV

Forty-three members of the Scudder family had answered the call to be missionaries in India when God also spoke to Ida Scudder to go as a doctor. She completed medical training and was preparing to sail when the mission board requested she raise eight thousand dollars for a medical facility in Vellore, India.

With no experience in fund-raising, Ida felt dizzy with fear when she received the news. Yet there was no way out and, much to her surprise, people listened as this young woman told them of her call and the need for a hospital.

Before Ida boarded the ship bound for India, she was handed a check for ten thousand dollars. The money was supplied and a hospital was built, where thousands of India's sick felt the healing touch of God's servant, Ida Scudder.

What do you need from God? He, who owns the entire universe, is not without resources and He promises to meet your need. Yet in wisdom, He also knows the difference between a want and a need. God desires the best for you. Claim His promise and rejoice in what He provides.

Giertrud Rask

Missionary Wife
1673–1735

> Suppose a brother or a sister is without clothes and daily food.
> If one of you says to them, "Go in peace; keep warm and well fed,"
> but does nothing about their physical needs, what good is it?
> JAMES 2:15–16 NIV

When Norwegian pastor Hans Egede announced to his wife in 1718 that he was called as a missionary to Greenland, Giertrud wondered if she had made a mistake to marry him. She was forty-five at the time; he was thirty-two. They had four young children. The couple agreed to pray before they made a decision.

After sincere prayer, Giertrud became convinced they should go. Then Hans had doubts. Should he expose his wife and family to the dangers of a new country? Now Giertrud encouraged him. Hans said, "She, a frail woman, showed greater faith and manliness than I."

In spite of not feeling called, Giertrud was an effective missionary. The Greenlanders, reluctant to listen to Hans's message, were impressed by her sacrificial love as she nursed the sick in her bedroom during a smallpox epidemic.

Moravian missionaries, also in Greenland, praised Giertrud, who shared her meager food supplies with them until they worried that she gave too much.

Giertrud felt no call, but her love for God, exhibited by good works, made her an effective partner with her husband in missionary endeavors. You don't need a special calling to express love to the hungry, the unprotected, or lonely. You only need a heart overflowing with Jesus' love.

Constance Padwick
Missionary
1886–1968

For I have a great sense of obligation to people in both the civilized world and the rest of the world, to the educated and uneducated alike.
ROMANS 1:14 NLT

When English-born Constance Padwick traveled to Palestine in 1910, she received a passion that consumed the remainder of her life—a desire to reach the Muslim world for Christ.

Constance wanted to be a front-line missionary, but instead she used her writing skills to reach Muslims, a field she felt had long been ignored by the Christian world. Proficient in Arabic, she edited a missions magazine, produced literature specific for Arabic-speaking people, and wrote biographies of missionaries who had evangelized Muslims.

Critics have questioned whether missionaries are wasting their energy by reaching out to a people who constantly reject Christ. However, the theme running through Constance's books and articles was the belief that the church has a solemn obligation to share Jesus' salvation with everyone—even Muslims.

The apostle Paul, too, felt a deep sense of debt to carry the Good News to all peoples. On one hand he saw his Savior. On the other hand, he saw a lost world. Paul felt an obligation to bring the two together. You can't repay Jesus for what He's done for you. But you can show your gratitude to God by reaching hands of love across every cultural, social, economic, and racial barrier.

Lottie Moon
Missionary
1840–1912

> "Mary has chosen what is better,
> and it will not be taken away from her."
> LUKE 10:42 NIV

Leaving behind the monotony of plantation life in post–Civil War Virginia, Lottie Moon sailed for missionary service in China in 1873. But her dream for a fulfilling ministry in evangelism was dashed when she was assigned to teach in a school. Lonely and disappointed, Lottie became engaged to a young man. However, when she learned he accepted Darwin's theory of evolution, Lottie had a choice to make. Would she marry and compromise her beliefs or break her engagement?

She chose the latter route and said she was left to "plod along in the same old way." Later, when referring to her choice, she said, "God had first claim on my life and since the two conflicted, there was no question about the result."

Choosing what is best when it means forfeiting security and companionship is difficult. Yet with an eye on eternal values, Lottie looked beyond the present and made the right choice. What choices are you facing? Even in small, everyday decisions, make your choices in the light of eternity. What is the highest and best? What choice will benefit the most people? Choose the part that cannot be taken from you.

Lilian Hammer
Medical Missionary
1912–1959

"What he opens no one can shut, and what he shuts no one can open.
I know your deeds. See, I have placed before you
an open door that no one can shut."
REVELATION 3:7–8 NIV

When Lilian Hammer, a young mill worker in England, told her
father she was going to nurses' school to prepare for missionary work
in China, he ordered her out of the house. With family ties severed,
Lilian set her sights on the foreign field. Much to her dismay, the
mission board did not accept her for service.

Disappointed, Lilian doubted if she had truly heard God's
voice. Yet if He didn't want her on the mission field, she would serve
faithfully in England. Within a year, however, the door opened for
her to go to China with the British Red Cross. While she worked
with this organization, missionaries befriended Lilian, recognized her
abilities, and suggested she reapply for a missionary appointment.
This time the door opened for her to go to the place of her calling.

You thought you knew God's plan. You spent years in preparation,
only to have the door slam shut. Don't be confounded by delays
or closed doors. God controls all your opportunities. Hold steady.
When you place your future in divine hands, He will open the right
door in His good time.

Annie Armstrong
Missions Organizer, Author
1850–1938

Christ suffered for you. He is your example,
and you must follow in his steps.
1 PETER 2:21 NLT

Having a star to follow, a pattern for your life, often shapes who you become. It did for Annie Armstrong. When she became a Christian in 1870, she immediately became involved in home and foreign missions work following in her mother's footsteps. Annie, a stately, six-foot-tall, fashionably dressed lady, cut an impressive figure and became a powerful church leader in the early twentieth century.

One of Annie's most lasting contributions to the work of God was her involvement with black women. Few white women of that era were interested in encouraging their black sisters to become Christian leaders. Yet Annie initiated black mothers' meetings and an industrial school for girls. She also brought black and white women together to cooperate in missions efforts. It was said no white woman of that era did more than Annie Armstrong to encourage Negro Baptist women in foreign and home missions.

Because of "Miss Annie's" vision, strong leadership, and independent methods she was sometimes criticized. Unmoved, she continued working to promote mission causes following her mother's example.

Mothers can be good patterns for our lives, but if they fail, we may also stumble. However, there is one example who will not cause us to err: Christ. Read the gospels; study His words and actions. Then walk in the Savior's steps.

Edith Moules
Missionary
1900–1949

> I want to know Christ—yes, to know the power of his resurrection
> and participation in his sufferings.
> PHILIPPIANS 3:10 NIV

The doctor confirmed an earlier diagnosis: veteran missionary Edith Moules had cancer throughout her body. She was advised to rest in hopes of extending her life a few years.

Instead of taking it easy, Edith traveled in the United States and Canada promoting her mission to Africa's lepers. Wherever she went revival fires ignited.

Prayers for her recovery were made by African Christians and coworkers, yet her health continued to deteriorate. A month before her death, she asked her friends to anoint her with oil and pray for her as instructed in James 5:14. About sixty friends gathered and prayed. On September 6, 1949, heaven's gates opened for Edith. Her last words were, "Jesus, Jesus." Because she knew Christ, Edith passed from this life to the next in peace.

It's not important for you to know famous personalities in politics, literature, or the sports world. However, to have a successful passage through death to heaven, it is necessary to know Jesus, God's Son. When your living rotates around this awesome goal, dying is the final step into the presence of One with whom you're well-acquainted.

Emma Whittemore
Minister to Fallen Women
1850–1931

> Jesus went through all the towns and villages,
> teaching in their synagogues, proclaiming the good news of
> the kingdom and healing every disease and sickness.
> MATTHEW 9:35 NIV

Emma Whittemore had it all. Born into wealth, she moved among the elite in New York City. After her marriage to Sidney, their lives were a succession of parties, dances, and expensive clothes. Emma's life took a drastic turn when, due to a back injury, she became an invalid. Medical help failed to relieve her suffering, and friends encouraged her to seek divine healing. Emma scoffed at the idea, but when she became acquainted with the healing ministry of Reverend A. B. Simpson, she sought God for a divine touch. After prayer, she was miraculously restored to health.

Renewed physically and spiritually, Emma reached out to young women caught in another kind of misery—prostitution. In 1890 she began Door of Hope, a mission for fallen women.

Are you or someone you know suffering in your body? Jesus opened the door for us to bring our pain and afflictions to Him. In the New Testament record He healed every type of disease and sickness. Hebrews 13:8 assures you, "Jesus Christ is the same yesterday and today and forever." Fix your eyes on Him. Jesus' power and love are available for your needs—spiritual, mental, emotional, and physical.

Lillias Underwood
Medical Missionary
1860–1927

Devote yourselves to prayer, being watchful and thankful.
And pray for us, too, that God may open a door for our message,
so that we may proclaim the mystery of Christ.
COLOSSIANS 4:2–3 NIV

Lillias Underwood went to Korea as a medical missionary in 1888. Soon after her arrival, she was appointed medical attendant to a Korean queen. Because of restrictions surrounding the treatment of royalty and language barriers, Lillias's job was challenging. But as the years passed, she became a familiar figure in the court and was able to speak to the queen without an interpreter.

Because of Korean royal etiquette, Lillias knew that if the gospel was to be presented in court, the opportunity would have to be opened by divine hands. She begged fellow missionaries to pray. The opportunity came one Christmas Eve when the queen asked Lillias the origin of the holiday. This was just what Lillias had prayed for. With an anointing that comes following prayer, she shared the story of Jesus with the royal woman.

Because believers devoted themselves to prayer, the way was opened for a heathen queen to hear the truth. To devote yourself to prayer means you do not give up praying when a door is shut. It means you pray confidently for answers you know are in God's will. It means even when you're tired of praying, you trust God. Doors will swing open, and hearts will soften as you remain devoted in prayer.

Corrie ten Boom
Author, Evangelist
1892–1983

And God is able to bless you abundantly, so that in all things at all times, having all that you need, you will abound in every good work.

2 Corinthians 9:8 NIV

As Betsie ten Boom lay dying in Ravensbruck prison in 1943, she told Corrie, her sister, "Your whole life has been training for the work you are doing in prison—and for the work you will do afterwards."

After World War II and the horrors of prison, Corrie built her life on those words. Her entire family perished in Nazi concentration camps, yet she bypassed anger and bitterness and went on to share the good news of Jesus with thousands. She traveled to sixty countries and told audiences, "No pit can be so deep that Jesus is not deeper still." She repeated "Jesus is victor" on university campuses, in town halls, and in churches. Corrie took a horrific situation and, with God's help, turned it around for the good of others.

Satan would like you to believe that no good can come from the unfortunate happenings of your past. You may believe you must wallow in grief and anger your entire life. That's not true. God is able to take the worst situation and turn it around for good. Allow His grace to abound until your negatives become positives, and Jesus turns your tragedies into abounding works.

Mary Slessor
Missionary
1848–1915

> "Do not be terrified; do not be afraid of them.
> The LORD your God, who is going before you, will fight for you,
> as he did for you in Egypt, before your very eyes."
>
> DEUTERONOMY 1:29–30 NIV

Mary Slessor learned courage as a young person growing up in the slums of Dundee, Scotland, and she would need it when she went as a missionary to Africa. This incident in her youth is an example of her courage.

As a group from Mary's church conducted an open-air service, a gang of boys determined to break up the meeting. The gang leader attached a piece of lead to a rope and began twirling it over his head, coming closer and closer to Mary. She refused to move even when the lead glazed her forehead. "She's game, boys!" the leader exclaimed as he lowered the rope. The gang came to church that night.

Calabar, the place of Mary's calling, was also a dangerous place. Slavers snatched natives from the jungles and swamps and sold them into slavery. Europeans who set foot on its soil usually met with a swift death from disease or violence. Yet for thirty-eight years Mary courageously worked to spread the gospel in this dark place.

Mary wasn't terrified by fearful situations. Neither should these frighten you. Whether it's starting a new job, moving to an unfamiliar city, or beginning a ministry, you need courage to face the unknown. You're not without resources. The Lord promises to go before you. That truth alone will give you plenty of courage!

Betty Olson
Missionary Martyr
1934–1968

> For we do not have a high priest who is unable to empathize
> with our weaknesses, but we have one who has been
> tempted in every way, just as we are.
> HEBREWS 4:15 NIV

Betty Olson grew up in Africa, the daughter of missionary parents. When she was in high school, her mother died. As her life changed, Betty became caustic, bitter, and rebellious.

She trained as a nurse and wanted to use her skills on the mission field, but no mission board would accept her. Instead, Betty went to Africa to help her missionary father and stepmother, but she caused so many problems, her father asked her to leave.

Returning to the United States, Betty sought counseling, turned her life around, and was accepted for work in Vietnam. In 1968 the Vietcong overran her mission, killed missionaries, and captured Betty and two other workers. During a time of severe torture in the jungle, one of the workers died, and Betty, with the other worker, Mike Benge, was reduced to a skeleton. At age thirty-three, Betty died from malnutrition.

Mike survived and told Betty's story. "She never showed any bitterness or resentment," he said. "To the end she loved the ones who mistreated her."

Anger and rebellion may also be part of your life, but you don't have to remain there. Jesus understands. He, too, was tempted in all these areas. Don't waste time condemning yourself. Approach His throne of grace. As Betty received divine help to change, so will you.

Edith Moules
Missionary
1900–1949

> Create in me a pure heart, O God, and renew a steadfast
> spirit within me. . . . Restore to me the joy of your
> salvation and grant me a willing spirit, to sustain me.
> PSALM 51:10, 12 NIV

Edith Moules, missionary to Africa, once told a story about the true nature of lives changed by the gospel. When revival fires began to burn in the hearts of the people in Ruandan, a man came to her carrying a bit of boxwood with two or three rusty nails hanging out. He confessed he had stolen it from the carpenter's shop. People were surprised when Edith took the minor infraction seriously. But she knew if the man was to experience a deeper work of God in his life, confession of any wrong was the first step.

What happened when the people at the mission honestly acknowledged their sins? Edith said the missionaries had been seeking to establish a church in a pagan leper settlement. Two or three attempts had been made without success. Yet after the Christians confessed their sins and asked God's forgiveness, two believing lepers went to the settlement and, with their own hands, built a church. Soon there was a thriving group of thirty-five worshiping lepers.

Empty lives God can fill. Broken vessels He uses to mend broken hearts. When you humbly confess your sins, you will hear God's voice. With a revived spirit, you'll experience the sweetness of His peace and presence in new, exciting ways.

Malla Moe
Missionary, Church Planter, Evangelist
1863–1953

You were cleansed from your sins when you obeyed the truth,
so now you must show sincere love to each other as brothers and sisters.
Love each other deeply with all your heart.
1 PETER 1:22 NLT

In the late 1890s, after only a two-week Bible course, Malla Moe sailed for a mission station in South Africa. Upon her arrival she accepted a native lifestyle. She said, "I felt so happy because I had taken this step to. . .live out in the native kraals."

At age sixty-five, Malla took a new approach to evangelism when she began traveling in a strange contraption called a gospel wagon. With a demanding schedule, driving her horse and wagon, she took the message of Christ into villages where the people had never heard it.

Colleagues criticized her unconventional methods of evangelism. They claimed she had a domineering personality, yet no one denied she truly loved the people. When she prepared to leave for her first furlough, it was reported that grown men wept like children.

Malla did not claim to be flawless, but for fifty years the people she worked among felt Christ's love through her. This love covered a multitude of her imperfections.

Like Malla, you may be aware of flaws in your personality such as temper, irritability, or impatience. Yet, with a heart cleansed of sin, it is possible for you to be filled with Calvary love so every person you meet feels His intense love through you.

Mary Lyon
Christian Educator
1797–1849

"Fix these words of mine in your hearts and minds; tie them as symbols on your hands and bind them on your foreheads. Teach them to your children."
DEUTERONOMY 11:18–19 NIV

Few people in early nineteenth-century America were in favor of higher education for women, but Mary Lyon was convinced women must be trained to teach. She said, "This work of supplying teachers is a great work and it must be done, or our country is lost, and the world will remain unconverted."

In 1830, Mary began raising money for a college, but the work was discouraging. The people from whom she solicited funds were poor. Friends told her to wait until the economy improved. Her health failed, yet she worked on, and in 1837 she founded Mount Holyoke Female Seminary, "to cultivate the missionary spirit among its pupils, the feeling that they should live for God, and do something as teachers."

By endurance and hard work, Mary attained her goal as her graduates went to cities, rural areas, and Native American schools. During the first twelve years of the school, twelve women went as missionaries to the Native Americans. At the time of Mary's death, seventy students had become foreign missionaries.

Instructing the next generation in Bible truth is the responsibility of every believer. Some are called to the classroom; all Christians teach with their lives. As you walk circumspectly, your life will effectively point children and young people to the One whom you serve.

Rosalind Goforth

Missionary Wife
1864–1942

> And since we are his children, we are his heirs. In fact,
> together with Christ we are heirs of God's glory. But if we
> are to share his glory, we must also share his suffering.
> ROMANS 8:17 NLT

When Jonathan and Rosalind Goforth arrived in China in 1888, the thrust of their ministry was evangelism. This involved traveling to villages in the interior. Jonathan expected his wife to accompany him, but as their family increased in number, it became more difficult for Rosalind to accept the hazards of inland travel.

After a furlough, Jonathan shared his extensive plans of evangelism with Rosalind. When she heard his scheme, her "heart went like lead." The plan was good, but it was entirely unsuited for a family. Traveling to the interior meant exposing their children to diseases of every kind. Rosalind refused to go. Jonathan persisted, telling her, "I am sure the Lord would keep my children from harm." She admitted she didn't have faith, vision, or courage to take the risk. Yet more times than not, she and the children went.

But the price was high; Rosalind buried five of her eleven children in Chinese soil.

Christians are called to suffer, some more than others. Scripture assures us that rewards await the faithful, but how do you remain unmoved in the face of severe trials? While there is no secret formula for enduring suffering, God gives you an open window into His presence through prayer, and the assurance, "I will never leave you."

Jessie Gregg
Missionary, Evangelist
1875–1942

> But where sin increased, grace increased all the more.
> ROMANS 5:20 NIV

The Boxer Rebellion that began in China in 1900 was a violent reaction of some Chinese to foreign influences. "Foreign devils" and Christians were killed. More than one hundred Protestant missionaries lost their lives in the conflict.

Jessie Gregg was one missionary who survived. She, with another couple and their children, hid in a temple for six days. For a month they stayed at an isolated farm and later in a cave. When the missionaries were finally captured, one was shot and Jessie was pushed in the mud, dragged by her hair, beaten, and tortured. However, the persecution did not squelch her missionary zeal. When released, she went to England for a time, but returned to China where she worked as an itinerant evangelist for another fifteen years. It is estimated that five thousand Chinese accepted Christ through her preaching.

How did Jessie survive the persecution? How does any saint of any age endure the wrath of men? God's grace is a powerful force He gives to believers for difficult times. The greater the trial, the more grace He gives. You will live to see value in your hardships, for His grace is always sufficient.

Frances Ridley Havergal
Hymn Writer
1836–1879

> I plead with you to give your bodies to God because of all he has done for you. Let them be a living and holy sacrifice—the kind he will find acceptable. This is truly the way to worship him.
>
> ROMANS 12:1 NLT

From early childhood, Frances Havergal had a deep longing for God. As a youngster she diligently memorized scripture verses. When she became a young adult, she studied Greek and Hebrew to better understand the Bible. Her musical talents could have brought her fame, but these she dedicated to God's service.

On one occasion Frances was spending a week with friends for whom she had been praying. Some were not Christians. Others were believers, but to Frances they didn't seem passionate in their faith. During her visit, she prayed, "God, give me all in this house." Before the week was over each person she had prayed for had received a blessing. As a result of this victory, Frances dedicated herself anew to God's purposes and in 1874, she wrote this hymn:

Take my life, and let it be
Consecrated, Lord, to Thee;
Take my hands, and let them move
At the impulse of Thy love,
At the impulse of Thy love.

The apostle Paul urged believers to periodically check their dedication to God and make new consecrations. In view of what Jesus did for us at Calvary, this seems the reasonable thing to do.

Anna Jarvis
Founder of Mother's Day
1864–1948

"Honor your father and mother." This is the first commandment with a promise: If you honor your father and mother, "things will go well for you, and you will have a long life on the earth."
EPHESIANS 6:2–3 NLT

As twelve-year-old Anna Jarvis listened to her mother conclude a study of Bible mothers, she heard Mrs. Jarvis pray, "I hope that someone, someday, establishes a memorial mother's day for mothers living and dead." Her daughter did not forget that prayer and when her mother died, Anna promised, "By the grace of God, you shall have that day."

Anna, a public school teacher, began her campaign for a national Mother's Day by writing letters to government officials and leading businessmen. A wealthy businessman, John Wanamaker, invited Anna to speak at his store's auditorium in Philadelphia. That day she told more than five thousand people of the need to honor the nation's mothers.

Through Anna's untiring efforts, in May 1914 a resolution passed the United States Congress, proclaiming the second Sunday in May as Mother's Day. When President Woodrow Wilson signed the resolution, Anna's promise to her mother was fulfilled.

It is not difficult to honor a faithful mother. It may be more difficult to honor her if she abandoned, failed, or betrayed you. The Word of God remains true: the blessing of God rests upon the child who honors her mother.

Sally Parsons

Preacher
1782–1838

> Watch ye, stand fast in the faith, quit you like men, be strong.
> Let all your things be done with charity.
> 1 CORINTHIANS 16:13 KJV

In 1792 revival fires swept through the village of Westport, New Hampshire. One young person, Sally Parsons, felt the flame. When she told her parents of her conversion, her mother was pleased, but her father ordered her out of the house. Sally knelt outside the door and prayed for him.

Through this experience, Sally became strong in her new faith, and she felt God call her to preach. A church took notice of her calling and voted to give her a horse, saddle, and bridle so she could minister in neighboring towns.

For four years, Sally preached up and down the state of New Hampshire. Her family noted her God-given gift, and, one by one, they became Christians. Even her father eventually became a believer, apologized to Sally, and promised her a dowry if she married.

Because a young girl acted heroically when facing persecution, God was able to bring many into faith, including her own family. You, too, may be ridiculed and treated shamefully as you stand for Bible principles. Watch how you react to these taunts. There's no telling what good things can happen when you respond courageously in love.

Eleanor Chestnut
Medical Missionary
1868–1905

> In the midst of a very severe trial, their overflowing joy and their extreme
> poverty welled up in rich generosity. For I testify that they gave
> as much as they were able, and even beyond their ability.
> 2 CORINTHIANS 8:2–3 NIV

After a miserable childhood in grueling poverty, Eleanor Chestnut found the purpose for her life when she answered the call to be a missionary. She prepared well by attending medical school, nurses' training, and Bible college. In 1894 she sailed for China.

As she served in the most primitive conditions, Eleanor's life as a medical missionary was one of continual sacrifice. On one occasion after she had amputated a man's leg, he needed skin grafts. Eleanor's leg later bore scars from where she took her own skin for the man's leg.

In letters home, she wrote that treating opium addicts was her most difficult challenge. As one victim "pursued demons," Eleanor stood guard to keep herself and the man from harm. Yet, her letters also showed signs of humor.

Sadly, Eleanor made the ultimate sacrifice in 1905 when the very people she loved murdered her while she bandaged the arm of an injured child.

Because she gave her all, Eleanor Chestnut's life impacted a generation of Chinese people for God. Christians today, too, are called to sacrifice for Christ's cause. How much does God ask you to sacrifice? The requirement is the same for every believer; He wants your all on the altar.

Mary Webb
Christian Organizer
1779–1861

> "The share of the man who stayed with the supplies is to be the same as that of him who went down to the battle. All will share alike."
> 1 SAMUEL 30:24 NIV

Because a childhood disease left Mary Webb crippled, she could not go to the foreign mission field. However, this did not stop her from becoming involved in reaching the world for Christ. At age twenty-one, while a student, she and thirteen other women students organized a missionary society—a revolutionary move in an era when only men were considered competent to direct such an organization.

For more than forty years, Mary served as the secretary-treasurer of the Female Society for Missionary Purposes. Farmers' wives saved a few cents from their egg money to donate to the cause, and maids gave sacrificially from meager wages. Mary could not be in frontline ministry, but from her wheelchair, she served as leader of a ministry that supported missionaries.

Perhaps you, for various reasons, can't serve God in an active role. Though the behind-the-scenes work may not seem glamorous, it is equally vital to the Christian cause. Helping, giving, and supporting in a less prominent place may very well be the work God intended for you to do. And don't worry about a reward; those who stay by the supplies will share equally with those who receive front-page acclaim.

Charlotte Tucker

Missionary to the Zenanas

1821–1893

I planted the seed, Apollos watered it, but God has been making it grow.
So neither the one who plants nor the one who waters is anything,
but only God, who makes things grow.

1 CORINTHIANS 3:6–7 NIV

At age fifty-four Charlotte Tucker, a wealthy woman and a successful author, felt God call her to the zenana work in India. Zenanas were places reserved for women not allowed in public.

Gaining entrance to share the gospel with these women was another matter. Often turned away and sometimes spit on, Charlotte persisted. Her work was described by an observer: "Miss Tucker. . . surrounded by a small crowd of women squatting on the floor, she was wont to show them Biblical pictures, talk a little, and end up with a hymn sung in Punjabi." With little visible result, she continued the work until her death.

Charlotte was a seed planter. While every believer has a part in the harvest, the jobs vary. You may have planted the gospel message in the hearts of children in a Bible class without seeing results. Others reinforced the message, and eventually the seed grew until fruit became evident.

Are you a planter of seeds or one who waters? It doesn't matter what phase of the harvest you are involved in. Faithfully do your part. It's up to God to make the seed grow.

Fanny Crosby
Hymn Writer
1820–1915

Great peace have they which love thy law: and nothing shall offend them.
PSALM 119:165 KJV

Fanny Crosby, the blind hymn writer, wrote over seven thousand hymns and gospel songs, making her the most prolific hymn writer of all time. Her verses set to music have been sung in almost every country of the world. Many of her hymns have endured over one hundred years and continue to be included in hymnbooks today.

In spite of her successes, at the height of her popularity, Fanny had critics. One evaluator claimed her hymns did not possess high poetic quality. Another person wrote, "Not withstanding the immense circulation given to Fanny Crosby's hymns, they are, with few exceptions, very weak and poor, their simplicity and earnestness being their redeeming features."

Fanny was not moved by these remarks; she agreed with them. She said she was not writing hymns for literary analysis. Rather, she wanted the words to be understood by common, ordinary people.

Criticism in any area is difficult to handle. We want to be well spoken of and accepted. Our natural reaction to criticism is to lash out and defend ourselves. When you find yourself under attack, take a lesson from Fanny; she agreed with the critics. Or better yet, follow Jesus' example: when He was accused, He answered not a word.

Eleanor Macomber
Missionary, Church Planter
1801–1840

> Be strong in the Lord and in his mighty power. Put on the full armor of God, so that you can take your stand against the devil's schemes.
> EPHESIANS 6:10–11 NIV

Eleanor Macomber was commissioned to serve the Ojibwa Indians in Michigan, but in four years her health failed. After a brief rest she was well enough to accept a call to the foreign mission field of Burma.

When she was shown her outpost at Dong-Yahn, Eleanor wept. With no knowledge of the Burmese language, she'd be alone in a drunken, idolatrous society. However, she quickly rallied and, as a result of her preaching, in a few months a church was established with twenty people.

Eleanor faced other hardships. Buddhist priests tried to burn her house while she was in it. She struggled to learn the language. Yet this missionary boldly announced worship services and prayer meetings. She eventually established a training school and sent the students to evangelize nearby tribes.

Alone, opposed, reviled, and persecuted, Eleanor Macomber established a successful church in a heathen land. How did she do it? With prayer, God's Word, and faith—the full armor of God. Fight your battles with these same spiritual weapons.

B. V. Subbamma
Writer, Women's Worker, Evangelist
20th Century

Therefore God exalted him to the highest place and gave him the name that is above every name, that at the name of Jesus every knee should bow.
PHILIPPIANS 2:9–10 NIV

As a child growing up in India, B. V. Subbamma, a caste Hindu, attended a mission-sponsored school, but she resisted Christian teaching and believed Jesus was only for outcasts. However, after reading the Bible, she became a believer and said, "The name of Jesus became so precious to me that I could hardly believe it. . . . I was supremely happy, having the assurance that Jesus had suffered for my sin and had forgiven me and blessed me with salvation."

B. V. wanted to be baptized, but her family opposed her new faith. After much turmoil, she at last identified with the name of Jesus through baptism in 1942. While working to bring other Hindu women into faith in Christ, B. V. was hindered by the dreaded caste system.

India's caste system divides people into high and low groups. The high group considers themselves superior and does not associate with or acknowledge other groups. The system has long frustrated missionaries, and B. V. wrote a book that explains to Christians the structure of caste.

No person is more important than another. Only one name is above all—the name of Jesus. His name means "Savior." No wonder B. V. Subbamma strove to teach people of the One who loves them, regardless of their social status. Repeat the name; cherish it. In that name is your eternal salvation. *Jesus.*

Sarah Doremus
Missions Organizer
1802–1877

"For I was hungry, and you fed me. I was thirsty, and you gave me a drink.
I was a stranger, and you invited me into your home. . . .
I tell you the truth, when you did it to one of the least of these
my brothers and sisters, you were doing it to me!"
Matthew 25:35, 40 NLT

Sarah Doremus was born into wealth. She married a prosperous New York businessman, bore eight children, and adopted other children. In spite of an affluent, busy life she did not spend her time in selfish pursuits. Rather, putting Christian values into practice, she reached out to almost every benevolent project in New York City—prisons, hospitals, orphanages, old-age homes, industrial schools, and tract societies.

On a Sunday afternoon in the 1830s Sarah could be seen walking New York City streets on her way to the jail to hold services for women prisoners. With a vision beyond her time, she organized a home for discharged female convicts.

Prison work among the city's poor uncovered another need—women with social diseases. Sarah worked with doctors and acquired a grant from the state to finance medical care for these women.

Sarah Doremus discovered it took no special talent to reach out to the needy. Neither do you have to be rich or highly educated to show kindness to a prisoner or a homeless person. And amazing as it seems, when you show love to someone in need, you're actually doing the kindness for Jesus!

Adele Fielde
Missionary Teacher, Author
1839–1916

> Even when I walk through the darkest valley, I will not be afraid,
> for you are close beside me. Your rod and your staff protect and comfort me.
> PSALM 23:4 NLT

Adele Fielde's desire to become a missionary came true when she married Cyrus Chilcot. When her husband sailed for mission work in Siam, Adele agreed to follow in a few months. In 1865, after a seven-month sea voyage, she arrived, but it was not Cyrus who greeted her: rather, she was told he had died. Most women in that situation would have returned home, but Adele stayed. Later, she went to China.

One problem early missionaries faced was reaching women. In most cultures of that time they lived behind closed doors. Adele believed the women could be reached by other Christian women. After her husband's death she trained about five hundred native women in personal evangelism. Her method: after one lesson, she sent students out two by two to share the gospel with village women.

Her involvement in the work had a dual purpose: Adele had an effective ministry to Asian women, and she was also comforted in the loss of her husband.

For a shepherd, the rod and staff are weapons against predators. For the sorrowing Christian, the scriptures and His work serve to comfort the grieving person's spirit, body, and soul. If loss has visited you, take the weapons God provides for grieving hearts; His Word and work.

Mildred Cable
Missionary
1877–1952

Francesca and Evangeline French
Missionaries
19th–20th Centuries

> "So is my word that goes out from my mouth:
> It will not return to me empty, but will accomplish
> what I desire and achieve the purpose for which I sent it."
>
> Isaiah 55:11 NIV

Mildred Cable, with Francesca and Evangeline French, placed scripture portions wherever they traveled in China's Northwest region. They left Christian books in heathen temples, nailed posters with Bible verses written on them on walls of homes and temples, and preached to whomever would listen. Did the efforts of three middle-aged women missionaries have any effect?

Five years after their initial visit, the women returned to a city they had earlier evangelized. *Will anyone attend the meeting?* they wondered. To their surprise the room was filled, and many stood to have their names recorded on a list of inquirers. The scriptures they had left in a remote Chinese city had pierced the darkness, and the people wanted to know more about Jesus.

Have you given a Bible to a child, a tract to an aged person or a homeless man? Do you wonder if sharing gospel literature does any good? The Bible assures us that whenever the scriptures are given out, there will be results. You may not see the effect immediately, but not to worry: God promises His Word, in His time, will accomplish His good purposes.

Mary Briscoe Baldwin

Missionary
1811–1877

> "He went to him and bandaged his wounds, pouring on oil and wine.
> Then he put the man on his own donkey, brought him
> to an inn and took care of him."
>
> LUKE 10:34 NIV

Born of Virginia aristocracy, Mary Baldwin at age twenty-one wrote, "For years I had felt a great desire to be directly engaged in some Christian work, especially in extending the knowledge of the gospel among my fellow creatures." Yet Mary believed being a missionary was too noble a vocation for her, a mere woman.

However, when a missionary from Greece appealed for help in a school, Mary volunteered. In Athens she taught sewing to the students, mostly poor girls, so they could use the skill to make their living. She also trained upper-class girls to be teachers.

In 1866 Athens became crowded with Cretan refugees displaced because of a revolt against Turkey. Mary met the emergency by initiating an extensive feeding program for the starving. She also began a Sunday school and a day school where she taught sewing and knitting to the refugees.

When confronted with people's needs in your community or church, do you look the other way? Do you offer a "God bless you" and move on? Or, like Mary Baldwin and the Good Samaritan, do you provide help?

Amy Carmichael
Missionary
1867–1951

This means that anyone who belongs to Christ has become a new person.
The old life is gone; a new life has begun!
2 CORINTHIANS 5:17 NLT

As a young woman growing up in Northern Ireland, Amy Carmichael loved pretty clothes and eating expensive foods. In 1886 she became a Christian, and her life changed.

She first noticed the difference when she went to lunch with a friend. They were served poorly prepared lamb chops, which ordinarily would have annoyed Amy. But that day it didn't matter.

Amy again noticed the difference when her mother took her shopping for dresses and Amy wasn't interested in buying new clothes. These subtle changes surprised her and let her know she had experienced an inner transformation.

Later, Amy went to India and began an orphanage for India's unwanted children. In 1945, after four decades of work, eight hundred children were being fed daily, clothed, and educated in her Christian orphanage. It began years earlier when a young woman's life was transformed by the gospel.

You, too, can begin again. The new birth is not a rehabilitation plan, reeducation program, or a reformation. You do not turn over a new leaf when you become a believer. Rather, you are given a new heart and a new start. It happened to Amy Carmichael. When you accept Jesus, it will happen to you.

Ethel Waters
Gospel Singer, Actress
1896–1977

And we know that in all things God works for the good of those
who love him, who have been called according to his purpose.
ROMANS 8:28 NIV

Ethel Waters was conceived after her twelve-year-old mother was raped. Ethel's grandmother adopted her, and the two lived in poverty in Philadelphia. Hungry most days during her childhood, in desperation Ethel often ate dog food. No wonder the child rebelled and was a menace at school! But God was watching over her, and at age twelve Ethel wandered into a revival meeting where she invited Jesus into her heart.

During her early childhood Ethel had sung in a children's church program and discovered she had a good voice. As a young adult she went into black vaudeville and sang blues music. In spite of a successful acting career and Academy Award nominations, Ethel's life lacked joy.

When the Billy Graham Crusade came to Madison Square Garden in 1957, Ethel attended. She said, "I was depressed, empty. I felt the Lord calling me back home." She joined the crusade choir. Later, she traveled with the crusade as a soloist and became known for her rendition of "His Eye Is on the Sparrow."

A miserable childhood, an empty existence! Can any good come from it? Yet when Ethel renewed her faith in Christ, much good resulted. If your past is a graveyard, give it to God. He fit the broken pieces of Ethel Waters's life together again, and He will do the same for you.

Maud Ballington Booth
General of the Volunteers of America
1863–1945

> "I was in prison and you came to visit me."
> MATTHEW 25:36 NIV

Maud Charlesworth's mother took her to a Salvation Army meeting in 1881, and Maud's life was forever changed. She later joined the army and accompanied General William Booth's daughter, Catherine, to France and Switzerland to establish Salvation Army posts. Upon her return to England she worked in London's slums.

Maud married Ballington, the son of General Booth, and took both his names. The couple was assigned to supervise the army in the United States, but resigned the organization in 1886 and founded the Volunteers of America. To help those in prisons, Maud began the Volunteer Prison League.

She held church services and Bible studies in prisons and implemented programs to help men and women upon their release. Her success rate for rehabilitating ex-prisoners was reported to be remarkable.

Maud recalled one letter she received after a visit to Joliet State Prison. A man wrote, "You said you loved us. Nobody ever said that to me before in my whole life, and I hardly know what the word means."

A visit, a few kind words, and a prisoner felt love for the first time. The real evidence of your faith is the way you treat people. View every person you meet as if he or she is Jesus and impact countless lives for good and godliness.

Jessie Gregg
Missionary, Evangelist
1875–1942

Then he [Jesus] said to the crowd, "If any of you wants to be my follower, you must turn from your selfish ways, take up your cross daily, and follow me."
LUKE 9:23 NLT

After surviving the Boxer Rebellion of 1900, missionary Jessie Gregg took a brief furlough and returned to preach evangelistic meetings in fifteen Chinese provinces. Travel for the missionary was dangerous and slow. Food was sometimes scarce. At night she slept in strange places.

In one city, Jessie announced plans for a women's conference. Chinese women of that era didn't venture far from their homes, yet over four hundred women attended Jessie's conference.

Before the meetings ended, half of the attendees professed faith in Christ. What drew people to this woman evangelist? A born storyteller, Jessie delighted audiences with a simple gospel message that often brought tears of repentance to her hearers.

Jessie Gregg took great risks to share the message of Christ. While we tend to remain in our comfort zone, Jesus said every believer needs to move out and bear his cross. This may mean when you'd rather keep things for yourself, you willingly share. When your human nature wants to get even, you choose to turn the other cheek.

Avoid a religion that costs you nothing. Shoulder your cross. Follow the One who knew all about a cross.

Susanna Wesley
Christian Wife and Mother
1669–1742

You need to persevere so that when you have done the will of God,
you will receive what he has promised.
HEBREWS 10:36 NIV

Year after year Susanna Wesley patiently instructed her nine children in reading, writing skills, and Christian conduct. One day her husband, Samuel, listened to the lessons and wondered at her patience. "You told that child the same thing twenty times," he said.

"If I had satisfied myself by mentioning it only nineteen times," Susanna said, "I should have lost all my labor. It was the twentieth time that crowned it."

Susanna's patient endurance was transferred to two of her sons, John and Charles. This attribute became a great asset when they preached to large crowds and instructed thousands of new converts— many who were illiterate—in the Great Awakening of the 1700s.

Patience is a godly attribute and a necessary ingredient in the life of a Christian. You pray, and the time between the request and answer stretches on and on. You ask God to bring a family member or friend to Christ, but it doesn't happen immediately. Neither are sicknesses always healed the minute you pray.

Because God's blessings aren't instantly handed to you, patience is necessary. If the answer to your prayer is delayed, pray on. Endure. You *will* receive what He promised.

Mary Fisher

Quaker Preacher
1623–1698

"But you will receive power when the Holy Spirit comes upon you.
And you will be my witnesses, telling people about me everywhere—
in Jerusalem, throughout Judea, in Samaria, and to the ends of the earth."
ACTS 1:8 NLT

Mary Fisher, an English servant girl, was converted through the preaching of George Fox, founder of the Quakers. Immediately upon receiving Christ, she began to preach. For this she was thrown into prison.

In 1655 Mary, with her family, sailed for America. In Boston she also preached and was beaten, accused of witchcraft, and jailed.

Upon her return to England, Mary felt called to preach to the sultan of Turkey, but it was no easy task to locate a Turkish leader hundreds of miles away. When she arrived in Smyrna, the British consul placed her on a ship headed back to England. Mary managed to disembark and traveled six hundred miles until she found the sultan and his army. Miraculously, she received an audience with him and, through a translator, Mary spoke all that the Holy Spirit had laid on her heart.

Mary Fisher was possessed of a rare, almost unbelievable boldness. All believers need a certain amount of fearlessness if they are to make Jesus known. While it is more difficult to be bold when one's testimony is opposed, many find it hard to share their faith even in ideal situations. This is where the Holy Spirit comes in. He lives in every believer, and as He helped Mary Fisher, He will also help you speak unashamedly for Christ.

Marie Monson
Missionary
Early 20th Century

> For God has not given us a spirit of fear and timidity,
> but of power, love, and self-discipline.
> 2 TIMOTHY 1:7 NLT

When missionary Marie Monson transferred to China's Honan province, she encountered spiritual darkness in the form of superstition, ignorance, and hatred for foreigners. As her mind filled with fear, she asked herself, "Am I throwing my life away?"

Marie recognized these thoughts as an attack from the enemy, and she countered them by affirming the power of the gospel to change situations. She was helped by reading the account of George Mueller's steadfast faith for the needs of his orphanages. In missionary Hudson Taylor's biography, she identified with his struggles to begin the China Inland Mission. Marie studied the book of Acts and availed herself of the same power used by the early church.

Gradually, a few people in the province became friendly to Marie. When some became believers, a church was formed. No less important, Marie had overcome the onslaught of Satan.

Christians suffer attacks from the enemy of their souls. These are not times for you to remain passive. Do as Marie did: focus on a promise in the Bible, meditate on the resurrected Savior, read spiritually inspiring books, and saturate yourself with prayer. Other believers have overcome attacks through the power in Jesus' name. So will you.

Andrew, Simon Peter's brother, spoke up, "Here is a boy with five small barley loaves and two small fish, but how far will they go among so many?"
JOHN 6:8–9 NIV

While Mabel Francis was in her teens the young man whom she hoped to marry died. Mourning her loss, she faithfully visited his grave every day until God reminded her, "Why are you weeping for this young man who is in heaven when the people in this town don't know My love?"

These words jarred Mabel, and she began Sunday afternoon meetings in a schoolhouse. A local pastor invited her to preach in his church, and soon a revival came to their New Hampshire town. Other communities heard of the young lady preacher and asked her to speak in their churches.

From this small beginning, at age nineteen, Mabel felt called to missionary service. In 1909 she went to Japan, and for fifty-six years preached and built churches in that country.

When a boy gave his little lunch to Jesus, a miracle resulted. And when an insignificant New England teenager gave God her abilities, she became a powerful instrument for advancing His kingdom.

A fish, a piece of bread, a word, a smile, an invitation to church, a song, your voice, a coin—all small things. When you offer even one of these to God, it can be the start of a miracle!

Katherine Zell
Author, Hymn Writer, Reformer
1497–1562

> How good and pleasant it is when God's people live together in unity. . .
> for there the LORD bestows his blessing.
> PSALM 133:1, 3 NIV

Feelings were high, opinions varied, and discussions became heated in the church during the time of the Reformation. One woman, Katherine Zell, was disturbed by the disagreements between those who professed to be of the same persuasion. She saw a need for unity and openly rebuked leaders who chose to magnify lesser theological issues.

Besides being a spiritual advisor to many, Katherine was also known for her hospitality to Protestant refugees fleeing for their lives. During a three-week period she housed and fed sixty homeless people, victims of religious persecution. Her kindness was not limited to those who agreed with her on points of doctrine; she welcomed anyone into her home "who acknowledges Christ as the true Son of God."

Jesus, in His prayer for the church, prayed that His followers "may be one as we are one" (John 17:11). The Father, Son, and Holy Spirit are united, and believers strive for this oneness. If you disagree with a Christian brother or sister, pray about the matter, then let the Holy Spirit do the speaking to all concerned. God's blessing rests on those who work for unity.

Barbara Heck
Church Builder
1734–1804

> "As long as it is day, we must do the works of him who sent me.
> Night is coming, when no one can work."
> JOHN 9:4 NIV

"Philip, you must preach to us or we shall go to hell and God will require our blood at your hands," Barbara Heck told her cousin.

When twenty-six-year-old Barbara and her family emigrated from Ireland to New York City, she became concerned with the sinful conditions around her. On one occasion she broke up a card game and threw the cards into a fire.

Barbara promised her cousin Philip Embury, a preacher, if he started a church, she would gather the congregation. Attending the first service in 1766 were Barbara, her family, and two servants. Through her hard work, in two years the group had outgrown Philip's home and she prayed for a new location.

Barbara designed the plans for a new building and solicited financial help from New York City citizens. In all, 250 people made pledges. A chapel was built and soon filled with thousands of worshipers. This early Christian work was begun and continued with the help of a woman.

We are given forty to sixty years in which to work for God. Think about the amount of time you have left. What can you do to further God's purposes in your home, church, and community in your remaining years?

Margaret King
Missionary, Evangelist, Teacher
1884–1930

"Repent, then, and turn to God, so that your sins may be wiped out,
that times of refreshing may come from the Lord."
ACTS 3:19 NIV

In the early 1900s, missionary Margaret King was used in a great way to help young Chinese women in their spiritual development. She also worked closely with Chinese Bible women, and as an evangelist-teacher.

In 1911 she attended meetings conducted by evangelist Jonathan Goforth and came away infused with a new joy and fervor for God. She shared her excitement with a group in the girls' school in Yangchow, and a similar revival broke out. As the girls shed tears and confessed their sins, they too experienced great joy. Soon news of the revival reached other missionaries, and Margaret was invited to speak in their schools. Wherever she preached, it was the same; believers honestly searched their hearts, confessed sins, and received new joy.

Has your fervor for God and His Word waned? Is your Christian joy running low? As Margaret and Chinese believers needed refreshing from the Lord, you, too, may need a spiritual renewal. While honest confession can be painful, the results are invigorating; your cleansed heart will overflow with new delight in your Savior.

Kathryn Kuhlman
Evangelist
1907–1976

> Why am I discouraged? Why is my heart so sad? I will put my hope in God!
> I will praise him again—my Savior and my God!
> PSALM 42:5–6 NLT

Banks failed, jobs were scarce, and many people lost their businesses and farms during the depression of the 1930s. In desperation, some ended their lives. People needed hope and Kathryn Kuhlman, a woman evangelist, ignited hope for many.

Kathryn received Christ in a revival meeting when she was fourteen. Two years later she began traveling with an evangelistic team holding tent meetings. At age twenty-one, in spite of a stuttering problem, she began to preach. Yet Kathryn didn't consider herself a preacher. "I can't preach!" she said. "I talk about the Lord and my own experiences." Her message was simple: "God said it, I believe it. That settles it."

For those without money, homes, family, or friends, Kathryn's message of an all-sufficient God—Savior, healer, baptizer, and soon-coming King—gave people hope for a brighter future.

Her ministry also gave hope to the sick as she prayed for their healing. Yet Kathryn denied being a faith healer. "I never healed anyone," she said. "It's just the mercy of God."

Has your faith run low because of losses, sicknesses, and failures? Talk to your soul as the psalmist did. He declared, "I will put my hope in God." You will never be disappointed when you confess hope in the living, all-sufficient Savior.

Mary Mueller
Wife of George Mueller
1797–1870

In the morning, Lord, you hear my voice; in the morning
I lay my requests before you and wait expectantly.
Psalm 5:3 NIV

Much has been written about the prayer life of George Mueller, the man who believed God to supernaturally supply the needs for the children in his orphanages. But what of Mary Mueller, his wife? She, too, knew how to pray and receive from God.

In 1836 the Muellers opened their first home for orphans in Bristol, England. Their philosophy for supporting the endeavor: "Don't tell anyone the need, but God." Soon over two thousand children were being fed, clothed, and educated through Mary and George's prayers. Not only did Mary pray, but she also used her bookkeeping skills to keep the orphanage accounts.

Mary also helped deal with the day-to-day problems of sickness and malnutrition. During a typhus and smallpox epidemic, Mary prayed and of the fifteen children who became ill, not one died. She prayed for the spiritual needs of the orphans, and God sent times of revival. During a divine visitation, one hundred girls and boys trusted Jesus for salvation.

Prayer was not a last resort for Mary Mueller. And it should not be for any Christian. As Mary learned to persist in prayer you, too, can have the joy of seeing needs miraculously supplied by the most powerful force in this universe—persevering prayer.

Frances Willard
Founder of WCTU
1839–1898

For we are God's handiwork, created in Christ Jesus to do good works,
which God prepared in advance for us to do.
EPHESIANS 2:10 NIV

While ill with typhoid fever, twenty-year-old Frances Willard said she heard two voices speak to her. One encouraged her to yield her life to Christ. The other told her not to give in to such weakness. Frances obeyed the first voice.

God had indeed prepared a work for this woman to do. She taught school, was president of a Christian ladies' college, directed the women's work for evangelist Dwight L. Moody, and became America's foremost spokesperson for temperance.

Americans in the nineteenth century, especially men, consumed large amounts of alcohol. Public drunkenness was a problem. Frances and others were concerned, and through the Women's Christian Temperance Union (WCTU), worked to make the public aware of the problems alcohol consumption created for the nation's women and children.

When Frances was president of the WCTU, the American membership reached thirty thousand. A "mover and shaker," she also worked for women's health, prison reform, international peace, and public kindergartens.

God has a good work for every follower of Christ to accomplish. Assess your talents and interests. Pray about your part. Then, like Frances Willard, pursue a work that will benefit people in your church, community, and country.

Elizabeth Prentiss

Author, Hymn Writer

1819–1878

> "People do not live by bread alone; rather, we live by every word that comes from the mouth of the Lord."
>
> Deuteronomy 8:3 NLT

In 1853 while caring for her three toddlers, Elizabeth Prentiss began writing books for children. Her Little Suzy series taught simple truths and set a new trend in children's literature.

However, Elizabeth's most successful book was a novel entitled *Stepping Heavenward*, published in 1869. At that time novels were condemned in Christian circles and considered a tool of the devil. Some mothers wouldn't allow their daughters to read them. But Elizabeth used her book "to incite patience, fidelity, hope and all goodness by showing how trust in God. . .will brighten the darkest paths."

This author managed to write at least one book a year. Her works included books for children, novels, and poetry—all with a Christian message. She also wrote hymns.

Do you need answers? Then read the Bible and writings based on Bible truth. Solutions for all of life's dilemmas are found within the pages of the inspired Word. The answer may not jump out at you the first time you read a Bible verse, but as you read consistently with an open heart, solutions will become apparent. An all-knowing, all-loving God has given you answers. It's up to you to pick up the Book and read them.

Lady Selina Huntingdon
Benefactor, Revivalist
1707–1791

He saved us, not because of the righteous things we had done,
but because of his mercy. He washed away our sins,
giving us a new birth and new life through the Holy Spirit.
TITUS 3:5 NLT

Lady Huntingdon, a young, wealthy English aristocrat, was committed to the Church of England. Hoping to please God, she contributed to its causes and gave to the poor. Yet, she felt unsure of her eternal destiny.

During an illness, Lady Huntingdon was visited by her sister-in-law, Lady Margaret. A vibrant Christian, Margaret shared her faith with Lady Huntingdon and ended the visit by saying that since she had became a Christian she was "as happy as an angel."

Those words had a profound effect on Lady Huntingdon. A battle raged in her heart and ended when she surrendered her life to Christ. The change was dramatic. Her health improved, and she began to use her wealth to support the Great Awakening in England and America.

Many people make the mistake Lady Huntingdon did; they join a church, keep religious rituals, or do good deeds, thinking it will put them in right standing with God. However, the only righteousness God accepts is that of His Son, Jesus. Abandon your own righteousness as Lady Huntingdon did. Accept Christ's and begin to live!

Civilla D. Martin
Hymn Writer
1869–1948

He tends his flock like a shepherd: He gathers the lambs in his arms and
carries them close to his heart; he gently leads those that have young.
Isaiah 40:11 NIV

While her family spent time at a Bible training school in New York,
Civilla Martin's minister husband, Stillman, accepted an invitation
to preach some distance away. During that time Civilla became ill,
and Stillman decided to cancel his preaching appointment. But
when he told his plans to their nine-year-old son, the child said,
"Don't you think if God wants you to preach, He will take care of
Mother while you're away?"

Civilla was touched by her son's words and jotted down her
thoughts. When Stillman came home, she showed him the poem,
and he went to a reed organ and composed a melody. The chorus of
Civilla's hymn reads:

God will take care of you,
Through ev'ry day, o'er all the way;
He will take care of you,
God will take care of you.

Often in scripture God is compared to a shepherd. Sheep are
defenseless animals; they need protection. People are like sheep—
unprotected, vulnerable to disease and mishaps of every kind. The
Lord, like a concerned shepherd, cares for you. And if necessary,
He will gather you close to His heart and carry you. Every day, all
the way, He will care for you.

Sue McBeth

Missionary, Teacher
1830–1893

He is the one we proclaim, admonishing and teaching. . .so that we
may present everyone fully mature in Christ. To this end I strenuously
contend with all the energy Christ so powerfully works in me.
COLOSSIANS 1:28–29 NIV

Sue McBeth had a specific call to bring the gospel to Native
Americans. She also had a dream: she would train converts to
evangelize neighboring tribes. When she went to the Nez Perce tribe
in Oregon Territory in 1874, in spite of partial paralysis of her lower
limbs, she preached with what was described as "apostolic zeal."

To realize her dream, Sue held classes in her home for converts.
The training period was from four to five years. She said, "I'd rather
have one thoroughly trained and tested Nez Perce minister and pastor
than half a dozen half taught and trained." Such was her efficacy as a
teacher, it was reported in the 1890s that two-thirds of the tribe had
been converted through the preaching of the pastors Sue had trained.

It is one thing to receive a God-given dream and purpose for
your life. It is quite another thing to make that dream a reality. By
hard work and determination, Sue McBeth realized her purpose.

What are you doing with the dream God has given you? You
may have intended to begin a new ministry, be a diligent student of
the Bible, or strive to be more Christlike. Write your goals on paper, then turn them over to God. With His help, begin now to make
these a reality.

Marie Monson
Missionary
Early 20th Century

"My grace is sufficient for you, for my power is made perfect in weakness."
Therefore I will boast all the more gladly about my weaknesses,
so that Christ's power may rest on me.
2 CORINTHIANS 12:9 NIV

Missionary Marie Monson had been in China only a few months when she fell down a staircase and lay in a coma. When she regained consciousness, she experienced constant headaches, and the doctor ordered no language study for two years.

In this depressing time, Marie called for the elders of the church to anoint her with oil and pray for her. The headaches subsided.

Soon after the fall, Marie became ill with malaria. *Is this the end of my missionary career?* she questioned. In desperation she cried out, "Your will be done, Lord!"

Miraculously her temperature dropped. Marie's physical trials continued as she suffered bouts of malaria and dysentery. Yet through prayer she was repeatedly helped.

Why should a person determined to do God's will have to suffer? The apostle Paul asked God to relieve him of a chronic condition, but he was not delivered (2 Corinthians 12:7–9). Rather, because of the affliction he learned to depend on God's supernatural strength.

If your life is plagued by repeated illnesses or discouraging situations, lean on God, His Word, and prayer. Your troubles can be a showcase where God reveals His mighty power either by healing or strengthening you.

Amanda Smith

Preacher, Musician
1837–1915

> Since God in his wisdom saw to it that the world would
> never know him through human wisdom, he has used
> our foolish preaching to save those who believe.
> 1 CORINTHIANS 1:21 NLT

"I was a colored servant girl sitting away back by the door," Amanda said, describing her conversion experience. A young white woman begged Amanda to come to Christ, and as she knelt, the woman placed her arms around the black girl and prayed. That night Amanda vowed to "be the Lord's and live for Him."

After two unsuccessful marriages and the births of three children, Amanda heard a holiness evangelist. "I felt the touch of God from the crown of my head to the soles of my feet," she said. "O what a mighty peace and power took possession of me!"

Later, she received a vision of the word GO and a voice said, "*Go, preach.*" Amanda, uneducated, yet articulate in the pulpit, began to share through "foolish preaching."

After successful evangelistic meetings in the United States, Amanda trekked across England and Scotland in meetings for twelve years. She stayed two years in India and Burma, then eight years in Africa—all the time preaching the gospel.

God has chosen preaching as a primary means of conveying the knowledge of His Son. Jesus preached, and through the centuries His disciples have done the same.

Carefully listen to those who preach. The Word they declare is not human wisdom, but God's thoughts, direct from His heart.

Mary Williams
Missionary Wife
Early 19th Century

> But when I am afraid, I will put my trust in you. I praise God for
> what he has promised. I trust in God, so why should I be afraid?
> PSALM 56:3–4 NLT

Soon after missionaries John and Mary Williams arrived in the South
Seas islands in 1817, Mary held daily Bible classes for native women
and taught them to sew.

She was content with their work until John announced he was
going inland to preach. Because of reports of cannibalism, Mary
begged her husband to reconsider. She finally consented with the
stipulation that he would not go to the island of Erromanga, where
the natives were reported to be "the most wild and cruel."

In 1839 John ventured inland, but he didn't listen to his wife.
Four months later Mary was awakened in the night with the news she
had feared; only her husband's skull and a few bones were recovered.

Was Mary out of God's will to ask her husband not to go inland?
Was John wrong to go to a dangerous island to die and leave his wife
a widow and his three children fatherless? No doubt Mary struggled
with these questions as she mourned her husband's death.

Do you have unanswered questions of faith? When there seem
to be no answers, you can trust God. In the face of tragedy, you can
trust Him. Even when you pray and the results aren't as you hoped,
you can trust. Trust is leaving all in the hands of an all-knowing,
loving Savior. He is with you. Trust on!

Lillian Trasher

Missionary
1887–1965

> "Man shall not live on bread alone, but on every
> word that comes from the mouth of God."
> MATTHEW 4:4 NIV

Missionary Lillian Trasher faced a monumental task when she began Assiout Orphanage in Egypt. With only a bare knowledge of the language, she wrote textbooks, taught classes, and sometimes rode a donkey to villages begging for food and clothes for the children. But what about the orphans' spiritual needs? Lillian was concerned for this need also, and in letters to her supporters, she begged them to pray for God to move in the children's hearts.

Those prayers were answered in 1927 when Lillian wrote, "I have witnessed the greatest revival I have ever seen." Scores of boys and girls were saved. Lillian sent for the older boys who had left the orphanage and lived nearby. When they attended the services, she said, "All twenty-five of them dedicated their lives to God."

Our physical bodies need food, clothes, and shelter. We also possess an eternal spirit in need of nurturing. This part of our being develops by feeding on nourishment provided by God. Though busy caring for your physical needs, recognize as Lillian did the unseen part—your spirit. Don't neglect this vital part. Feed it daily with God's Word, prayer, and thanksgiving.

Dr. Jessie McDonald
Medical Missionary
1887–1980

> Then people brought little children to Jesus for him
> to place his hands on them and pray for them.
> MATTHEW 19:13 NIV

Jessie McDonald's interest in missions began at age seven when she helped her mother teach English to Chinese immigrants. One day as young Jessie helped a Chinese man, it dawned on her that he did not know Jesus. Her mother explained that many people in China had never heard of Jesus. "When I get big," Jessie said, "I'm going to China."

The McDonald family often entertained missionaries and on one occasion a missionary from New Hebrides recounted the dismal conditions of his field. As Jessie listened, she thought, *Do I really want to be a missionary?* "What we desperately need is a doctor," the missionary added, and Jessie decided she'd become a missionary doctor.

Dr. Jessie McDonald sailed for China in 1913, the first woman missionary-surgeon to serve under the China Inland Mission. Her services were invaluable to Asian women who did not allow male doctors to treat them.

A serving, fruit-bearing life began when a child was exposed to positive influences. Expose your children's soft, pliable minds to good things, and they will gravitate toward good. By the voices they hear, by the places you take them, allow Jesus to place His hand upon them so they will experience the glorious future God has planned for them.

Helen Steiner Rice

Poet
1900–1981

> "Look at the birds of the air; they do not sow or reap or store
> away in barns, and yet your heavenly Father feeds them.
> Are you not much more valuable than they?"
> MATTHEW 6:26 NIV

"He was the gentlest man I've ever known," poet Helen Steiner Rice said of her father. "He never raised his voice at me. . . . He had no need to because I wanted to please him more than anything."

From her childhood, Helen had fond memories of going fishing with her father. When her father died in the 1918 influenza epidemic, her plans to attend college had to be abandoned. Yet, for her entire life, the word "Father" evoked pleasant memories for her.

Helen's love for her father is reflected in her poem, "Fathers Are Wonderful People."

For the only reason Dad aspires to fortune and success
Is to make the family proud of him and bring them happiness
And like our Heavenly Father, he's a guardian and guide,
Someone that we can count on to be always on our side.

Make a list of the attributes you'd desire most in an earthly father. All these good qualities and more reside in God. This is a picture of the One who cares for you, who guides your life, who is always on your side—your kind, gentle, heavenly Father.

Amanda McFarland
Missionary
1837–1898

And God has placed in the church first of all apostles,
second prophets. . .then gifts. . .of helping, of guidance,
and of different kinds of tongues.
1 CORINTHIANS 12:28 NIV

Upon her husband's death in 1875, the Presbyterian Board sent Amanda McFarland to Fort Wrangel, Alaska, a town reported to have no doctor, no church, and no law or order. Her job was to establish a home for native girls attempting to escape from white traders who took the girls in exchange for goods.

Amanda began with twenty-one girls. She held Bible classes and taught them to sew. Soon she had one hundred girls in her care. Funds were scarce and when Amanda needed more room, she purchased a larger home with her own money. She claimed no special gifts, but when she became aware of a need, she rolled up her sleeves and did something about it.

Tucked away in the list of gifts given to the church is the gift of helps—giving practical assistance where needed. Women like Amanda excel in this gift as they help in kitchens and nurseries; by cooking, cleaning, and doing laundry.

No gift is superior to another. Neither are God's gifts for self-exaltation. Rather, they are to help the entire body of believers. Look around you. What needs do you see? Now use the gifts God has given you to ease the load for someone in your church or community.

Marilyn Kunz
Bible Study Organizer, Writer
1927–1999

I am not ashamed of the gospel, because it is the power of God that brings salvation to everyone who believes: first to the Jew, then to the Gentile.
ROMANS 1:16 NIV

"What do you believe about Jesus?" Marilyn Kunz asked her high school English teacher one afternoon. Using simple words, the Christian teacher, Vera Ehnbom, explained the gospel to Marilyn. She accepted Christ and began attending the teacher's Sunday school class.

After college Marilyn and her friend, Kay Schell, saw the need for home Bible study and the two women started a neighborhood group. They developed study guides, and in five years, two hundred groups were meeting in New York City suburbs to study the Bible.

From there, Neighborhood Bible Study spread across the country and around the world. Eventually Marilyn and Kay's guides were translated into over thirty languages and dialects. It began when one teacher unashamedly shared the truth about Jesus with a student.

Don't discount the few words you may share about Christ with an unsaved person. Because all of heaven's power stands behind your witness, the little you say has the potential to begin an avalanche of blessings. It did for teacher Vera Ehnbom. It will for you, also.

Evelyn LeTourneau
Wife and Mother
1900–1987

From inside the fish Jonah prayed to the LORD his God.
He said, "In my distress I called to the LORD, and he answered me."
JONAH 2:1–2 NIV

Evelyn was almost seventeen years old when she eloped with R. G. LeTourneau, a man twelve years her senior. During the first years of their marriage the couple lived in a single room, then in a rat-infested farmhouse while R. G. worked at menial jobs. But their greatest challenge came when their first child, a son, died in 1919. Stunned with grief, Evelyn and R. G. turned their lives over to God, started attending church, and began living by biblical principles.

R. G., an eighth-grade dropout, developed large earth-moving machinery, and his inventions revolutionized road building and jungle clearing. Success and wealth, however, did not deter Evelyn and R. G. from their earlier commitment. In fact, they remained focused on God's purposes and became known for their liberality by contributing ninety percent of their income to Christian work.

Death, loss, and disappointments also may have sent you reeling. As Evelyn and R. G. LeTourneau did, make a new commitment to godly purposes. God can then transform your distress and set you on a new, unwavering course for your life.

Nellie Fowler McCormick

Philanthropist
1835–1922

Honor the LORD with your wealth, with the firstfruits of all your crops.
PROVERBS 3:9 NIV

Nellie Fowler, a tall, handsome woman with brown hair and eyes, married Cyrus H. McCormick in 1858. When her husband, the inventor of the famous grain reaper, died twenty-six years later, she was left with a large estate. She could have used her great wealth to live in ease and pleasure, but Nellie chose to share her resources. She was reported to be one of the most generous Christian philanthropists of her time.

A deeply religious woman, Nellie believed the money had been given her by God and should be used wisely and for good purposes. Much of her giving went to benefit the world's youth, from seminary students to pupils in southern mountain schools and churches. Her three-story brownstone home in Chicago became a haven for missionaries going to and coming from mission fields. She said, "The greatest gift comes from self-sacrifice and devotion to the missionaries themselves."

Whether you have little or much, honor God with your possessions. The "firstfruits" speaks of placing the first and best portion at God's disposal. By giving to Him first, you *honor* God. This principle is an antidote for the human tendency to greed.

Be blessed; honor God with your wealth.

Henrietta Mears
Christian Educator, Author
1890–1963

> While they were worshiping the Lord and fasting, the Holy Spirit said,
> "Set apart for me Barnabas and Saul for the work to which I have called them."
> ACTS 13:2 NIV

In 1927, Henrietta Mears had a critical decision to make: Should she continue in her present occupation of teacher in a public school or consider full-time Christian ministry? She asked the Lord to use her talents where they would benefit His kingdom the most.

During a sabbatical from teaching, Henrietta spent time in California. There she was offered the position of Director of Christian Education in a church. Henrietta had a lunch appointment with the pastor and, as they approached the restaurant entrance, the door opened silently. It was the first time Henrietta had seen a door controlled by an electric eye. As she and the pastor talked, it became apparent to Henrietta a door for Christian service was also automatically opening.

When she began to work at the church, the Sunday school had about four hundred attendees. In two years' time, the number had multiplied to thousands. She began writing Sunday school lessons and eventually formed a publishing company, Gospel Light Press. It happened when a woman asked God for His highest and best for her life.

Do you have a decision to make? Are you confused about which path to take? Use the electronic door to the will of God: prayer. By your asking God to guide you, in time, the right door will effortlessly swing open.

Isobel Miller Kuhn
Missionary, Author
1901–1957

And without faith it is impossible to please God,
because anyone who comes to him must believe that he
exists and that he rewards those who earnestly seek him.
HEBREWS 11:6 NIV

While she was in college, Isobel Miller's faith was shaken when a professor said, "You just believe in God's existence because your papa and mama told you so." Doubts of God's reality increased, and she became a campus socialite. While engaged to be married, she discovered the young man was unfaithful to her and she thought of ending her life.

As she studied Dante, she read, "In His will is peace." Isobel raised both hands and said, "God, if there is a God, prove to me that You are, and if You will give me peace, I will give You my whole life."

With that prayer, Isobel became a believer. Later, she served God for twenty-nine years as a missionary in China. She was diagnosed with breast cancer in 1954. As treatment continued, she used the time to write eight books telling of her struggles of faith.

Have you, like Isobel, struggled to believe in God? This is where faith enters the picture. Saving faith looks at the claims of the Bible, and the evidence of an orderly creation. Then taking a leap of faith, it embraces the One who made it happen. God is not an entity or an influence, but a Person easily within reach. Embrace Him as your Savior. Such faith is rewarded with *Life*!

Clara Swaim
Medical Missionary
1834–1910

Sing and make music from your heart to the Lord,
always giving thanks to God the Father for everything.
EPHESIANS 5:19–20 NIV

Clara Swaim went to India in 1870, the first woman physician to serve on a mission field. She trained nurses and midwives and built the first women's hospital in that country. Though she treated up to seven thousand patients a year, she considered herself primarily an evangelist and worked to distribute the Hindustani Bible to her patients.

After Clara had been in India fifteen years, a Muslim prince asked her to become the physician to palace women. Again, her main concern was the spiritual needs of her patients. To her astonishment, Clara's hymnbook became the means of communicating the gospel to the royal women and children. She wrote, "There are more than thirty persons singing our hymns here already, for we have taught them to every one who would learn." She added, "We often find that we can sing Christianity to these people when we cannot preach it."

Joyous Christian songs wafting through a heathen court! What a unique way God chose to reach this royal family! The Bible encourages us to sing various kinds of Christian songs. These may celebrate a victory or simply bless God's Son, Jesus. Even if you don't claim a melodious singing voice, use yours to praise God. As Clara Swaim discovered, you will find that joyful Christian music pushes back the darkness of evil when nothing else avails.

Laura Askew Haygood
Missionary Teacher, Evangelist
1845–1900

> But God chose the foolish things of the world to shame the wise;
> God chose the weak things of the world to shame the strong.
> 1 CORINTHIANS 1:27 NIV

"Foolish! You can't do it!" friends told Laura Haygood when she considered going to China as a missionary. Although she taught in a girls' high school in Atlanta, Georgia, and spent every Saturday instructing Sunday school teachers from several denominations, Laura was in poor health and walked with crutches. But when the superintendent of a Chinese mission needed an experienced person to develop a Christian education program in the Shanghai area, Laura took the plea to heart. In spite of limitations, she went to China in 1884.

Laura faced opposition to the education of Chinese young women, but through her efforts soon two-thirds of the school's students were girls. She taught Bible classes, did house-to-house visitation, opened a girls' high school, began a training school for new missionaries, founded two training schools for Bible women, and raised money to begin new schools. In spite of a disability, Laura ably served at her post. She was appropriately called "the teachers' teacher."

Have you sensed a call to do something that seems out of your reach because of a disability? Look to God. Strange as it seems, He actually *chooses* to use those who are weak so they will operate in His divine strength.

Susannah Spurgeon
Author, Book Supplier
1832–1903

She opens her arms to the poor and extends her hands to the needy.
PROVERBS 31:20 NIV

Charles Spurgeon, pastor of London's Metropolitan Tabernacle, is considered one of the great preachers of all time. His natural gift of oratory attracted crowds in the thousands. But what of his wife, Susannah?

As the pastor's wife, Susannah did not sit idly by, but when she saw a need, she did something about it. Attending her husband's college were numerous young men training for the ministry. One of their needs was for expensive theological books that were beyond the reach of most students. Susannah solicited donations for books in her husband's monthly magazine, *The Sword and the Trowel*. Then she invited needy ministerial students to purchase books at reduced rates. From there, Susannah's book ministry spread to provide books for missionaries. By 1902, she had given out more than ten thousand volumes. It happened when one woman saw a need and did something about it.

Needs abound all around. Pray about what you can do. Offer your knowledge, expertise, and money as Susannah Spurgeon did. God's special blessing rests on those who extend generous hands to the needy. The psalmist said, "Oh, the joys of those who are kind to the poor" (Psalm 41:1 NLT).

Phoebe Cary
Hymn Writer
1824–1871

Andrew, Simon Peter's brother, spoke up, "Here is a boy with five small barley loaves and two small fish, but how far will they go among so many?"
JOHN 6:8–9 NIV

Two gamblers were playing cards in a casino near Hong Kong when the younger man began to softly sing, "One sweetly, solemn thought comes to me o'er and o'er, I am nearer home today than I've ever been before."

An older man looked up in surprise and asked, "Where did you learn that hymn?"

"Oh, Sunday school," he replied.

His partner threw down his cards. "There's my last game," he said. "That's the end!" The change in the man was reported to be permanent.

When the story was told to Phoebe Cary, the writer of the hymn, she said, "It makes me happy to think that any word I could say has done a little good."

A little good! Jesus' disciples were not impressed with a boy's small lunch. What good would that little do for such a great need? Jesus took the lunch in His hands, and all of heaven's blessings came upon the "little bit."

When you look at the array of human needs, you may be tempted to think the little you do won't make a difference. Your offering is small. Your witness is weak. Your influence is limited. You are wrong! Place your "scrap of bread" in Jesus' hands and watch what happens. With it He will feed a multitude!

Eliza Gillett Bridgman
Missionary
1805–1871

> So when Peter went up to Jerusalem, the circumcised believers criticized him and said, "You went into the house of uncircumcised men and ate with them."
> ACTS 11:2–3 NIV

Eliza Gillett, appointed as a missionary to China at age forty, expected to remain single her entire life. Elijah Bridgman, already on the field, thought he'd never marry, but shortly before Eliza arrived he changed his mind and prayed for a wife. When Eliza came to his mission in 1845, romance blossomed, Elijah proposed, and she accepted.

Not everyone was happy for the newlyweds. When word of their marriage reached the mission board, they were shocked and wrote Eliza. Hadn't she intimated when she went to China she would remain unmarried? They charged her "with breach of contract."

Eliza's return letter was respectful, but firm. She reminded the board that she had not taken a monastic vow. She also believed the mission was better off for her marriage. Members of the mission board eventually relented and became friends with the Bridgmans.

The early church also had its difficulties. The Christian leaders in Jerusalem criticized Peter for eating with Gentiles—not an accepted practice for a Jew. However, when they heard the whole story, their criticisms turned into praises.

When you experience conflicts with your Christian brothers and sisters, hear them out. Then resolve matters quickly—before you must answer to God.

Carol Terry Talbot
Missionary
Early 20th Century

> About midnight Paul and Silas were praying and singing
> hymns to God, and the other prisoners were listening to them.
> ACTS 16:25 NIV

Carol Talbot was headed for missionary work in India when her ship docked in Manila and the Japanese bombed Pearl Harbor. As World War II began, Carol was captured and remained a prisoner for three and a half years.

Food was scarce in prison. Because of poor nutrition Carol contracted impetigo, a communicable disease. She said, "As the disease spread over my body, people. . .were afraid to touch anything near me."

One day Carol told a fellow prisoner, "I suppose someday I'll see God's purpose in this and thank Him for it." The woman responded, "How much better it would be if you thanked Him for it now by faith." This was Carol's wake-up call. She said, "I thanked God for giving me. . .a heart to understand why I had become the 'camp leper.' "

Through this experience Carol learned a spiritual principle: as she thanked God in the circumstance, blessings were released upon her. The next day the nurse changed her treatment. Friends and even strangers offered to wash her sheets and clean her cubicle.

Carol's experience was similar to that of Paul and Silas. Stripped, beaten, in stocks in an inner prison, yet they praised God and the prison door flew open.

Often our prayers are like shopping lists. How much better if we first raised our eyes heavenward with praise and thanksgiving.

Anne Askew
Christian Martyr
1521–1546

> There were others who were tortured, refusing to be released
> so that they might gain an even better resurrection.
> HEBREWS 11:35 NIV

As Anne Askew studied the Bible and listened to the preaching of a reformer, she became a Christian. From then until her death, she refused to compromise her beliefs in Christ.

Anne, at age twenty-four, was arrested, accused of denying biblical truth, and tried for heresy. During this time her husband renounced her. Yet she remained firm in her Christian commitment.

The second time Anne was arrested, she was placed in the Tower of London and condemned to die as a heretic. During her imprisonment she wrote in her diary, "They put me on the rack because I confessed no ladies or others to be of my opinion. . . . I lay still and did not cry out. . .they took pains to rack me. . .till I was nigh dead."

On the day of her execution a weakened Anne was brought to the stake on a chair because of the effects of her tortures. At the last minute, the Lord Chancellor said the king would pardon her if she denied her faith in Christ. She refused. The fire was lit and Anne Askew died.

A steadfast faith does not guarantee a life free of suffering. Arm yourself with the commitment of Anne Askew so whether you are delivered or not, God's strength will keep you unwavering in faith.

Helen Steiner Rice

Poet

1900–1981

> Let the message of Christ dwell among you richly as you teach and admonish one another with all wisdom through psalms, hymns, and songs from the spirit, with gratitude in your hearts singing to God.
>
> COLOSSIANS 3:16 NIV

"When I was a child I attended Sunday school and sang 'Jesus loves me,' " said greeting card writer, Helen Steiner Rice. "I believed the words then, and I believe them now."

Helen recalls sitting on her mother's or grandmother's knee and having them read to her from the Bible. One of her favorite passages was the twenty-third Psalm. "My advice," Helen wrote to a troubled person, "read that chapter when you first wake up. Read it very slowly and carefully and with deep meditation. . . . It is the most powerful piece of writing in the world and it can heal any hurt the world inflicts."

Hurts and disappointments are part of the fabric of life. No one escapes. Helen felt the ugly sting of death when her husband took his life after the stock market crash of the 1930s. The Word of God was the soothing balm she poured into her bruised soul.

Often the Word is put to music, and we sing Bible truth. Whatever way you choose, do as Helen recommended; meditate on the Bible. Read it regularly. Life's deepest wounds are healed by the powerful Word of God.

Julia Ward Howe
Hymn Writer
1819–1910

> Righteousness exalts a nation, but sin condemns any people.
> PROVERBS 14:34 NIV

In 1861, during the Civil War, Julia Howe visited a military camp near Washington DC, and watched Union soldiers march to the song "John Brown's Body." A friend expressed a wish that someone would write Christian verses for the lilting melody. The next morning words tumbled into Julia's mind and, in the predawn darkness she quickly scribbled them on paper. The song, "Battle Hymn of the Republic," was published in *Atlantic Monthly*, and sung by Union soldiers during the war.

Julia Howe was born into a prominent New York City family and received an excellent education. By age seventeen she was writing poetry for publication. She later worked for prison reform, woman's suffrage, and world peace. But today she is remembered as the author of a popular patriotic song. The last verse and chorus of Julia's hymn read:

> *In the beauty of the lilies, Christ was born across the sea,*
> *With a glory in His bosom that transfigures you and me;*
> *As He died to make men holy, let us live to make men free;*
> *While Christ is marching on.*
> *Glory! Glory, hallelujah! Glory! Glory, hallelujah!*
> *Glory! Glory, hallelujah! Our God is marching on.*

Julia Howe's words remind us that each person has an obligation to improve her country. We do this, in part, by keeping the laws, voting in elections, and praying for those in authority (see 1 Timothy 2:1–2). A nation is only as good as each individual citizen.

Abigail Adams
Wife of a United States President
1744–1818

> So I will very gladly spend for you everything
> I have and expend myself as well.
> 2 Corinthians 12:15 NIV

When Abigail Smith married John Adams in 1764, little did she realize the sacrifices she would be called to make. As John became involved in establishing the new nation, Abigail was left to care for their farm, family finances, four children, elderly parents, and sick relatives. Alone she endured the birth of her stillborn child. At one time the couple was apart ten years while John took care of America's interests in Philadelphia and abroad.

In the face of these hardships, Abigail remained steadfast in her faith as seen in her letters to John. "The only certainty of life is God," she wrote. Repeatedly she said, "Only righteousness can exalt a nation."

Love for God, her husband, and the nation motivated Abigail Adams. Such devotion is needed in every age. Is your patience being stretched to the limit by separations, family problems, or difficult people? Have you become weary as you care for elderly parents or a sick spouse? Unselfish Christian love is willing to go an extra mile. Now is a good time for you to pray: "God, I am willing to spend myself for others without thought of any return except Your love and approval."

Rachel Saint
Missionary, Bible Translator
1914–1994

"I tell you that if two of you on earth agree about anything they ask for,
it will be done for them by my Father in heaven."
MATTHEW 18:19 NIV

Rachel Saint's interest in missions began when she read missionary stories as a child. However, it wasn't until she was in her thirties that she felt called to a mission field.

Rachel studied to be a Bible translator, and her first assignment was to the Piro Indians in Peru. Yet she felt a strong desire to work with tribes unreached by the gospel.

While visiting her brother Nate, a missionary pilot in Ecuador, she became aware of a fierce, warlike people living in the jungle, the Huaorani Indians, a tribe untouched by the gospel. However, Wycliffe, the group sponsoring Rachel, had no work in Ecuador.

The urge remained strong, and she shared her desire with a Peruvian pastor. The two agreed in prayer that the way would open for Rachel to go to this people. Within a year, the Ecuadorian ambassador to the United States invited Wycliffe to work among the native tribes. Rachel went to the Huaoranis, learned their language, and lived to see the Bible translated into their language.

A successful missionary career to an unreached people began as a result of agreeing prayer. What dilemmas do you face that need God's intervening hand? Determine what God's will is, then, together with another believer, agree in prayer for the work to be done. God honors sincere prayers of agreement.

Dale Evans Rogers
Actress, Author, Songwriter
1912–2001

> We are hard pressed on every side, but not crushed; perplexed, but not in despair; persecuted, but not abandoned; struck down, but not destroyed.
>
> 2 CORINTHIANS 4:8–9 NIV

When Dale Evans and her husband, Roy Rogers, announced in 1950 they were expecting a child, the world took notice and rejoiced with the cowboy actress and actor. Their child, Robin Elizabeth, lived only two years, however.

The famous couple loved children, and over the next years adopted four children, making a total of eight in the family. But tragedy was never far from Dale and Roy. In 1964, Debbie, their Korean-Puerto Rican child, was killed in a church bus crash. Sandy, whom the Rogers had adopted when he was five, died at age eighteen while serving with the military in Germany.

"Once more we made the sad journey to Forest Lawn Memorial Park," Dale said. She wrote a book to honor each deceased child. In memory of their son, Dale and Roy performed for United States servicemen in Vietnam and told the soldiers of God's peace.

When tragedy beat at Dale Evans, she drew from an inner well of comfort and it sustained her. You, too, have an inexhaustible source of strength in Christ. You may be struck down, but no—never are you abandoned or defeated.

Lillian Trasher
Missionary
1897–1965

For he will command his angels concerning you to guard
you in all your ways; they will lift you up in their hands,
so that you will not strike your foot against a stone.
PSALM 91:11–12 NIV

Lillian Trasher went to Egypt as a missionary in 1910, and eventually began an orphanage for neglected children. By 1916 she had fifty children in her care. But obstacles developed as she cared for their needs. Often with nothing to feed the children, she rode from village to village on a donkey begging for food.

A perilous time occurred during a political outbreak against British rule in 1919. As hostilities increased, Lillian and her children survived for three days hiding in an abandoned brick kiln. Buildings all around the orphanage were destroyed but miraculously the buildings on orphanage property stood intact.

In 1933 Lillian suffered another blow when Muslim authorities removed seventy children from the orphanage, the only home many of them had known.

Dangers, dire needs, and anxious moments haunted this woman for years. Through it all, God supported Lillian Trasher. No doubt at times, angels came to her rescue.

Are you in a precarious situation? Call on God. You also may be directed to ask Him to send His angels to support you spiritually, mentally, physically, and emotionally—in all your ways.

To the one who is victorious, I will give the right to sit with me on my throne,
just as I was victorious and sat down with my Father on his throne.
REVELATION 3:21 NIV

Missionaries Mary Porter and Maria Brown went to China in 1871 well aware of the injustices imposed upon Chinese women. Female infants were sometimes killed at birth. Girls were denied education and often forced into cohabitation and slavery.

Although the binding of little girls' feet had been practiced for centuries, the missionaries agreed they would not allow this in their Christian school. Foot binding could cause severe pain, broken bones, and permanent deformities.

When Mary and Maria began Peking Boarding School, 150 girls applied for admittance. Because of the missionaries' stand against bound feet, only seven could enroll. Yet the women stood firm. They believed the body was the temple of the Holy Spirit and was defiled by this practice.

In the 1880s Mary and Maria led an effort to ban all customs detrimental to women. At a Christian women's conference in 1894, a leading Chinese woman unbound her feet before attendees and encouraged others to do the same. Finally, in 1907, the Chinese government passed a law forbidding foot binding.

Are you aware of an injustice that needs correcting? If two women missionaries—with persistence and prayer—could help overcome a centuries-old custom, you, too, can address problems that need changing in your neighborhood, your town, or even in the world.

Mary Slessor
Missionary
1848–1915

I am glad to boast about my weaknesses, so that the power of
Christ can work through me. That's why I take pleasure in my weaknesses,
and in the insults, hardships, persecutions, and troubles that
I suffer for Christ. For when I am weak, then I am strong.

2 CORINTHIANS 12:9–10 NLT

At age eleven Mary Slessor worked in a Scottish textile mill half the day and attended school the other half. Three years later she became known as a "factory girl," working twelve hours a day at a loom.

When her father died, Mary became the sole support of her mother and six younger brothers and sisters. She learned to get along with little food and clothes. She had no luxuries. Her only social outlet was the church she attended.

While Mary's early life was bleak, it prepared her for mission work in Africa, where she went in 1876 at age twenty-eight. Calabar was known for its slave trade. Witchcraft and human sacrifice were routine. Newborn twins were instantly murdered. Women were treated like cattle. In this heathen darkness, Mary successfully preached the gospel and founded a home to train girls to carry on the work. Her efforts came to the attention of the British government, and she was appointed vice-consul in Okoyong.

An all-knowing God knows what is ahead. Present hardships, trials, persecutions, and rejections are training for future usefulness in God's kingdom. As you are content in your present situation, you will someday look back and see this time as a stepping-stone to the greater responsibilities God had for you.

Mrs. Charles Jones Soong
Christian Mother
1869–1931

> Be still before the LORD and wait patiently for him; do not fret when people succeed in their ways, when they carry out their wicked schemes.
> PSALM 37:7 NIV

Mrs. Charles Soong was known as China's great Christian Mother, and gave that country four of its most distinguished public figures. Her daughter, Mayling, became the wife of China's statesman, Chiang Kai-shek.

Mrs. Soong gave generously to the needy. She daily gathered her family for Bible reading, hymn singing, and prayer. But her greatest legacy to her six children was her prayer life. Her daughter, Madam Chiang said, "Whenever Mother prayed. . .the undertaking invariably turned out well."

Her family learned not to disturb their mother's prayer time, which often began at dawn and continued for hours. "Asking God was not a matter of spending five minutes to ask Him to bless. . . . It meant waiting upon God until she felt His leading," Madam Chiang said.

On one occasion her family felt the impact of their mother's prayers when her son-in-law Chiang and his army were trapped by enemy soldiers with no possible escape. Mrs. Soong's prayers were answered when a snowstorm broke and held up the enemies' advance. Chiang's life was spared and a seeming defeat turned to victory.

You, your family, or your friends may be trapped by various "enemies." You see no way out. Now is the time to take prayer to the next level; wait on God. Wait until you are confident of a positive outcome.

Corrie ten Boom
Author, Evangelist
1892–1983

> But thanks be to God! He gives us the victory through our Lord Jesus Christ.
> 1 CORINTHIANS 15:57 NIV

Ninety-six thousand women perished in Ravensbruck prison during World War II, including Corrie ten Boom's sister, Betsie. Other family members perished in other camps. Yet Corrie's life was spared and in the aftermath of the war, she comforted the weak, discouraged, and maimed, working to help them forgive their captors and move on with their lives.

After a church meeting in Munich where Corrie preached, a man extended his hand to her. She recognized him as a former SS guard at Ravensbruck, and Betsie's pale face flashed before her.

"How grateful I am for your message, *Fraulein,*" the man told Corrie. She, who taught others to forgive their persecutors, kept her hand at her side while angry thoughts surged through her mind. "Jesus, I can't forgive him," she silently prayed. Yet when Corrie extended her hand, something happened; a current seemed to pass from her to him. She couldn't forgive him, but Christ in her could. No wonder the words, "Jesus Is Victor" are etched on Corrie's gravestone.

What will be written on your gravestone? Will you forgive those who have betrayed, mistreated, and used you? Or will you take an unforgiving heart with you into eternity? There was plenty of love at Calvary, and if you ask Him, Jesus will share unlimited amounts with you.

Lilias Trotter
Missionary
1853–1928

Wait for the LORD; be strong and take heart and wait for the LORD.
PSALM 27:14 NIV

Lilias Trotter, an artist and wealthy socialite, enjoyed travel, education, and the friendship of men and women of renown in London's social scene. In 1888 she put this aside to become a missionary to the Muslims of Algeria. Realizing Muslims could not be reached by traditional methods of evangelism, she used her knowledge of art and literature to write and design attractively illustrated tracts.

Beginning with three workers, she organized evangelistic teams to distribute the literature. Eventually she employed thirty full-time workers. One of her major accomplishments was translating the New Testament into the Algerian dialect.

The task of converting Muslims to Christ was slow work. Lilias said, "Time is nothing to God—nothing in its speeding, nothing in its halting." Over and over she wrote in her diary, "Blessed are all they that wait for Him."

Does God understand the urgency of our prayers? Yes, but for reasons unknown to us, there are delays. In Psalm 40, David rehearsed what he learned in his waiting times: He was lifted from despair, his feet were set upon a rock, and God gave him a new song.

Be assured, God has heard your prayers. While you wait for God to act, use the time to learn about the character of your great God. His answer is worth waiting for.

Lettie Cowman
Author, Missionary
1870–1960

Do not love the world or anything in the world.
If anyone loves the world, love for the Father is not in them.
1 John 2:15 NIV

Lettie Cowman, a new convert, wrote in her diary concerning the books in her library, "I can't continue to have companionship of the blessed Trinity while reading these." So book after book went into the fire.

Lettie, an excellent pianist, also had stacks of sheet music from operas and popular songs. The Holy Spirit whispered to her, *"Does all this glorify your Lord?"* Much of her music was also burned as God directed her to separate herself from lesser things for God's higher purposes.

Later, Lettie and her husband, Charles, went as missionaries to Japan. After Charles's death, Lettie became president of a missionary society, befriended world leaders, preached around the world, and wrote Christian books and articles. Indeed, it was necessary for Lettie Cowman to put to death much of her self-life as God prepared her for greater things.

The world is under the influence of Satan. God calls Christians to separate themselves from a worldly lifestyle. Think about what society says about marriage, the home, and raising children. Compare this with God's standard. Be open as Lettie Cowman was to choose higher, better, and eternal values.

Sally Thomas
Generous Giver
1769–1813

> They gave as much as they were able, and even beyond
> their ability. . .they gave themselves first of all to the Lord.
> 2 CORINTHIANS 8:3, 5 NIV

Little is known of Sally Thomas except what Joseph Rowell, her pastor's son, wrote about her in a magazine article. She lived in Cornish, New York, and for over twenty years worked for fifty cents a week as a domestic servant. After a few expenses, she gave everything she earned to mission causes. Sally's offering was the first gift donated to the American Board of Commissioners for Foreign Missions. She managed to save over three hundred dollars during her lifetime, which she willed to foreign mission causes at her death.

Paul urged the Corinthian Christians to excel in the grace of giving (2 Corinthians 8:7). He went on to explain principles to follow when you give. First, give in proportion to what God has given you. Second, follow through with your promises. Third, give sacrificially and cheerfully. God allows you to earn money so you can share with others. Generous giving also frees the hand of God to shower His blessings upon you.

Jesus said of one woman, "This poor widow hath cast in more than they all. . .she of her penury hath cast in all the living that she had" (Luke 21:3, 4 KJV). She and Sally Thomas truly excelled in the grace of giving. You can, too.

Betty Stam
Missionary Martyr
1906–1934

> I know whom I have believed, and am convinced that he
> is able to guard what I have entrusted to him until that day.
> 2 TIMOTHY 1:12 NIV

Betty Scott was raised in China by missionary parents. As a young person she took as her life motto, "To me to live is Christ, and to die is gain."

At Moody Bible Institute the "no-frills" girl with dark hair met John Stam. Both were preparing for missionary service. They fell in love and as they talked of their future, both agreed, "God first." They married in China in 1933.

Betty was bathing the couple's three-month-old daughter when the message came that Communist forces had captured their city. When rebels burst into their home, the Stams were prepared. Before the soldiers took John away, Betty served them tea and cake. Later, the men returned for Betty. She used the delay to conceal her child.

Bound, stripped of their outer clothes, Betty and John were paraded through the streets to the taunts of onlookers. Led up a hill, the couple knelt, and their lives ended. Later, a woman brought the Stam's daughter, Helen, to a missionary.

An earlier commitment gave Betty Stam courage to face death and trust God to take care of her child. Our commitments are important, and often life-changing. Are you willing that God's plan for you be done, whether "by life or by death?"

Evangeline Cory Booth

Salvation Army General
1865–1950

> "Call to me and I will answer you and tell you
> great and unsearchable things you do not know."
> JEREMIAH 33:3 NIV

General William Booth, founder of the Salvation Army, once said of his workers, "Some of my best men are women!" This was true of Booth's daughter, Evangeline.

When she became National Commander of the United States Salvation Army in 1904, workers were often pelted with ridicule and rotten tomatoes as they preached and sang on street corners. But through Evangeline's efforts, the army received worldwide recognition, and she was awarded the Distinguished Service Medal by President Woodrow Wilson.

With the onset of World War I, Evangeline wanted to help the soldiers in France. She handpicked men and women officers to go to the front to read the Bible to the troops, pray with the men, and give weary soldiers encouragement. Her "Doughnut Girls" became world famous as they served coffee and doughnuts to soldiers behind the front lines.

While Evangeline's only motive was to encourage the troops, her efforts served a dual purpose. Returning soldiers praised the Salvation Army workers and in turn, the army's image improved. Much of the respect the world now gives to the Salvation Army is due to the wise decisions of Evangeline Booth.

When you determine to do a good deed, you never know how God will bless and do greater things than you'd ever dream possible. When we call, He always responds in amazing ways!

Mary Lee Cagle
Evangelist
1864–1955

> "Obey me, and I will be your God and you will be my people.
> Walk in obedience to all I command you, that it may go well with you."
> JEREMIAH 7:23 NIV

"God, if You'll heal my husband, I'll preach!" Mary Cagle prayed. A voice responded, "Will you preach if I don't heal him?" This was Mary's wake-up call. "Yes, Lord," she finally said. "Whether he lives or dies, I'll do what You want me to do."

At age fifteen Mary Lee had been converted and called to Christian work. She decided to be a foreign missionary, but as she sought God during a revival meeting, she became convinced God wanted her to stay in America and work as an evangelist. Not willing to face the reproach women preachers of that era endured, instead she married a minister and helped him in ministry. Yet, she didn't have peace of mind.

After three years of marriage, her husband became critically ill and eventually died. Mary gave total allegiance to God's will and became an evangelist. In 1927 she reported, "I've held thirteen revival meetings, preached 175 times, and saw 216 converted."

Has God asked you to do a work for Him, and you're attempting to strike a compromise? Lay your reluctance, pride, and will at Jesus' feet. As Mary Cagle discovered, total obedience brings His total peace.

Elizabeth Bunyan
Second Wife of John Bunyan
1630–1692

> Say to those with fearful hearts, "Be strong, and do not fear, for your
> God is coming to destroy your enemies. He is coming to save you."
> ISAIAH 35:4 NLT

When Elizabeth married John Bunyan, the man who later authored *Pilgrim's Progress*, she took upon herself the care of John's four children from his first marriage. This included Mary, a blind child. Elizabeth also knew her husband would continue to preach the gospel although it was against the law for men not ordained by the Church of England.

Shortly after their marriage John was arrested and thrown into prison for preaching. With no way to make a living, Elizabeth and the children survived on charity. During this time she also delivered a stillborn infant.

However, Elizabeth did not bemoan her fate, but traveled to London and with boldness pled for John's release before the House of Lords. When she burst into tears before the assembly, she said it was "for the account the men will have to give at the coming of the Lord." In spite of her efforts, John remained in prison for twelve years.

Elizabeth faced injustice, hardship, and poverty, yet she endured. You don't know what you can withstand until you go through a difficult experience—but God knows. When you arrive on the other side of the hardship, you will marvel at the unseen hand of Christ that sustained you all the while.

Mildred Cable
Missionary
1877–1952

Francesca and Evangeline French
Missionaries
19th–20th Centuries

> Paul had a vision of a man of Macedonia standing and begging him,
> "Come over to Macedonia and help us." After Paul had seen the vision,
> we got ready at once. . .concluding that God had called us to
> preach the gospel to them.
> ACTS 16:9–10 NIV

After twenty-one years of routine missionary work in China, Mildred Cable and Francesca and Evangeline French, now middle-aged women, felt called to carry the gospel to Northwest China where the name of Jesus was not known.

When they shared their plans, fellow missionaries said, "Why leave a successful work in a school to roam deserts?" After a year of prayer, the three decided they had heard from God. For several months they traveled by cart on muddy mountain trails to arrive in Suchow, a city inhabited by criminals, traders, and merchants. In the winter they were isolated by heavy snows, but for eight months of the year the women gave out tracts and held meetings. In one season they conducted 656 services, entered over two thousand homes to preach, and sold thousands of scripture portions.

The Holy Spirit had indeed called Mildred, Francesca, and Evangeline to the uttermost parts. God continues to speak. Listen to Him when you read the Bible. Keep an open ear for the Spirit's voice as you pray. God will direct you to give, pray, or go as you listen.

Dorothea Dix
Author, Teacher, Nurse
1802–1887

"So too, a Levite, when he came to the place and saw him,
passed by on the other side. But a Samaritan, as he traveled,
came where the man was; and when he saw him, he took pity on him."
LUKE 10:32–33 NIV

In 1840 Dorothea Dix volunteered to teach a Sunday school class of twenty inmates at a women's prison in East Cambridge, Massachusetts. She found the prison conditions appalling. The women, many mentally ill, were confined in unheated rooms in "cages, closets, cellars, stalls, pens; chained, naked, beaten with rods and lashed into obedience."

This discovery led Dorothea to visit three hundred other jails and five hundred almshouses. She took the case to court and pled for improved treatment for the insane, mentally retarded, and criminals. Her efforts led to new laws that benefited the unfortunate in Massachusetts and other states.

When commended for her work, Dorothea said, "I am merely acting in obedience to the Voice of God."

Dorothea Dix reached out in compassion to those who could not help themselves. Where can you make a difference? Pray for Christ's compassion and look for opportunities to showcase it to the unfortunate in your community.

Cynthia Farrar
Missionary Teacher
1795–1862

God's love has been poured out into our hearts
through the Holy Spirit, who has been given to us.
ROMANS 5:5 NIV

The mission board had questions when they sent Cynthia Farrar to India in 1827. What will the American public think of a single woman going to the mission field—something that had not been done before. And who will Miss Farrar teach in India? It was common knowledge that most Hindu fathers opposed education for their daughters.

Miss Farrar began a girls' school in Bombay, and there were problems. Attendance of the pupils was erratic as mothers withdrew their daughters for petty reasons or the girls left school to marry.

Cynthia Farrar persisted. It was said of her, "It was chiefly by gaining the love of her pupils, and making it pleasant for them to attend her school, that Miss Farrar could keep them long enough to learn to read."

By 1851 high caste Indian men invited Cynthia to begin schools for their daughters. Later, primary and secondary mission schools were built upon the foundation she had laid.

When Cynthia Farrar died after thirty-four years of service in India, hundreds of Hindu women honored her by attending her funeral. Her life is proof that the best way to influence people is to love them.

Whom are you attempting to win to Christ? Try love. By your actions and words, show them a heart full of Calvary love.

Lucie E. Campbell

Hymn Writer
1885–1963

> "On this rock I will build my church,
> and the gates of Hades will not overcome it."
>
> MATTHEW 16:18 NIV

Shortly after Lucie's birth, her father was killed in a train accident and her mother went to work to support her nine children. When Lucie graduated from high school she received a teaching certificate, but suffered the injustices of unequal pay and benefits for black teachers.

Although she had little musical training, Lucie composed over eighty hymns. Many of her songs encourage those who endure prejudice, racism, and injustice. They also speak of conversion and commitment to Christ. The first verse of her song, "He Understands, He'll Say Well Done," reads:

If when you give the best of your service,
Telling the world that the savior is come;
Be not dismayed when men don't believe you;
He understands; He'll say, "Well done."

While the world for Lucie was an unjust place, in her church she found love, appreciation, and fruition of her musical gifts. On one occasion she accompanied world-famous soloist Marian Anderson at a religious convention. In 1915 she was selected music director of the National Sunday School and Baptist Training Union Congress. Lucie also found an outlet for her teaching skills in training Sunday school teachers.

The church is not only our solid rock in an unstable and harsh world, it is also a venue where we develop our gifts and put them to use. Boldly take your place in God's glorious church!

Lillian Dickson
Missionary
1901–1983

How beautiful on the mountains are the feet of those who bring good news, who proclaim peace, who bring good tidings, who proclaim salvation.
ISAIAH 52:7 NIV

At the beginning of her missionary work in Taiwan, Lillian Dickson heard about aborigine tribes living in the mountains who remained untouched by the gospel. Many of these tribespeople were afflicted with leprosy, tuberculosis, and dysentery. They had no crafts or skills. The word "God" was not in their vocabulary, and they had no written language.

"Lil" took it upon herself to reach the forgotten people. Walking miles in the unexplored mountains, she became a one-woman medical missionary service to the former headhunters.

On one occasion, Lil took medicine to villagers who suffered from worms. When the aborigines became sick after taking the medication, Lil watched as they gathered in circles and quietly argued. Feeling danger, she and her friends smiled and sang hymns to keep up their courage. The next day the chief's assistant told Lil several tribesmen had been in favor of killing the missionaries. "We waited and now we're not sick," he said.

Lil's feet became dirty and tired while walking the Taiwan jungle trails. Yet God's Word describes them as beautiful because of the message they carried. Use your feet to bring good tidings to the suffering in hospitals, jails, and nursing homes, and join the ranks of those whose feet qualify to be called lovely.

Mahalia Jackson

Gospel Singer
1911–1972

> O come, let us sing unto the LORD:
> let us make a joyful noise to the rock of our salvation.
> PSALM 95:1 KJV

Mahalia Jackson sang for presidents and her recordings brought her worldwide fame, yet she never compromised her commitment to "make a joyful noise to the Lord."

As a little girl growing up in her father's church in New Orleans, Mahalia sang in a children's choir, and the jazz influence of the city found a permanent place in the rhythm and beat of her music.

When she was five, her mother died and Mahalia's father sent her to live with an aunt who did not allow secular music in her home. There Mahalia sang hymns and gospel songs and never abandoned this spiritual heritage.

At age sixteen Mahalia moved to Chicago, where she worked in a food plant and as a maid. When she became a soloist in a church choir, recording and performance opportunities came her way. Yet, obedient to her high calling, she sang only gospel music.

By the 1950s she had achieved world fame. Her recording "I Can Put My Trust in Jesus" won a prize from the French Academy, her recording of "Silent Night" a bestselling single in Norway.

As Mahalia Jackson made it her guiding star to sing only praises to God, make it your goal to do what pleases God, what best utilizes your God-given talents, and what brings glory to His name.

Fannie Edna Stafford
Hymn Writer
Early 20th Century

> "Then Jesus went around doing good and healing all
> who were oppressed by the devil, for God was with him."
> ACTS 10:38 NLT

"The great need of this weary world is to know that somebody cares," the pastor told his congregation. The message burned into one listener's heart—Fannie Stafford.

Later that day Fannie pondered the pastor's words and decided, "Yes, people need to know someone cares for them." She wrote some verses and sent them to a publisher. When her poem was published, a musician recognized their beauty, wrote music for the words, and it became the hymn "Somebody Cares."

Somebody knows when your heart aches,
And ev'rything seems to go wrong;
Somebody knows when the shadows
Need chasing away with a song;
Somebody knows when you're lonely,
Tired, discouraged and blue;
Somebody wants you to know Him,
And know that He dearly loves you.

Fannie Stafford was right—the world has seen enough indifference. People need to know that at least one person cares for them. And Jesus cares. But there is just one way that truth can be communicated; those who have felt His care showing it.

You may be prompted to make a call, write a note, or give a plate of cookies. You can teach a class, sing a song, give a hug, take someone to lunch, say "I love you," or write a hymn. It is not difficult to show that Christ cares; it takes only a little effort and some of your time.

Ann Hasseltine Judson
Missionary
1789–1826

> Mary responded, "I am the Lord's servant.
> May everything you have said about me come true."
> LUKE 1:38 NLT

After a revival in New England in 1806, young Ann Hasseltine resolved to devote herself to godly purposes. She wrote in her journal, "Direct me in Thy service, and I ask no more. I would not choose my position of work, or place of labor. Only let me know Thy will, and I will readily comply."

Little did Ann know that this prayer would lead her to become the first American woman to go with her husband to a mission field. She did not know that with this prayer her infant child would die from jungle fever. Neither did she know her prayer would lead her to hide the translation of the Burmese New Testament in a pillow while her husband was imprisoned and tortured. She did not know that after her death at age thirty-seven, Burma would have sixty-three Christian churches, and her life would inspire many to go to difficult mission fields.

One prayer—Ann's prayer—helped change the destiny of an entire country. Mary, the mother of Jesus, prayed a prayer of submission to do God's will, and the salvation of the entire world was made possible. Be careful how you pray. God takes you at your word.

Dr. Anna S. Kugler
Medical Missionary
1856–1930

> For there is one God and one mediator between God and mankind,
> the man Christ Jesus, who gave himself as a ransom for all people.
> 1 TIMOTHY 2:5–6 NIV

From childhood Anna Kugler had dreamed of going to the mission field. In her teens she felt called to be a missionary doctor, and in 1882 she went to Guntur, India, an area of twenty million people where no women's hospital had ever existed.

On the field Dr. Kugler faced the question that has disturbed missionaries from the beginning of medical missions: should she be concerned only for people's physical problems or should her mission also attend to their spiritual needs? Her medical facility provided excellent care, but also proved effective in evangelism.

All people regardless of caste, even outcasts, received equal medical help at the hospital. Doctors and nurses took an active part in evangelism, praying at the bedside and explaining the gospel to the sick. Dr. Kugler taught native women to instruct patients in the scriptures. Regardless of patients' religion persuasion, they were offered Bibles when they left the wards.

In the midst of overwhelming physical needs, Anna Kugler kept her focus on what really mattered; each person's eternal soul. In all your efforts for good, give priority to the only hope for eternity to come—Jesus Christ.

Annie Johnson Flint
Poet
1866–1932

"Your kingdom come, your will be done, on earth as it is in heaven."
MATTHEW 6:10 NIV

As a young adult, Annie Johnson experienced symptoms of arthritis. Soon she was forced to give up her teaching job. With no way to make a living, Annie turned to writing poetry to support herself and a frail sister.

As the pain increased, often she could write only a few words at a time. Yet God used her writings to encourage other suffering people. When she received a letter telling of a woman's struggles with depression, Annie wrote the poem, "What God Hath Promised."

God hath not promised skies always blue
Flower-strewn pathways all our lives through;
God hath not promised sun without rain,
Joy without sorrow, peace without pain.

But God has promised strength for the day,
Rest for the labor, light for the way,
Grace for the trials, help from above,
Unfailing sympathy, undying love.

Did Annie ask God to take away her pain? No doubt she did. Jesus, too, when faced with the cross, asked for another way. Yet He surrendered His will to God. Every time you repeat the Lord's Prayer, you also surrender to God's perfect will. Sometimes—only God knows the reason—He wants you to go through the trial in His strength.

Lilian Hammer
Medical Missionary
1912–1959

And I was delivered from the lion's mouth. The Lord will rescue me from every evil attack and will bring me safely to his heavenly kingdom.
2 Timothy 4:17–18 NIV

As word of missionary Lilian Hammer's medical knowledge spread from one Thai village to another, calls came for her to treat the sick. She gained the people's confidence, and when the natives saw that she was able to help opium addicts come clean with minimal suffering, many sought her care. Grateful former addicts in one village built her a hut and invited her to live among them.

While treating recovering addicts, Lilian became keenly aware of their spiritual needs. What hope did a former addict have of remaining clean if the cure did not include spiritual healing? She knew that while demon worship and false gods remained in a hut, the craving for the pipe would soon return. Hindered by a language barrier, but armed with Bible pictures, Lilian worked with addicts and prayed for their spiritual deliverance until her death.

The message of the Bible is one of total deliverance—physical, emotional, mental, and spiritual. Don't write anyone off as hopeless in any area. Jesus is alive! The power of God is available to deliver you, your family, and your friends from every evil work and carry each one safely to heaven.

Isobel Miller Kuhn

Missionary, Author
1901–1957

> "In my distress I called to the LORD; I called out to my God.
> From his temple he heard my voice; my cry came to his ears."
> 2 SAMUEL 22:7 NIV

While attending a Bible conference in Washington state, Isobel Miller heard a missionary tell of fierce tribes living on the China-Burma border, a people yet unreached by the gospel. The Lisu had no words in their language for mercy or compassion, but they had hundreds of words to describe the best way to skin a person alive. Isobel knew she must bring Christ to them.

At Moody Bible Institute Isobel met John Kuhn, who shared her vision for missions. The couple went to the Lisu, but the people were unresponsive to the message. Then Isobel had an idea; why not hold a Bible school during the rainy season. The Rainy Season Bible School was a huge success. About thirty students became evangelists and pushed through the jungles to reach distant villages with the gospel.

Little progress in the work was just one of the obstacles Isobel overcame. During World War II, Kathryn, her young daughter, attending a mission school, was interned by the Japanese and the parents did not hear from her for three months. Speaking of the hardships, Isobel said, "I would fall on my knees and weep before the Lord, asking for His help. And never did He spurn me."

With nowhere to turn, Isobel often took leaps of faith into God's mercy. Are you at a place of no return? Do as Isobel often did: fall into the arms of the One who hears your faintest distress call.

Fanny Crosby
Hymn Writer
1820–1915

"And in the proper season I will send the showers they need.
There will be showers of blessing."
EZEKIEL 34:26 NLT

Fanny Crosby, the blind hymn writer, was once in a church service when it was evident God's Spirit was moving in an unusual way. People sensed Jesus' presence, and a deep conviction of sin came upon the congregation.

Fanny, too, felt the Holy Spirit tugging at her heart and she silently prayed, "Include me! Do not pass me by, Lord!" When she later recounted this experience, she wrote a song that is often used by pastors and evangelists when they invite people to come to Christ.

Pass me not, O gentle Savior, hear my humble cry:
While on others Thou art calling, do not pass me by.
Savior, Savior, hear my humble cry;
While on others Thou art calling, do not pass me by.

Do you want to be included in the moving of God? Do you long for the scriptures to leap off the page and touch your spirit? Do you want to feel a holy awe as you worship? Do you yearn for the pastor's message to stir your heart and challenge your lifestyle? Do you want to sense Jesus beside you as you pray?

If this describes you, sincerely pray, "Pass me not, O gentle Savior!"

Do not merely listen to the word, and so deceive yourselves. Do what it says.
JAMES 1:22 NIV

Born into slavery, Katherine Ferguson was wrenched from her mother at age eight and never saw her again. A kind mistress allowed her to attend church, and Katherine became a Christian. Later, she bought her freedom for two hundred dollars and paid back the money by baking and selling cakes.

Although she could not read or write, Katherine saw the value of Christian education and while living in New York City, she began a Sunday school in her home for poor children. Because she had memorized much of the Bible and numerous hymns, she was an able teacher. The average attendance reached forty to fifty black and white children and adults. To Katherine goes the honor of beginning New York City's first Sunday school.

Empathy for the neglected and abused led Katherine to take forty-eight children from almshouses and care for them until suitable homes were found. She also opened her arms to unwed mothers. A home for these women was named in her honor.

It is easy to talk about what should be done to improve the world. It is quite another matter to span the bridge from theory to doing. Katherine jumped all the hurdles and become a "doer." You, too, can find ways to put Bible principles into practical, everyday use.

Elizabeth Peterson
Missionary
Early 20th Century

> Above all, love each other deeply,
> because love covers over a multitude of sins.
> 1 PETER 4:8 NIV

In 1897, missionaries Elizabeth Peterson and Alma Strand entered a Chinese city to begin a Christian work. Their initial effort was a school for children. However, this did not meet with the approval of the townspeople, who circulated lies about the women, saying they worked by magic and when the missionaries blew on the children they were transported to other lands.

As the lies increased, so did Elizabeth's love for the children. Soon the school had twenty-three students, and some of the pupils became earnest Christians.

The missionaries fled the city during the Boxer Rebellion, but when Elizabeth returned, she again gave special attention to the young. Described as tactful, wise, and motherly, so effective were her loving efforts that the townspeople were eventually won over. No longer did they tell lies about the missionaries or ask why the foreigners were among them. By 1914, Elizabeth reported twenty-one children had become Christians.

In a remote Chinese village Christ's love triumphed over Satan's lies. However, it makes no difference where you live: make love your aim. The enemy has nothing to counter with when you simply love!

Anne Dutton

Author
1692–1765

> I will give thanks to you, LORD, with all my heart;
> I will tell of all your wonderful deeds.
> PSALM 9:1 NIV

During the great spiritual awakening of the 1700s, Anne Dutton felt an urgency to share Christ. Knowing there were few opportunities for women to preach and teach, she instead helped her husband, a pastor in England. When he was lost at sea, Anne devoted herself to religious writing.

She published a periodical, *The Spiritual Magazine*, and wrote over sixty hymns and poems. But Anne found her greatest ministry in writing letters to new converts. When she became acquainted with evangelist George Whitefield, he recognized the value of such letters and encouraged her to increase her correspondence, especially to new believers in South Carolina where he had recently held meetings. What did Anne write to the new Christians? In simple words, she told of the wonders of God.

In 1735, Anne authored *A Discourse upon Walking with God*, containing insights for practical daily living. She also wrote a book of poetry that was widely circulated. Her writings were so effective that she became well known on both sides of the Atlantic.

Do you know children or adults who have recently committed their lives to Christ? New converts are especially vulnerable to attacks of doubt and discouragement. Reach out to these as Anne Dutton did. Write them encouraging letters or e-mails. Share how God has helped you. Tell a new believer of the wonders you've discovered in Christ's salvation.

Mary Dorr
Originator of the Gold and Silver Angel Awards
1918–2004

> But I do not want you to be ignorant, brethren, concerning those who
> have fallen asleep, lest you sorrow as others who have no hope.
> 1 Thessalonians 4:13 NKJV

Mary Dorr, a radio and television personality, once heard a Hollywood producer say, "If you want to be successful in the media, break five of the Ten Commandments every fifteen minutes." Mary, a Christian, was grieved by the statement and created the Gold and Silver Angels, awards for people in radio, television, and film who advance decency and morality. Winners include: Dr. Norman Vincent Peale and his wife, Ruth; Art Linkletter; Roy Rogers and Dale Evans; Steve Allen; and Jayne Meadows.

While Mary fought for improved public media, she faced personal tragedy at home when her husband died in 1969 and she was left to raise their five children. The family's grief was alleviated when Mary reminded them that Christians have hope. She said of that time, "I knew that God was watching out for us. I didn't despair."

Three years later Mary's twenty-year-old son, Denny, died in his sleep. Then her mother also passed away. The family needed comfort, and they found it as together they quoted Bible verses, memorized scriptures, and read God's Word.

Sooner or later we face the loss of those we love. But a Christian's sorrow is not the same as those without Christ; we have hope. When Jesus returns, all believers—living and dead—will be together forever. How comforting!

Leila Naylor Morris

Hymn Writer, Author

1862–1929

Offer yourselves to God as those who have been brought from death to life;
and offer every part of yourself to him as an instrument of righteousness.
ROMANS 6:13 NIV

While attending a camp meeting, young Leila Naylor gave her life to Christ. When she returned home she wrote a hymn, "I Cannot Tell It All," describing her salvation experience. She married Charles Morris and became a homemaker, yet a pen and paper were always close at hand when she felt inspired to write a song.

Leila went on to write hymns of commitment and dedication such as "Nearer, Still Nearer," "Fully Surrendered," and "Can the World See Jesus in You?" It was her firm belief that her life must be consistent with the words she wrote. And it was, as she served in her church, assisted in Holiness camp meetings, and maintained a Christian home.

Unlike most hymn writers, Leila wrote both the words and music for her songs. In her forties she began to lose her eyesight, and her son built a twenty-eight-foot blackboard with staff lines so she could continue writing music. At age fifty-one she was totally blind.

Your life is a reflection of the Holy One you serve. To maintain an exemplary Christian walk, sincerely pray Leila Morris's hymn.

Nearer, still nearer, close to Thy heart,
Draw me, my Savior, so precious Thou art;
Fold me, O fold me close to Thy breast,
Shelter me safe in that "Haven of Rest,"
Shelter me safe in that "Haven of Rest."

Florence Nightingale
Nurse
1820–1910

Be kind and compassionate to one another.
EPHESIANS 4:32 NIV

Two heroes emerged from the Crimean War of 1853: the soldier and the nurse. Before this time, nursing was dishonorable work practiced by drunkards and prostitutes. Soldiers also were treated with little respect by their officers and governments. Wounded soldiers especially endured horrifying conditions. Florence Nightingale single-handedly transformed public estimation of both professions.

When Miss Nightingale walked through the gateway of the hospital in Turkey, she reportedly said, "Abandon hope all ye who enter here." The place was overrun with fleas and rats. The food was not edible. Cholera and dysentery killed more men than wounds did.

Through the efforts of Miss Nightingale and her nurses, incredible changes occurred. The soldiers called it, "Nightingale power." One observer said of her treatment of the injured, "I much admired her manner. . . . It was so tender and kind."

Because of her kind treatment of British soldiers, the public's estimation of them rose, and they were no longer treated disrespectfully. "Christ is the author of our profession," Florence said of nursing and it, too, became an honorable vocation as she raised the standards for nurses.

Jesus touched dreaded lepers, healed blind beggars, and restored degraded prostitutes. Follow His example as Florence Nightingale did. With your words and actions, treat all people as you'd like to be treated—with kindness and respect.

Lucy Waterbury Peabody

Teacher, Missionary Leader
1861–1949

I ask you, my true companion, help these women since they have contended
at my side in the cause of the gospel, along with Clement and the
rest of my co-workers, whose names are in the book of life.
PHILIPPIANS 4:3 NIV

A strong leader and an able speaker, Lucy Peabody worked zealously for twenty-five years to promote missionary causes around the globe. For example, in 1921 Lucy took on the monumental project of raising three million dollars to build seven Christian women's colleges in Asia. Lucy called the project "College Days," and philanthropist John D. Rockefeller promised to donate a million dollars if American women raised two million.

Beginning in Washington DC, she held luncheons in leading cities to promote the project. Christians of all denominations rallied behind the cause.

In a radio address in December 1922, Mrs. Peabody made one last appeal before the year ended and called it "Dollar Day." Joining her on the broadcast were Mrs. Coolidge, wife of vice president Calvin Coolidge, and Dr. Ida Scudder, a missionary to India. The listeners were urged to give one dollar on December 9th toward the Christian colleges. The goal was exceeded, Mr. Rockefeller added one million, and the colleges were built.

What challenges are you facing? Like Lucy Peabody, use creative ways to address the problems. Share your project with others and allow them the privilege of participating in helping you achieve your God-inspired goals.

Elizabeth (Betty) Greene
Aviation Missionary
1920–1997

> I have become all things to all people so that by all possible means
> I might save some. I do all this for the sake of the gospel.
> 1 CORINTHIANS 9:22–23 NIV

Betty Greene took flying lessons while she was in high school, and when the Army Air Corps opened the way for women to train as pilots, she applied. Though the requirements were difficult, she was accepted.

Why did Betty want to fly? "I am looking forward to being a missionary," she said. "I think flying is going to be very useful in the work of spreading the message of Christ."

During World War II she enlisted in the WASP program and flew four-engine B-17 Flying Fortresses. But she knew military service was only a stepping-stone. She moved to Los Angeles and founded Mission Aviation Fellowship. When Wycliffe Bible Translators needed a pilot in Mexico, Betty flew the mission. From there she helped in Peru, the first woman pilot to soar over the Andes' rugged peaks.

Betty Greene loved flying, yet it was more to her than that—it was a way to bring people to Christ. For this cause she risked her life every time she climbed into the cockpit.

What are you willing to risk to win people to Christ? Are you ready to learn a new skill, expose yourself to danger, or live in a third world country? If what you do helps even one person hear the gospel, it is a good cause.

Maria Fearing

Missionary
1838–1937

> What things soever ye desire, when ye pray,
> believe that ye receive them, and ye shall have them.
> MARK 11:24 KJV

Maria Fearing, a house slave on a plantation in Alabama, listened to her mistress read the Bible to her children and tell them stories of missionaries in Africa. This had a profound affect upon Maria, and it became her secret desire to serve those of her own race who lived on the dark continent.

After the emancipation of slaves, Maria, at age thirty-three, learned to read and write. She was fifty-six when a missionary from the Congo came to her church and pled for recruits. Maria volunteered, but when she applied to the mission board, they said she was too old.

Maria sold her house, received a one-hundred-dollar gift from the women in her church, and with her small savings, she again appealed to the mission board, prepared to pay her own way. In 1894 Maria received an appointment.

Maria proved to be an effective missionary. She quickly learned the Buluba-Lulua language, and in two years the mission board reappointed her with full support. Later, she established a home for kidnapped girls and orphans and acted as the director.

A consuming desire! Maria Fearing was possessed of an inner flame that could not be extinguished. What fervent desire do you have? Do you long to write a book, be an effective Bible teacher, or see a friend healed? God placed that fire in your heart. Now fan the flame with prayer and action.

Edith Moules
Missionary
1900–1949

> For this is what the high and exalted One says. . . "I live in a high and holy place, but also with the one who is contrite and lowly in spirit, to revive the spirit of the lowly and to revive the heart of the contrite."
> ISAIAH 57:15 NIV

Missionary Edith Moules, her husband, Perry, and other missionaries were treating up to five thousand patients a week at the mission dispensary in Africa. They traveled to outlying mission stations and conducted weekly Bible studies. But Edith felt something was missing.

When a leprous Christian woman angrily refused to be separated from those not infected, Perry said, "If Christians behave this way, what can we expect of pagans?"

Edith and other workers admitted their need for personal revival and went to God with their concerns. She came to the realization that as Christ died for her, with the same dedication she must be willing to die to pride and selfishness and become alive to the Holy Spirit's voice. The missionaries' prayers eventually led to a revival in several African mission stations.

If your Christian walk lacks joy, if the Bible is just another book to you, you also need reviving. Spiritual renewal comes as you humbly admit your need and dedicate yourself to loving God and doing His will. God promises to visit the contrite person with vigorous spiritual energy and joy.

Mary Pennington

Christian Woman
1616–1682

> Like newborn babies, crave pure spiritual milk,
> so that by it you may grow up in your salvation.
> 1 PETER 2:2 NIV

In search of spiritual light, Mary Pennington asked, "Lord, what is prayer?" When visiting a church, she heard the preacher pray and for the first time, Mary felt she had heard true prayer. Yet she was unable to address God herself.

"I kneeled down morning after morning and night after night and had not a word to say," Mary wrote. After her husband died she gave up her spiritual quest altogether and went after "many excesses and vanities. Yet. . .my heart was constantly sad," she said.

After Mary's second marriage, she again began to seek God. "The groans and cries in secret that were raised in me that I might be visited by the Lord," she said. Later, she and her husband sought God in earnest and joined a church. In this fellowship Mary enjoyed spiritual growth and happiness.

Do you want to grow spiritually? God is concerned this occurs and He provided the fuel to make it happen. Regularly expose yourself to good "helpings" of Bible reading, gospel preaching, and sincere prayer. Then experience His supernatural, divine strength surging in your spirit.

Jennie Faulding Taylor
Missionary Wife
1843–1904

> A cheerful heart is good medicine,
> but a crushed spirit dries up the bones.
> PROVERBS 17:22 NIV

In 1866, an excited young woman, Jennie Faulding, sailed for China with missionary Hudson Taylor, his family, and twenty-one other new missionaries.

Possessing an unusually happy disposition, Jennie quickly learned the language and adopted Chinese dress. Soon she was chatting with Chinese women and received invitations to visit wives of high-ranking officials. Her cheerful demeanor did not go unnoticed, and the Chinese named her *Fah,* which means happiness.

When Hudson Taylor's wife died, he and Jennie married and she became mother to his three children. Soon the couple had three children of their own. During a furlough in England, Hudson became aware of a famine in China. The situation required a woman fluent in Chinese to begin an orphanage in a ravished province. Jennie was the choice person to go, but she recoiled at the thought of leaving her children. Yet, she went.

Armed with a happy disposition, supported by prayer, she established the orphanage and three years later reunited with her children.

Would Jennie have been able to survive the rigors of missionary work without a cheerful attitude? Probably not. Writing to Philippian believers, Paul told them to think true, noble, right, pure, lovely, admirable, and excellent thoughts (Phillippians 4:8). Like Fah, Jennie Taylor, fill your mind with happy thoughts. It is a healing medicine to your body, spirit, and mind.

Dorothy Leigh Sayers
Novelist, Playwright, Christian Apologist
1893–1957

> Whosoever shall confess that Jesus is the Son of God,
> God dwelleth in him, and he in God.
> 1 JOHN 4:15 KJV

Described as one of the most brilliant and fascinating women of the twentieth century, Dorothy Sayers, a successful writer of mystery novels, was also a bold Christian whose friends included authors C. S. Lewis and J. R. R. Tolkien.

Because she believed man made in God's image has the ability to be creative, she felt a sacred responsibility to use her abilities in productive ways. She said, "The only Christian work is good work, well done." Dorothy spent every spare moment writing and, as a result, published fourteen detective novels, numerous short stories, poems, plays, and essays, and translated Dante's *Divine Comedy*. Her famous radio play on the life of Christ, *The Man Born to Be King*, presented Jesus speaking modern English and brought loud protests from audiences. But Dorothy thrived on controversy. Her favorite subject to debate was Christianity, and she loudly proclaimed to all, "The man we hanged on the cross was God Almighty."

Every person will eventually answer the question, "Who is Jesus?" When Jesus asked Simon Peter who He was, Peter said, "You are the Christ." Ponder carefully your answer to that question. The answer determines your future.

Eugenia Price

Author

1916–1996

> "Salvation is found in no one else, for there is no other name under heaven given to mankind by which we must be saved."
>
> Acts 4:12 NIV

Before her conversion, Eugenia Price was captivated by cigarettes, alcohol, and drugs. She detested the word "saved" and professed to be an atheist. After moving from West Virginia to Chicago, she became a successful script writer of radio serials and met Ellen, a Christian friend, who talked to Eugenia about accepting Christ. She resisted.

Later, she confessed, "The more real He became, the more I wanted Him to be mine." In 1949, Eugenia became a Christian. She said, "My simple theology: I belong to Him and He belongs to me!"

She devoted her scriptwriting skills to *Unshackled*, a Christian radio show, which led to invitations for Eugenia to speak in churches and conferences.

After visiting Saint Simons Island in Georgia, Eugenia began writing Christian historical novels of the area. The president of the Georgia Historical Society said, "Her books are wholesome reading. Grandmothers can recommend the books to their granddaughters." In all Eugenia wrote fourteen novels that magnify the name of Jesus.

Let the beauty of the person of Jesus captivate you as it did Eugenia. That name frees you from the shackles of destructive habits and attitudes. That name allows you to be all God intended you should be. *Jesus!*

Margaret Fell Fox

Wife of the Founder of the Quakers
1614–1702

> In Joppa there was a disciple named Tabitha (in Greek her name is Dorcas);
> she was always doing good and helping the poor.
>
> ACTS 9:36 NIV

Margaret Fell, a member of England's nobility, met George Fox, founder of the Quakers, when he visited her home in 1652. She described him as "dressed in a rough leather suit" and said of him, "He turned our minds toward the light of Christ." They married in 1669.

At that time Quakers were often persecuted, so it was a risk for Margaret to cast her lot with the despised group. When she held religious meetings on her spacious estate, she was arrested, tried, and convicted. Her first imprisonment was four years.

At age seventy, Margaret traveled to London to appeal to the king to relieve the persecution of Quakers, and in 1689 King James II signed the Tolerance Acts.

One of Margaret's greatest services was to Quaker women as she trained them in midwifery, preaching the gospel, and caring for widows, prisoners, and the poor.

Margaret Fox's impact in her community was much like that of Tabitha in the scriptures who helped the poor in Joppa. You, too, have influence in the place where you live and work. By simply "doing good," you are following in the pathway of these godly women.

Mary C. Crowley
Christian Entrepreneur
1915–1986

> "Give, and it will be given to you. A good measure, pressed down, shaken together and running over, will be poured into your lap."
> Luke 6:38 NIV

Home Interiors and Gifts, a business that now has millions of dollars in assets, employs over eighty thousand sales representatives, and covers forty-eight states and Puerto Rico, is built upon a scriptural premise. What is the principle that guided its founder, Mary Crowley?

"Honor God; and bless and serve others," she said. Mary started a one-woman operation out of her garage, and from the beginning, she practiced tithing—giving ten percent of her income to the Lord's work. Hospitals, churches, young people's clubs, and numerous organizations also benefited from Mary's gifts. Her sales representatives were blessed by her generosity when they enjoyed free shopping at Christmas.

"Give for the joy of giving" she said. "If you only 'give to get' you are not giving, you are trading."

Tithing began with Abraham (see Genesis 14:20 and Hebrews 7:1–6). During the time of the prophet Malachi, the people had stopped tithing. He said they were robbing God.

Everything you have comes from God. He asks you to return a small part to advance His causes and to honor Him. And you are sure to benefit; tithing carries with it a powerful promise: "I will. . . pour out so much blessing that you will not have room enough for it" (Malachi 3:10).

Lena Shoffner

Evangelist
Early 20th Century

> For he himself is our peace, who has made the two groups one and
> has destroyed the barrier, the dividing wall of hostility.
> EPHESIANS 2:14 NIV

On a warm summer evening in 1897 folks gathered at an Alabama camp meeting to hear evangelist Lena Shoffner. As the custom was, black people sat on one side of the aisle and white folks on the other side. Between them ran a thick rope. Mrs. Shoffner walked to the pulpit and for one hour and thirty minutes preached against the evils of prejudice. Her text: "He. . .destroyed. . .the dividing wall."

As she preached, people on both sides of the rope began to weep. Someone loosened the rope and as it fell, black and white people on both sides streamed into each others' arms. United at last, race no longer mattered as they prayed and sang. Such was the effect of the preaching of this woman evangelist.

Little else is known about Lena Shoffner, who lived in the South in a time rife with racism. God no doubt revealed to her the freeing truth of equality in Christ.

Many barriers divide people. Racial prejudice is one of them. Other roadblocks to Christian unity are political issues, doctrine, age, appearance, and economic status. Jesus abolished all barriers. You, with every other person stand equal—under His cross.

Lottie Moon
Missionary
1840–1912

> There are different kinds of service, but we serve the same Lord. . . .
> A spiritual gift is given to each of us so we can help each other.
> 1 CORINTHIANS 12:5, 7 NLT

When Lottie Moon arrived in China in 1873, she quickly learned the language and was assigned to teach what she called forty "unstudious" children. Her heart was in evangelism and church planting, but the mission board allotted those ministries to men.

However, after assessing her calling, Lottie determined to go to China's millions as an evangelist. In spite of opposition from fellow missionaries and field directors, she conducted evangelistic meetings and established what was said to be a "great evangelistic center." Her talents and love for the lost made her a successful soul winner. She wrote, "Surely there can be no deeper joy than that of saving souls."

God has given specific talents to every person. These are to be used to build up His church. What are your talents? Teaching, helps, hospitality, friendliness, giving, faith, praying for the sick—the list goes on. All God's gifts are not as spectacular as Lottie Moon's; some function unnoticed behind the scenes. Assess your gifts. Develop them. Then use them to contribute to the good of Christ's body, the church.

Hannah Whitall Smith

Author
1832–1911

The Lord isn't really being slow about his promise, as some people think.
No, he is being patient for your sake. He does not want anyone
to be destroyed, but wants everyone to repent.

2 PETER 3:9 NLT

When Hannah Whitall Smith, the author of *The Christian's Secret of a Happy Life,* was in her thirties she became extremely troubled because people around her seemed unconcerned for their eternal destiny. She had recently experienced God's glorious salvation and she could not conceive that some people would be lost.

One day while riding the streetcar, two men especially caught her attention, and an overwhelming anguish gripped her heart. She pulled her black veil across her face to conceal her grief. "Lost! They're lost," she silently cried. "Oh, God, how canst Thou bear it?" An inward Voice gently said, "*It is not My will that any should perish.*" Hannah stepped off the streetcar relieved, the burden lifted.

How do you see the people around you? Either they are believers, prepared for an eternity in heaven with Christ, or they are lost and will be forever punished in hell. As you see as God sees, your prayers will be more fervent, your concern for others will grow until the lost near you will feel Jesus' love and confess, "Yes, I believe."

Fidelia Fiske
Missionary
1816–1864

> And the Lord's servant must not be quarrelsome but must be kind to everyone. . . . Opponents must be gently instructed.
> 2 TIMOTHY 2:24–25 NIV

Upon her graduation from Mt. Holyoke Female Seminary, Fidelia Fiske became a teacher at the school. Mary Lyon, the school's founder, was concerned for the spiritual condition of those in foreign lands and she encouraged the students and teachers to consider becoming missionaries. When the call went out for a young woman to fill the post left by the death of a missionary in Persia, Fidelia wrote, "If counted worthy, I should be willing to go."

Though willing, she received fierce opposition from her family to the point where she withdrew her offer and another woman was appointed to the post. At the last minute, however, the volunteer was unable to go, and Miss Lyon begged Fidelia's mother to allow her daughter to go. Finally consent was given and Fidelia sailed for Persia.

The apostle Paul instructed the young pastor, Timothy, not to quarrel with those who resisted him. When Fidelia followed this scriptural injunction, good family relationships were maintained and God overruled her opposers. In the face of opposition you may be inclined to push your point, but strife is not God's way. As He did for Fidelia Fiske, God will work out His perfect plan for you in His own time.

Jeannette Rau

Moravian Missionary

1722–1749

> So I am willing to endure anything if it will bring salvation
> and eternal glory in Christ Jesus to those God has chosen.
> 2 TIMOTHY 2:10 NLT

Jeannette Rau grew up in New York near a Mohican settlement where she learned the Mohican language and several dialects. When Count Zinzendorf, leader of the Moravians, came to America in 1741, she went with his group into the wilderness to bring the gospel to the Native American tribes in what is now Pennsylvania and New York.

Jeannette's husband, John, who wrote an account of their trip, spoke of "frightful mountains, streams swollen by heavy rain." He said, "We imperiled our lives by fording the creeks." In Wyoming Valley, they pitched their tents close to a Shawanese village and John described the encounter. "The savages were unfriendly, painted with red and black each with a large knife in his hand they came in crowds around the tent again and again."

Zinzendorf gathered the crowds, mostly Mohicans, and with Jeannette as interpreter, told them "words spoken by their Creator."

Nothing of worth comes without sacrifice. Jeannette Rau imperiled her life to carry God's truth to the Native American people. The apostle Paul endured imprisonment, beatings, and shipwrecks to bring the gospel to the Gentiles. Someone paid a price so you could come to Christ. What are you willing to endure so others can be saved?

And God is faithful; he will not let you be tempted beyond what you can bear. . .he will also provide a way out so that you can endure it.
1 CORINTHIANS 10:13 NIV

Annie Olson, a single missionary, faced discouraging situations when she went to China in the late 1800s. Alone in a remote village, no communication with other missionaries, and little progress in the work plagued her.

After the Boxer Rebellion she returned to a city where the people were described as lawless. However, God blessed her efforts and by 1902, three people had committed their lives to Christ. Six years later, eight more believers had joined the church.

Then Miss Olson became discouraged; she wanted to go home. But at the same time an opium addict asked the missionary to pray for the return of his stolen mule. She prayed, and when the mule returned on its own, the entire town was stirred. As a result, a wealthy man, disillusioned by his heathen gods, came to Miss Olson and asked to know the God who answered prayer.

Other townspeople became interested, and soon Miss Olson's church had 250 members. She overcame the discouraging season and continued to work in the city for many years.

Discouragement is one of the most common temptations we face. Recognize these facts: God *promised* no trial exceeds His grace—He will provide a way. God is faithful! Even now courage is flowing in your direction.

Eliza Lucas Pinckney

Agriculturalist, Colonial Woman
1722–1793

> Fear God and keep his commandments,
> for this is the duty of all mankind.
> ECCLESIASTES 12:13 NIV

When sixteen-year-old Eliza Lucas's father, a British army officer, went to the Caribbean, he left her in charge of three plantations, the slave labor, and a younger sister. Undaunted by the responsibility, Eliza also began cultivating and creating strains of new crops, and helped neighbors with their legal affairs.

In her journal Eliza declared her determination to "honor God and obey His commandments." She wrote, "Not to regard the frowns of the world, but to keep a steady upright conduct before my God, and before man, doing my duty."

Duty was at the core of Eliza's being, who upon her marriage resolved "to make a good wife to my dear husband. . .to be a good mother to my children. . .to make a good sister. . .to make a good mistress to my servants. . .to make their lives as comfortable as I can . . .to be a faithful friend. . .and a universal lover of all mankind." Eliza Pinckney concluded doing one's duty was the essence of a fulfilled life.

Someday we will give an account of our lives to God (Romans 14:12). By doing our duty now, we can fearlessly look forward to that day.

Vibia Perpetua
Christian Martyr
181–203

> Do not be afraid of what you are about to suffer. . . . The devil will put some of you in prison to test you, and you will suffer persecution for ten days. Be faithful. . .and I will give you life as your victor's crown.
> REVELATION 2:10 NIV

The church in North Africa endured a time of severe persecution in the third century. Vibia Perpetua, a Christian woman, fell victim to the attack and from prison wrote of her experiences.

Well educated, of a high-ranking Carthage family, Vibia's father was humiliated when his daughter was arrested, and he begged her to renounce Christ. She refused and he threatened to whip her. But her father pled for her life when he heard she was condemned to die. He also attempted to rescue Vibia when she was sentenced to be thrown to wild beasts.

The prisoners were stripped and sent to face a ferocious bear, leopard, and wild boar. As Vibia went into the arena, she called to her friends, "Give out the Word. Stand fast in the faith, love one another." The slaughter was too much for even the bloodthirsty crowd, who shouted, "Enough!" The beasts were unable to kill Vibia, and she was finally beheaded.

Faithful Christians of every century have been persecuted. Satan can harm the body, but he can't destroy the soul. God remains in control, and trials have their limits. Regardless of the future, be faithful. In heaven with Christ, our sufferings will seem as nothing.

Ruth Paxson
Bible Teacher, Missionary, Author
1889–1949

For everyone born of God overcomes the world.
This is the victory that has overcome the world, even our faith.
1 John 5:4 NIV

As a child growing up in Iowa, Ruth Paxson became a Christian. In 1911, she began working with the YMCA in China. Later, she ministered as an evangelist and Bible teacher to missionaries in China.

The people attending her deeper life conferences asked Ruth to publish her teaching notes. She assembled these and published several books, now considered classics on the Christian life. Her best-known work is *Life on the Highest Plane*. She said the purpose of her books was "to show the Biblical pathway to victory through union with Christ by way of the cross and the throne."

Life on a higher plane! Here are excerpts from Ruth's book to ponder:

"Christ was made like us that we might be made like Him."
"As we are in Christ in the heavenlies so is He in us on earth."
"Christ in us can live this life anywhere and that is what He longs to do."
"The exalted Christ lives now to bestow upon us in all of its fullness His own triumphant, joyous, holy life."

Don't allow ignorance or neglect to rob you of the fullness of God. Jesus intended the believer's life to be one of continuous, overcoming victory. That victory is a person: Christ.

Elizabeth Clark Garrett
Philanthropist
1805–1855

> "The LORD gave and the LORD has taken away;
> may the name of the LORD be praised."
> JOB 1:21 NIV

When Augustus Garrett, mayor of Chicago, died, he left a large real estate fortune to his widow. *How can I use this money to the best advantage?* Elizabeth Garrett wondered.

She believed giving to Christian colleges would eventually benefit the most people, and in 1855 she gave $250,000 to begin Garrett Bible Institute. This was the largest amount of money given to the Methodist church by a woman up to that time.

However, Elizabeth's generosity did not come without pain. Earlier she had lost her four-year-old daughter to cholera. Then, after a son also died, Elizabeth began to look at money differently. Next she experienced a series of business failures and, in spite of the losses, she gave half her income to religious causes.

Elizabeth's story serves as an example of the good that can come from tragedy. Reasoning and analyzing what happens to us doesn't always bring answers. Sometimes we simply accept what God allowed and worship Him. That worship can be words of praise or, as in Elizabeth Garrett's case, it may take the form of gifts to worthwhile causes.

Fanny Crosby
Hymn Writer
1820–1915

> When he [Jesus] saw the crowds, he had compassion on them,
> because they were harassed and helpless, like sheep without a shepherd.
> Then he said to his disciples, "The harvest is plentiful but the workers are few."
> MATTHEW 9:36–37 NIV

On a hot summer night in 1869 Fanny Crosby, the blind hymn writer, was taken through New York City's Bowery district, a place for the poor, the homeless, and the jobless. A companion described to Fanny the needs of the people on the streets, many of them outcasts from society.

Though she was sightless, Fanny's spiritual eyes saw more than the filth and drunkenness around her; she saw people's souls. She knew they were lost unless someone would tell them of Christ.

So Fanny told them. When she was over sixty years old, she began spending several days a week speaking and counseling at the city missions. From these experiences Fanny wrote a hymn that encourages Christians to reach out in love to lost people.

Rescue the perishing, care for the dying:
Snatch them in pity from sin and the grave;
Weep o'er the erring one, lift up the fallen,
Tell them of Jesus the mighty to save.

How do you see the people around you? View them through Christ's eyes, in need of His transforming salvation. Pray for them and find opportunities to tell them of Jesus, who is "mighty to save."

Dorothea Dix
Nurse, Author, Humanitarian
1802–1887

> The LORD our God will we serve, and his voice will we obey.
> JOSHUA 24:24 KJV

As a young woman, Dorothea Dix wrote, "The theater and tea parties are my aversion and I look with little envy on those who find their joy in transitory delights." Perhaps her bent toward more serious endeavors was influenced by her grandmother, who revered the Word of God and sent Bibles to every newly married couple in nearby Maine towns.

At the onset of the Civil War, Dorothea offered her services to the Union and served as superintendent of nurses in the army. She stirred Northern women to make bandages and hospital gowns for the men and, following her example, many women volunteered to serve in army hospitals.

However, the war took a toll on Dorothea; after thirty months of nursing, the sixty-five-year-old nurse weighed ninety-five pounds. And her work wasn't done as she helped locate missing soldiers.

She wrote, "I must work the work that is given me to do, and how is my soul straightened out until it is accomplished?"

Dorothea Dix had a deep sense of purpose for her life. Your life, too, has been planned by God. While you may not sense as specific a call as Dorothea, seek to obey Him day by day. Obedience to God is the ultimate calling and purpose.

Sarah Pierrepont Edwards

Wife of Early American Church Leader
1710–1759

> But whose delight is in the law of the LORD,
> and who meditates on his law day and night.
> PSALM 1:2 NIV

Sarah Pierrepont met Jonathan Edwards when she was thirteen. They were married four years later and began a marriage Jonathan described as an "uncommon union."

While Jonathan, a preacher, spent up to thirteen hours a day preparing sermons and writing books, Sarah managed the parsonage, made clothing, candles, and brooms, fed the poultry, and raised eleven children. She was also innkeeper to the hundreds of visitors who came to consult her famous husband.

In the 1730s, a revival swept through New England, and Sarah became keenly aware of the nearness of God. Jonathan wrote of her, "God fills her mind with exceeding sweet delight, and that she hardly cares for anything, except to meditate on Him."

Sarah's busy life improved through meditation. It was said of her, "She sometimes goes about from place to place, singing sweetly, and seems to be always full of joy and pleasure."

Meditation can also ease your frantic pace. Sing, praise, and pray as you go about your work. Use sleepless nights to meditate and worship (Psalm 63:6). Meditating on "whatever is noble. . .right . . .pure. . .lovely. . .admirable" (Philippians 4:8) will bring sure delight to your soul.

Rachel Joy Scott
Student
1981–1999

> Remember your Creator in the days of your youth,
> before the days of trouble come.
> ECCLESIASTES 12:1 NIV

"Everyone was there at the altar, and I felt so drawn to it. . .to be drawn that way, it was nothing short of God. . .that night I accepted Jesus into my heart. I was saved," wrote twelve-year-old Rachel Scott.

Two years later, her mother remarried, and during the time of adjustment, Rachel became withdrawn and private. Her mother gave her sixteen-year-old daughter a journal, and Rachel began to record her life's journey.

She was active in church, she played a role in a school play; yet her writings tell of lonely times. "I have no personal friends at school. . . . If I have to sacrifice everything, I will," she wrote.

On April 20, 1999, Rachel and a friend were eating lunch near the school cafeteria when two gunmen fired at them. Rachel sustained wounds to her head, chest, arm, and leg. One of the gunmen then asked her, "Do you believe in God?" Rachel answered, "You know I do." He shot her in the temple.

Anticipating a long life and in pursuit of pleasure, young people often don't seriously consider God. But it was young people who died that day in the Columbine High School massacre. The Bible pleads with the young to remember God before troublesome days come. The perfect time for you to accept Christ is now.

Cecil Frances Alexander
Poet, Hymn Writer
1818–1895

> Peter got down out of the boat, walked on the water and
> came toward Jesus. But when he saw the wind, he was afraid.
> MATTHEW 14:29–30 NIV

Cecil Alexander and her husband, an archbishop, helped care for Ireland's poor. She and her sister also operated a school for the deaf, but today Cecil is remembered for the hymns she wrote. At a young age she dedicated herself to writing sacred verse and composed a series of verses set to music that explain to children the Apostles' Creed. *Hymns for Little Children* was published in more than one hundred editions. In all, she wrote over four hundred hymns, tracts, and poems.

In her hymn "Jesus Calls Us," Cecil addresses a problem common to all: the storms we encounter in life. When Peter, the Lord's disciple, got out of the boat and attempted to walk on the water, he saw the crashing waves and began to sink. Then he caught sight of the Lord and heard Him beckon, "Come."

Jesus call us; o'er the tumult
Of our life's wild, restless sea.
Day by day His sweet voice soundeth,
Saying, "Christian, follow Me."

In our joys and in our sorrows,
Days of toil and hours of ease,
Still He calls, in cares and pleasures,
"Christian, love Me more than these."

No need to face the storms on your own. Jesus wants to hold your hand in the tumult and walk beside you on the "wild and restless sea."

Priscilla Stewart Studd

Missionary
Early 20th Century

> The LORD is my strength and my shield; my heart trusts in him,
> and he helps me. . . . The LORD is the strength of his people.
> PSALM 28:7–8 NIV

While serving with the Salvation Army in China, Priscilla Stewart met missionary C. T. Studd. The two fell in love and were married. While Priscilla did women's evangelistic work, her husband ministered to opium addicts. However, the first years were difficult for the young missionaries. Mr. Studd said of that time, "We never went outside our door without a volley of curses from our neighbors."

While on furlough in England in 1894, Mr. Studd became aware of tribes in Central Africa who had never heard of Christ and he determined to go. Priscilla objected and for good reason. At age fifty, her husband's health was poor and he had no financial backing. She also suffered from a heart condition. Although Priscilla protested, her husband left England and spent sixteen years in Africa.

During this time Priscilla suffered further heart complications. But when her husband returned in 1916, he found his wife active and busy in mission work. Reverend Studd's health had also improved while he was in Africa. What happened to the Studds? No doubt, God strengthened them in answer to prayer.

Are you limited by physical problems? God's power is available to help with our bodily weaknesses. He created your body. Now ask Him to renew it. Our almighty God is ready, willing, and able to give you His supernatural strength.

Joanna Bethune
Pioneer in American Sunday School Movement
1770–1860

> "Therefore go and make disciples of all nations, baptizing them. . .
> and teaching them to obey everything I have commanded you."
> MATTHEW 28:19–20 NIV

Beginning in 1803 Joanna Bethune and her mother taught poor children in Sunday school. But after Joanna and her husband observed the successful Sunday school work of Robert Raikes in Scotland and England, they decided to organize schools in America on a larger scale.

In January 1816, one hundred women from various churches in New York City met at Joanna's invitation and, after her plea for the need to teach American children the Bible, there was "not a dry eye in the room." That day the women organized the Female Union for the Promotion of Sabbath Schools.

The following week the women began holding classes. By July, 250 teachers were instructing more than three thousand pupils in the Bible. Joanna supervised the budget, established policy, oversaw publication of curriculum, and coordinated a large staff of teachers. Later, the women were joined by interested men, and from this group the American Sunday School Union emerged. Joanna wrote a book on teaching children and taught a class until she was past eighty.

God has written one Book, the Bible. It is eternal truth. Jesus' last message before leaving earth was that His followers teach all His commands. Seriously consider His words, then look for opportunities to fulfill the command to "go teach."

Mrs. Wang & Mrs. Chang

Bible Women
Early 20th Century

> They signaled their partners in the other boat to come and help them,
> and they came and filled both boats so full that they began to sink.
> LUKE 5:7 NIV

"How can we reach the women?" nineteenth-century missionaries asked when they arrived on foreign soil. In most cultures of that era women did not leave their homes nor were they allowed to speak to men. This is where Bible women entered the picture.

Native Christian women functioned as interpreters, teachers, Bible readers, and evangelists. Helen Barrett Montgomery described these workers: "One of the humblest, she is at the same time one of the mightiest forces of the Cross in non-Christian lands."

Missionary Rosalind Goforth, who went to China in 1888, said of a Mrs. Wang, "My dear Bible woman in whom I have complete confidence." Mrs. Goforth also had great admiration for a Mrs. Chang and said, "During the terrible ordeal of 1900, she was faithful almost unto death, being strung up by her thumbs by the Boxers, but saved through intervention of neighbors."

Besides helping the missionaries, these women went from house to house teaching women and girls to read. Their hours were long, the pay low, and their lives were often in danger.

Consider the power of two and link with another person to pray, study the Bible, or visit in hospitals and jails. How much greater the results when two or more work together to "pull in the net."

Sybil Bingham
Missionary
Early 19th Century

> "You shall not make for yourself an image in the form of
> anything in heaven above or on the earth beneath. . . .
> You shall not bow down to them or worship them."
>
> Exodus 20:4–5 NIV

Sybil Bingham, one of fourteen young American missionaries to go to the Hawaiian Islands in 1819, was shocked by the dirty, naked savages who greeted them. *Can these be human beings?* Sybil asked.

However, the missionaries had arrived at an opportune time. A new king had come into power and outlawed idolatry and human sacrifice. Sybil Bingham took advantage of the recent laws and organized a school. Several female chiefs wanted to know more about the Christian faith and they enrolled. Among those converted through Sybil's able teaching was a priestess, Kapiolani.

At that time Hawaiians lived in fear of the goddess Pele, who was supposed to reside in a fuming volcanic crater. After becoming a believer, Kapiolani climbed to the top of the mountain and, before a crowd, defied the idol by throwing rocks into the lava and descending into the crater. This one act was said to do more to pave the way for Christianity in Hawaii than all the sermons preached against idols.

Idolatry comes in many forms; it can be money, work, fame, people, or pleasure. Check your life. John, the apostle, pleads with Christians, "Dear children, keep yourselves from idols" (1 John 5:21).

Johanna Veenstra
Missionary
1894–1933

> "But take this staff in your hand so you
> can perform the signs with it."
> Exodus 4:17 NIV

Johanna Veenstra, a young stenographer in New York City, felt called to city missions. But while a student at a Bible institute in Brooklyn, she heard a missionary speak of the urgency of getting the gospel to tribes in Central Africa. As he told of the danger of false religions reaching the people before missionaries came, Johanna, a very ordinary woman, made an extraordinary commitment: She would go to Nigeria.

After taking a midwifery course, in 1919, Johanna went to the Dzompere tribes. She wrote of the hardships of the primitive field. "I took one trek through the hills. . .for nine days," she said. "We planned to stay over Sunday. . .but we were not welcome."

Another time she said, "Rains came down in torrents. . .the whole place was flooded." In this harsh place she set up a boarding school to train young men as evangelists. In spite of living in a crude hut inhabited by rats and ants, Johanna said she never regretted leaving New York City.

God uses ordinary people and things to accomplish His extraordinary deeds. Moses, a sheepherder, used a shepherd's staff to work miracles before Pharaoh. With a common sling and rock, young David slew a giant. And Johanna, a stenographer, became an effective Christian witness to the Dzompere people. Give your ordinary talents to God and watch what miracles He will do with that "stick" in your hand.

Emily H. Tubman

Philanthropist, Emancipator
1794–1885

> All the believers were one in heart and mind. No one claimed that any
> of their possessions was their own, but they shared everything they had.
> ACTS 4:32 NIV

Emily Tubman was born into wealth and married into riches. With wealth came social status in her Southern community. One Sunday morning as she met with believers for worship, she thought of the fortune she had inherited from her husband. Shouldn't she, a Christian and a student of the Bible, use it to further the gospel?

Churches and colleges, black and white communities alike, received from this generous woman who lived during the terms of twenty-one United States presidents from George Washington to Grover Cleveland.

After the Civil War, Emily, with other railroad shareholders, agreed to provide free transportation for thousands of Confederate soldiers returning home. She also quietly gave money to help poor families of veterans recover from the war's devastation.

When thanked for her generosity, Emily often said, "I am a steward of the Lord, and only hold this money in trust."

How do you view your possessions? After the outpouring of the Holy Spirit in the book of Acts, the believers freely gave to one another. Like Emily Tubman and those early Christians, recognize your source and generously share what God has entrusted to you.

Irene Webster-Smith
Missionary
20th Century

> Whether you turn to the right or to the left, your ears will
> hear a voice behind you, saying, "This is the way; walk in it."
> ISAIAH 30:21 NIV

"What are you going to do when you return to Japan?" a woman
asked missionary Irene Webster-Smith during her furlough in the
United States.

Irene had been praying about her future ministry, and with
the question her mind was suddenly filled with images of Japanese
children. Often young girls were sold to unscrupulous men who
promised the girls a glorious future. Instead they were trained in a
life of vice as geishas.

Is this the work You want me to consider, Lord? she prayed.

When Irene presented the new venture to the mission board, they
told her to go ahead. Upon her arrival in Japan she told a Christian
doctor of her plan. "What took you so long?" he asked. The doctor
explained that he had prayed for fifteen years for a missionary to
begin this work.

Irene went on to establish Sunshine Home, a place where girls,
rescued from a life of evil, could be raised in a Christian atmosphere.

How do you know God's plans for your life? He will lead you
step by step, just as He did Irene Webster-Smith. And if you get off
track, God promises the Holy Spirit will tap you on the shoulder and
point you in the right direction.

Lucy G. Thurston
Missionary, Author
1795–1876

"Be strong and courageous. Do not be afraid; do not be discouraged,
for the LORD your God will be with you wherever you go."
JOSHUA 1:9 NIV

In 1820 newlyweds Lucy and Asa Thurston, with fifteen others, set sail in a small trading vessel for missionary work in Hawaii. After 157 days at sea, they reached their destination.

Lucy Thurston could scarcely believe what she found in Kailua. The people worshipped volcanoes, sharks, wood, and stones. They had no written language or organized government. The villagers lived in filthy thatched huts. In this setting, Lucy led a women's Bible study and instructed women in sewing, reading, writing, and singing.

When it was discovered Lucy had breast cancer, she lay on a couch with her Bible and hymnbook at her side and was operated on without the aid of anesthetic. She survived the ordeal and lived twenty-two more years.

For forty-eight years Lucy Thurston courageously worked for God in this primitive place. No doubt at times she felt overwhelmed. There's no telling how many times Lucy Thurston had to "take courage."

God has appointed certain tasks for you to do because He knows you can do them. However, at times you may be fearful. Avail yourself of God's courage; He has plenty to share with you.

Esther Edwards Burr
Colonial Woman
1732–1758

Therefore, there is now no condemnation for those who are in Christ Jesus. . .
the law of the Spirit who gives life has set you free
from the law of sin and death.
ROMANS 8:1–2 NIV

Esther Edwards, daughter of Jonathan Edwards, the revivalist of colonial New England, married Aaron Burr, a preacher and the president of Princeton University. In a series of letters Esther wrote to a friend, we catch a glimpse into the life and spiritual struggles of this young wife and mother.

Esther confessed to feelings of depression and wrote, "A strange gloom has possessed my mind for some weeks past." She wrote of struggles of conscience, "I am carnal, fleshly, worldly-minded and devilish. Oh, I long for a Sabbath's frame of mind. . . . My heart I see is on the world and not on God."

Yet in the same letters, Esther told of an exhausting schedule. "Spent a.m. visiting some sick and the poor prisoners that you know are very near to me." She said, "Dined eight ministers." "Company stayed yet, the weather being very bad." "No sooner house emptied but filled again."

Although Esther Burr lived in years past, she fought the same battles that have always besieged Christian women; in the face of life's many demands, how can I live pleasing to God?

Thanks to God! In Jesus, you're free from condemnation. Move on! Enjoy your life in Christ!

Maude Cary
Missionary
1878–1967

> When Cephas came to Antioch, I opposed him to his face,
> because he stood condemned.
> GALATIANS 2:11 NIV

In 1901 a Kansas farm girl, Maude Cary, set sail with forty others for mission work in Morocco. They spent the first months learning the Arabic language. In the summer Maude, with other new missionaries, went into the villages as itinerant evangelists. It was hard work, especially dealing with the fierce dogs most Moroccans kept. But this paled in comparison to Maude's next problem.

When a meeting of mission workers was opened for complaints, Maude was accused of being selfish. Another person said she was guilty of idle talk and that she took undue pride in her appearance. A fellow worker accused her of not praying with Muslims when she witnessed to them. As a result of the confrontation, Maude was asked to leave the mission field. Later, she was allowed to stay, but Maude's heart was broken by the humbling experience.

Petty misunderstandings may occur in Christian circles. Here are some scriptural principles to help you deal with these problems. Gather all the facts and with a gentle spirit go to the person with whom you differ. Affirm the good in them and talk over the matter in a way so as not to destroy the person's spirit. Differences of opinion need not shake your faith or cause disharmony in the church when they are handled in a Christlike manner.

Margaret Blagge Godolphin

Christian Woman
1652–1678

> Where sin increased, grace increased all the more.
> Romans 5:20 NIV

Margaret Blagge was born into an English royal family and as a young woman she moved in the court of pleasure-loving King Charles II. Margaret, a Christian, voiced distress over the influences around her. "I have no time for my soul. Cards we play for hours every day. I can scarce say my prayers and seldom read." However, in this worldly environment, she successfully maintained a walk with God, and her good reputation remained untouched by the corruption of the scandalous court.

Eager to devote herself to spiritual matters, Margaret considered not marrying, but a friend reminded her that Mary, Jesus' mother, was married. As a wife Margaret viewed the union through spiritual eyes. "It will be to serve God and to encourage one another daily," she said.

After marriage, she left the pomp of the English Royal Court and devoted herself to the pursuit of godliness. A writer said of Margaret, she "seemed to thirst after nothing more than to be with God."

Perhaps you find yourself living or working in a place saturated by indifference to God's standard of righteousness. Christ's grace and constant presence makes it possible for you to live above evil influences. Think about it: After the cross, Jesus went to hell and took the keys from Satan (Revelation 1:18). He reigns as victor over every adversary, and so do you.

Harriet Tubman
Emancipator
Early 19th–Early 20th Century

> Be alert and of sober mind. Your enemy the
> devil prowls around like a roaring lion looking for
> someone to devour. Resist him, standing firm in the faith.
> 1 PETER 5:8–9 NIV

They called her Moses and, like the Bible deliverer's, after Harriet Tubman's escape from slavery, her goal was to lead others out of bondage.

Harriet told this incident from her slave days: She had worked all day in the fields and when evening came, she was called to the main house. The mistress's sick infant wouldn't stop crying, and she instructed Harriet to rock the cradle through the long night.

Of course she fell asleep. The baby cried and the mistress whipped Harriet with a horsewhip on her neck and back, leaving scars that lasted a lifetime.

After Harriet escaped and led slaves North to freedom, she applied the lesson learned from the happening. The slaves fleeing with Harriet often became tired and wanted to rest or go back. Remembering her vigil and its aftermath, she admonished them, "Be alert! Stay awake! Don't rest!"

The Bible, too, uses words of warning to alert believers to the dangers of spiritual lethargy. We have an enemy. Like a lion stalking his prey, the devil attacks the weak and those off guard. His goal is the destruction of our souls. We are to resist him using the weapons of prayer and the Word of God. In the power of Jesus' name, be vigilant!

Irene Webster-Smith
Missionary
20th Century

> Although I want to do good, evil is right there with me.
> For in my inner being I delight in God's law; but I see
> another law at work in me. . .making me a prisoner.
> ROMANS 7:21–23 NIV

When Irene Webster-Smith first felt a stirring in her heart to be a missionary, she rebelled and stopped going to church. Then she read a notice requesting secretarial help for a missionary in Japan and Irene sensed she should apply for the job. But there were obstacles to overcome to arrive at the place of her calling.

Upon hearing of the plan, Irene's mother objected. Unknown to Irene, her mother had terminal cancer and missionary service was put on hold until after her mother's death.

Then there was Al to consider. He and Irene were in love. They agreed to wait to be married until she returned to Ireland in two years. Another obstacle was obtaining passage in 1917 during World War I. Finally she sailed on a Japanese ship.

As Irene's love for Christ matured, she soon jumped the hurdles that loomed in her way of fulfilling God's purposes. In Japan she established a home for girls, taught the Bible to college students, began a center for American soldiers, and led Japanese war criminals to faith in Christ.

Our carnal and spiritual natures compete for control of our lives. "Thanks be to God—through Jesus Christ" (Romans 7:25). With His help, we can break out of the prison of a selfish nature into freedom and life.

Evelyne Brand
Missionary
1879–1974

> "I am still as strong today as the day Moses sent me out. . . .
> Now give me this hill country that the LORD promised me that day."
> JOSHUA 14:11–12 NIV

"Please send me back for one more year! I promise not to make any trouble," sixty-four-year-old Evelyne Brand begged the skeptical mission board in England.

When Evelyne and her husband, Jesse, went to India as young missionaries they had vowed to bring the gospel to the people living on five mountain ranges. Jesse died after they had evangelized one mountain, and Evelyne, in spite of her age, wanted to complete the task. A reluctant mission board relented.

After a year Evelyne resigned from the mission and went out on her own. Riding on a pony, she traveled to villages, camped out, gave medical care, and told people about Jesus. Because of an earlier accident, she wobbled about with the aid of bamboo canes. Yet her joy knew no bounds. Granny Brand, as she was called, continually exclaimed, "Praise God!"

After her "retirement," Evelyne worked for twenty-four more years until she had established mission stations on all five mountains. At age ninety-five she tore ligaments in her leg and while being treated, she died.

God has given countless promises in His Word to believers: peace, health, and the salvation of family members are only a few of them. Pursue your God-inspired goals even into your old age. Like Evelyne Brand, claim that "mountain"!

Grace Livingston Hill

Author
1865–1947

> Lord, you are my strength and fortress, my refuge in the day of trouble!
> JEREMIAH 16:19 NLT

It seemed like a perfect match when author Grace Livingston married Frank Hill, a young pastor. Soon after their marriage, Grace noticed her husband sometimes became fidgety and agitated.

One Sunday morning Frank was especially nervous as he sat on the church platform. When he suddenly left the building, Grace followed him and watched as he swallowed two pills. Then he returned to the pulpit and delivered the sermon.

Later, when Grace questioned Frank, he confessed to a drug addiction that had began when a doctor prescribed a medication for headaches. He told Grace, "I've tried to keep the problem from you. I've confessed the sin of using it. But I can't stop."

There was little understanding of drug addiction in 1892, and there were no drug rehabilitation centers. A shadow had entered their marriage, yet Grace told no one. Seven years later, Frank died from a ruptured appendix. Twenty-five years after her husband's death, Grace told her daughter of the father's problem.

Burdens too heavy to bear, struggles with no answers. Perhaps you, like Grace, are carrying a distressing secret that clouds your very existence. This is not the time to abandon hope. When there are no answers, commit the situation to God. When there is no other place to turn, turn to God. He is a sure refuge.

Sarah Johnson
Colonial Christian Woman
1741–1845

> Jesus said to her, "I am the resurrection and the life.
> The one who believes in me will live, even though they die;
> and whoever lives by believing in me will never die."
> JOHN 11:25–26 NIV

While a friend read to her from the Bible, 104-year-old Sarah Johnson slipped away to heaven. The funeral sermon, delivered by her pastor, gives insight into the faith of this colonial black woman.

The pastor related that after taking Communion one Easter, he asked Sarah if she was getting ready for heaven, and she replied, "I am not only willing to die, but I am anxious to be gone." On another occasion, he asked if she was perfectly sure of heaven, and Sarah answered confidently, "I am safe not in myself but in my Savior." The last time the pastor visited Sarah, he asked how the great work of salvation had been accomplished in her life, and she replied, "Not by me, but by faith in Jesus Christ, my Savior."

Sarah Johnson fearlessly approached death, not because of any work she had done but because of what Jesus did for her on the cross.

What is the basis for your hope of eternal life? If you trust in your good deeds or a religious rite, you will be disappointed. Only in the merits of another—Jesus—can you stand righteous before God.

Sarah Broadman Judson

Missionary, Translator, Author
1803–1845

> Who shall separate us from the love of Christ? Shall trouble
> or hardship or persecution. . . . No, in all these things we
> are more than conquerors through him who loved us.
> ROMANS 8:35, 37 NIV

Sarah and George Broadman went to Burma as missionaries knowing they would be exposed to jungle fevers and work among a people unresponsive to the gospel. They were also aware that missionary Ann Judson's recent death was related to the difficult conditions of the country. Yet Sarah and George sailed in 1826.

The Broadmans had a fruitful ministry to the Karens, a mountain tribe, but in the tropical climate George's health declined, and he died after less than five years in Burma.

Sarah had established a girls' school and, fearful it would dissolve if she abandoned it, she stayed on with her two-year-old son. When missionary Adoniram Judson visited Sarah in 1834, they were married. In the next eight years Sarah had eight children, made new translations of the Bible into the Burmese language, translated about twenty hymns into native languages, and at the time of her death was translating John Bunyan's *Pilgrim's Progress*.

Sarah had numerous opportunities to turn aside from the risks of a difficult calling, but she didn't. What hard trial do you see on the horizon? It may appear your next mountain will be too painful to climb or even impassable. Yet nothing—no, nothing—can separate you from God. Calvary's love causes you always to triumph.

Hannah Whitall Smith
Author
1832–1911

> And what does the LORD require of you? To act justly and
> to love mercy and to walk humbly with your God.
>
> MICAH 6:8 NIV

When Hannah Whitall Smith and her family moved to Millville, New Jersey, in 1864, she missed her Christian friends and Bible study group in Philadelphia. A pastor advised her to befriend the poor people in her neighborhood.

Hannah's dressmaker, a Christian, invited her to attend a Saturday evening testimony meeting in the woman's church, but Hannah hesitated. The people attending would be factory workers. *What do they have to offer?* she thought. "I had studied and taught the Bible a great deal," she said. "I felt I had more to teach them than they, me."

Hannah, filled with "importance and superiority," decided to go. When she entered the meeting, a factory woman with a shawl on her head was speaking. "My whole horizon used to be filled with this big 'Me,'" the woman said. "But when I got sight of Jesus as my Savior, this great big 'Me' melted to nothing."

Hannah thought, *I cannot imagine my "Me" melting down to nothing.* Yet the words touched her and the conviction came that "this is real Christianity, the kind I long for."

Part of "real Christianity" is being clothed with humility. Jesus is your example. He rubbed shoulders with the debased of society: lepers, tax collectors, and prostitutes. As day after day you walk with the carpenter from Nazareth, choose His way of humility.

Mary Smith Moffat
Missionary
1795–1870

> He [Jesus]. . .took off his outer clothing, and wrapped a
> towel around his waist. After that, he poured water
> into a basin and began to wash his disciples' feet.
> JOHN 13:4–5 NIV

When Mary Smith went to South Africa to marry missionary Robert Moffat, she wrote, "I am now united to one who counts not his life dear to himself."

Neither did Mary count her life dear as she set out with her husband by oxcart for a jungle location where she spent the next forty years. There she washed clothes in the river, ground wheat to make bread, cleaned the dirt floor of her home with cow dung to kill the fleas, and taught native children about Jesus.

Mary Moffat's humble attitude served as an example to her children. Mary, her oldest daughter, married missionary-explorer David Livingstone. Children Elizabeth, Ann, Robert, and John also became missionaries. Mary Moffat wrote, "Our gracious God has been very condescending to spare the lives of His unworthy servants to witness some fruit of missionary labor." Part of that fruit was seen in the lives of her godly children.

When Jesus washed His disciples' feet, He wanted this humble act to translate to every facet of their future ministry. Would they communicate the gospel with arrogance? Or would they, like Jesus, wrap a towel about themselves and "wash feet"?

Mary Moffat chose to "wash feet," and her family followed her example. Live your life as a humble servant and see this quality reflected in your loved ones.

Dinah Hardenbergh
Colonial Christian Leader
1725–1807

> So all of us who have had that veil removed can see and reflect
> the glory of the Lord. And the Lord—who is the Spirit—makes us
> more and more like him as we are changed into his glorious image.
>
> 2 CORINTHIANS 3:18 NLT

Between the morning and afternoon services in their New England church, Dinah Hardenbergh, the pastor's wife, gathered the women and further explained the scriptures her husband had preached from that day.

In 1747 Dinah began to keep a diary, and from it we learn of this colonial woman's spiritual journey. One subject she wrote about was becoming Christlike. She said, "It is my inmost desire that. . .the precious image of the Lord Jesus be more fully transferred to and impressed upon me, and all things become more and more new."

While Dinah taught the women in her church, she saw the bigger picture—her life was a reflection of Jesus. Her spiritual quest was rewarded with insight and maturity. In later years her counsel was sought by pastors and she was called "a pastor to pastors."

As a Christian, your old nature is dead. The new nature you received at the new birth is alive to godly purposes. The greatest of these is that you become more like your Savior. This is a progressive work. We aid the Holy Spirit in our growth by exposing ourselves to the right influences. To speed your progress, today pray, "Jesus, stamp Your likeness on my life."

Lucy Webb Hayes
Wife of United States President
1831–1889

> "But as for me and my household, we will serve the LORD."
> JOSHUA 24:15 NIV

Daily prayers were observed in Lucy and Rutherford Hayes's home when they lived in Ohio. When Mr. Hayes became president of the United States and their family moved into the White House, they maintained the custom. Mrs. Hayes said, "Exalt the home and you lift up the nation." On Sunday evenings during her time as first lady, Lucy, described as the perfect hostess, handed out songbooks to guests and they sang the hymns of the church.

Before becoming president, Mr. Hayes had served as governor of Ohio for three terms and in those years the Hayes had served no alcoholic beverages at state functions. In the nation's capitol, they maintained the habit. For this Mrs. Hayes was nicknamed, "Lemonade Lucy."

She explained to a friend, "I have three sons just coming to manhood. . . . I do not feel as if I could be the first to put the wine cup to their lips."

To maintain a Christian home there are certain things you will do: You will attend church, read the Bible, and pray with your family. To the best of your ability you will eliminate ungodly influences. Declare with Joshua, the Old Testament leader, "In our home, we will serve the Lord!"

Helen Steiner Rice

Poet
1900–1981

> But our citizenship is in heaven. And we eagerly await a Savior from there,
> the Lord Jesus Christ, who. . .will transform our lowly bodies
> so that they will be like his glorious body.
> PHILIPPIANS 3:20–21 NIV

"What are you going to do in heaven?" the visitor asked Helen Steiner Rice when he called on her during her last days.

"Sit and rest and listen to the heavenly music," she said wearily.

"And write a few poems," the visitor added.

"Yes, I'm sure I'll do some writing," Helen said. "We'll have time to do the things we love."

Helen loved writing poems. She once estimated she had written more than two million poems. In her employment by Gibson Greeting Cards, her writings appeared on greeting cards and in books for five decades. From 1960 until her death, her poems focused on faith, love, and hope.

Because she belonged to Christ, Helen longed for the eternal city and talked about it with fondness. The Bible describes heaven as a better place. Our prayers are said to ascend to heaven. Jesus is preparing us a place in heaven, "that you also may be where I am" (John 14:3). And in heaven you will have a perfect body, free of infirmities and limitations—like Christ's glorified body. No wonder Helen was eager to go!

Lilias Trotter
Missionary
1853–1928

> I saw a throne in heaven and someone sitting on it. The one sitting on the throne was as brilliant as gemstones—like jasper and carnelian.
> REVELATION 4:2–3 NLT

Lilias Trotter established the Algerian Mission Band and worked for four decades to bring the gospel to Muslims in North Africa. As she lay dying, friends gathered around her bed and while they sang a hymn, Lilias looked out a window. "A chariot and six horses!" she said. "You are seeing beautiful things?" a friend asked. "Yes, many, many beautiful things," Lilias said. Raising her hands to God, she took her last breath and entered heaven.

Through a vision, God gave Lilias a view of her new home. The heavens also were opened for John the apostle, and he caught a glimpse of Christ's glory. This prepared him to face the frightening events of the last days.

As events progress toward the end of the age, sordid world conditions will cause believers distress. To counteract these effects, read the book of Revelation and Bible references to heaven. You can't know or understand all there is to know about the future home of believers. Rather, concentrate on knowing the One who has gone to prepare a place for you. When Jesus becomes your quest, you will eventually find out what heaven is all about. And it will be far greater than your expectations. The best *is* yet to come.

Bertha Smith
Missionary
1888–1988

Come near to God and he will come near to you.
JAMES 4:8 NIV

Missionary Bertha Smith arrived in China in 1917 and spent the first two years studying the Mandarin language. She said of that time, "I was lonesome and homesick enough to die."

To counteract the loneliness she took long walks. While walking she repeated Bible verses and sang hymns. She found the spiritual exercise a tremendous help for her homesick heart, but it also served another purpose: Bertha experienced the wonderful presence of Jesus in a new way.

She faced another dilemma in those early years in China; what about marriage and children? Could she live alone all her life? On her walks, Bertha entered into an agreement with the Lord. "I am here to win souls," she said. "I am willing to go through as much self-denial to see children born into the family of God as is necessary for a mother to endure for her children to be born." After this experience, Bertha gave herself fully to language study and there were no more tears.

Bertha Smith learned how to glean spiritual stamina for life's challenges. In James 4, the Bible mentions other "secrets" to an overcoming life. We are encouraged to submit to God, resist the devil, purify our hearts, and humble ourselves. There is no better cure for loneliness, homesickness, or any other problem you may encounter than to draw near to God.

Lilian Hammer
Medical Missionary
1912–1959

"But the time is coming—indeed it's here now— when you will
be scattered, each one going his own way, leaving me alone.
Yet I am not alone because the Father is with me."
JOHN 16:32 NLT

When Lilian Hammer, a missionary nurse, transferred to Thailand to work among the tribespeople, word of her healing abilities spread throughout the villages. With only a bare knowledge of the language, Lilian trudged through the jungle to treat the diseased and show them Bible pictures. As she gained the confidence of the people in one village, they built her a hut and invited her to live among them. From this lonely spot she treated the sick and preached the gospel.

The mission board recognized Lilian's need for a companion and sent her a helper, but the woman was forced to leave because of illness and again Lilian was alone. She wrote, "I find it very hard to endure. . . . I am hoping to have a fellow worker some day. For twelve months I have been alone. However, whether alone or with a companion, the Lord is able to work." Lilian's life came to an end when, alone in the jungle, she was attacked and murdered.

Jesus, too, endured the greatest trial of His life—alone. Great heroes of faith such as David, Jeremiah, Paul, and Daniel also had times of loneliness. You, too, may be suffering from this malady. Take comfort in Christ's words, "The Father is with me."

Lettie Cowman
Author, Missionary
1870–1960

> "Unless a kernel of wheat falls to the ground and dies,
> it remains only a single seed. But if it dies, it produces many seeds."
> JOHN 12:24 NIV

Lettie and Charles Cowman went as faith missionaries to Japan in 1900 and founded the Oriental Missionary Society. Their goal was to place a scripture portion in every home in the empire. In seventeen years, more than ten million homes had received a gospel message through their efforts.

Then Charles became seriously ill. The couple returned to Los Angeles in hopes he would recover. During his lengthy illness, Lettie began writing and compiling poems and prose to encourage him. She also shared her writings with missionary friends, and later these became the book, *Streams in the Desert*.

Charles did not survive, but out of this difficult situation, God used Lettie's book to help thousands. Her devotional book has been published in fifteen languages and had more than one hundred English printings and several editions. The renowned Chinese leader, Chiang Kai-shek, was said to have requested the book be buried with him.

This is a principle of nature: A seed must die to produce fruit. Jesus' death brought life to millions, so through Lettie's testings, good things resulted.

What hard trials are you experiencing? Sickness, death, and loss can be opportunities to come alive to God's purposes and produce an abundant harvest.

Edith Moules
Missionary
1900–1949

"What is more pleasing to the LORD: your burnt offerings and sacrifices or your obedience to his voice? Listen! Obedience is better than sacrifice."
1 SAMUEL 15:22 NLT

Edith Moules was content with her work as a medical missionary in the Belgian Congo. In a three-month period she reported treating fourteen thousand people suffering from twenty-five different diseases.

One day as she examined patients, Edith looked up and saw a man staring at her. The man's fingers and toes were rotted off, his feet swollen. He was a leper. Edith found leprosy repugnant. She didn't want to help him, but she agreed to let him stay at the mission for a time.

The leprous man came day after day and watched Edith. She conveniently ignored him and later confessed, "I didn't want to handle leprosy because I was scared lest I contract it." As she prayed about the man's condition, God let her know He wanted to do a new thing that would require her obedience. "Foolish!" she realized. "What does the body matter?" Obedient to the voice of God, Edith expanded her medical work to include lepers. By 1931, the mission housed over sixty lepers.

Is God also asking you to do something you consider distasteful, unreasonable, or beneath you? Have you bargained with Him, looking for a way out? Did you offer Him an alternative plan? Perfect obedience pleases God; it's what He expects from you, His servant.

Evangeline Booth
Salvation Army Leader, Evangelist
1865–1950

Then the disciples went out and preached everywhere, and the Lord worked
with them and confirmed his word by the signs that accompanied it.
MARK 16:20 NIV

Evangeline Booth's parents, Catherine and William, were impressive
preachers, and Evangeline also had a commanding presence in the
pulpit. For thirty years, she led the Salvation Army in the United
States. When she preached to retreats in Maine and New Jersey,
she held large audiences spellbound for hours, and following her
sermons, many sought salvation.

After becoming general of the army in 1934, she conducted
"World for God" meetings in many countries of the world. A service
in India attracted more than twenty thousand people. An observer
wrote, "General Evangeline spoke for an hour on 'His Name Shall
Be Called Wonderful'. . . . At the General's invitation five thousand
seekers lifted their voices in prayer."

God has chosen to communicate His life-changing message of
redemption through preaching. The instrument used to propel the
powerful message is a weak human vessel.

However, the Lord has given the Holy Spirit to help the minister.
Whether you are called to preach, teach, or witness, how comforting
to know the Lord works with you to accomplish the work.

Betsy Stockton
Missionary
1798–1865

> "The greatest among you will be your servant.
> For those who exalt themselves will be humbled,
> and those who humble themselves will be exalted."
> MATTHEW 23:11–12 NIV

The first single American woman to serve as a foreign missionary was Betsy Stockton, a former household slave. Before her conversion, Betsy was described as "wild and thoughtless." After she was saved in 1816, she felt called to be a missionary in Africa. But when a plea went out for workers to go to Hawaii, in spite of her slave status, she applied to the mission board. They agreed to send her, not as a missionary but as a domestic servant who would also teach. About the same time, Betsy was given her freedom.

In a recommendation to the mission board, Betsy was described as "intelligent, pious, she reads well, knows sacred history and has conquered English grammar."

Despite her servant status, Betsy taught in a school in Hawaii and cared for the sick. She kept a diary that revealed a gifted woman—a true servant of Christ.

No matter what title we bear, the Bible reminds us to maintain a servant's attitude. A servant obeys and is willing to do menial tasks. He or she is not haughty or proud. As our example, Jesus washed the disciples' feet and said, "For even the Son of Man did not come to be served, but to serve" (Mark 10:45).

Katherine Zell

Author, Hymn Writer, Reformer
1497–1562

> Praise the LORD, for the LORD is good;
> sing praise to his name, for that is pleasant.
> PSALM 135:3 NIV

During the Reformation many people sought advice from Katherine Zell, a wise pastor's wife who worked to bring unity to the church in transition. She was also known for her good works as she visited in prisons and cared for the sick and dying during plagues.

Aware of the power of music, Katherine wrote, published, and sold hymns in pamphlet form for one cent apiece. With her songs, she hoped to help people center their minds on God and counter the godless influences of the day. She said, "When so many filthy songs are on the lips of men and women and even children, I think it well that folk should with lusty zeal and clear voice sing the songs of their salvation."

Moses led the Israelites in songs of celebration after miraculously crossing the sea (Exodus 15:1). With a song, Deborah and Barak gave God credit for victory (Judges 5). In prison, with their feet in stocks, Paul and Silas sang hymns and the prison doors flew open (Acts 16:25–26).

Whether you're celebrating a victory or in the throes of despair, follow Katherine Zell's advice: sing praise to God. Besides positively affecting your body, soul, spirit, and mind, you'll find "prison doors" swing open when you praise Him.

Marian Anderson
Musician
1902–1993

"I have told you these things, so that in me you may have peace. In this world you will have trouble. But take heart! I [Jesus] have overcome the world."
JOHN 16:33 NIV

Marian Anderson's musical talents transcended race, yet she daily confronted racial prejudice. On one occasion, she was paid to sing at the premiere of a film, but was refused a room in the city's leading hotel. In Atlantic City she was given the key to the city, but she couldn't spend the night there. Marian waited in separate train station waiting rooms and was refused admittance to restaurants. Before one concert a committee woman refused to shake the musician's hand.

In 1939 Marian was scheduled to give a concert in Constitution Hall in Washington DC, but the owners of the hall had a clause in their rental contract prohibiting blacks from appearing there. Other auditoriums also denied Marian use of their facilities. Instead, an outdoor concert was scheduled for the Lincoln Memorial on Easter Sunday, where seventy-five thousand people, black and white, gathered before the figure of the Great Emancipator as Marian sang hymns, Negro spirituals, and arias.

Marian's gentle nature and Christian upbringing prevented her from lashing out at these injustices. Instead, she used her music to conquer inequality.

Struggles of various kinds are inevitable. Instead of retaliating in anger, follow Jesus' teachings and example. Remember, He overcame an unfair world using peaceful means.

Dorothy Ann Thrupp

Hymn Writer, Editor
1779–1847

"I am the good shepherd: I know my sheep and my sheep know me."
JOHN 10:14 NIV

The hymn "Savior, Like a Shepherd Lead Us" was first published without a composer's name, but it is believed Dorothy Ann Thrupp penned the words. She was known to have written several hymns using the pseudonym "Iota" or her initials.

Dorothy Ann never married or had a family, but she loved children and wrote songs for them. Her "shepherd" hymn appeared in a volume published in 1836 and was intended for the young. However, the hymn, which uses metaphors of sheep and a shepherd, is sung and appreciated by all ages.

Savior, like a shepherd lead us, much we need Thy tender care;
In Thy pleasant pastures feed us, for our use Thy folds prepare:
Blessed Jesus, Blessed Jesus, Thou hast bought us, Thine we are;
Blessed Jesus, Blessed Jesus, Thou hast bought us, Thine we are.

Sheep are completely dependent upon the shepherd to lead them to water and pasture. Because they have no defenses to fight against attacks of wild animals, sheep need protection. A good shepherd will endanger his life to keep the sheep safe.

On the other hand, sheep have a duty to their shepherd; they listen to his voice and follow him (John 10:27). The good Shepherd *has* laid down His life for you. Now be a wise "sheep"; listen to His voice and follow where He leads.

Marie Monson
Missionary
Early 20th Century

> I have heard all about you, LORD. I am filled with awe by your amazing works.
> In this time of our deep need, help us again as you did in years gone by.
> HABAKKUK 3:2 NLT

In 1907, Marie Monson, missionary to China, heard that revival fires burned in Korean churches and she made plans to visit Korea. Before she went, God impressed on her that she could remain where she was and experience the same powerful move of God. With this revelation, she began to pray for a spiritual awakening in her life and in the Chinese church.

Marie joined with others in prayer, standing on the promise, "If two of you on earth agree about anything they ask for, it will be done for them by my Father" (Matthew 18:19 NIV).

"The Holy Spirit uses the scriptures in revival," Marie declared, and she studied the Bible and taught it to study groups. Marie's prayers were answered when Chinese believers could not sleep or eat until they had confessed their sins.

Does your spirit need renewing? It will happen when you admit your need, rediscover the power of God's Word, and sincerely pray, "Revive me, God, so I find my joy in You."

Catherine (Kitty) Plackett Short
Sister of Missionary Dorothy Carey
Mid-18th Century

> I commend to you our sister Phoebe, a deacon of the church in
> Cenchreae. . .for she has been the benefactor of many people, including me.
> ROMANS 16:1–2 NIV

Fearful to take her young family to a foreign land, Dorothy Carey refused to go to India with William, her missionary-husband, and he set out without her. However, while the ship waited in port, the captain told William and his son to disembark because he suspected they could not lawfully enter India.

When William returned to England's mainland, he again begged his wife to go with him. She finally consented if Kitty, her thirty-year-old sister, would accompany her. Kitty agreed to go.

In India, the two women shared household duties. Kitty sympathized with Dorothy over the appalling conditions they endured in India. Together they cared for the Careys' young sons. The family moved frequently in the first years and at one location, they stayed with Charles Short, a salt agent. Kitty fell in love with Charles and they married.

Historians give little space to Kitty Short. Yet, by accompanying Dorothy to India, by supporting and helping her in a difficult setting, Kitty played a key role in the overall picture of world missions.

You may also function as a helper. In this role you are not recognized by the throngs, but as part of the whole, your job assists with the church's overall success. No work is insignificant if it helps even one person.

Lottie Moon
Missionary
1840–1912

> When I am with those who are weak, I share their weakness,
> for I want to bring the weak to Christ. Yes, I try to find common
> ground with everyone, doing everything I can to save some.
> 1 CORINTHIANS 9:22 NLT

Missionary Lottie Moon effectively ministered as an evangelist in China for forty years. Her letters to America during that time pled with church leaders to send more missionaries and financial help. In 1888 the Lottie Moon Christmas offering was established, and the first year provided three additional missionaries. Much of her success was because she went where the people lived and, with concern and love, won their friendship.

When a famine struck the area after the Boxer Rebellion, Lottie gave her food and funds to the starving at the expense of her health. Fellow missionaries, concerned for her welfare, sent for a doctor. He concluded she was starving herself. Lottie was on her way to the United States to recover when she died in Japan from complications related to malnutrition.

While most Christians won't be called upon to sacrifice to the point of endangering their health, the Bible outlines principles for effective ministry. Find a common interest with those you are trying to win to Christ. Work to make people feel accepted, avoid a superior attitude, listen to their concerns, and seek opportunities to express Christ's love.

Lottie Moon fulfilled all these criteria and more. As Christ's disciples, we can, too.

Carry A. Nation
Activist, Preacher, Author
1846–1911

> Wine is a mocker and beer a brawler;
> whoever is led astray by them is not wise.
> PROVERBS 20:1 NIV

Carry Nation discovered firsthand what liquor can do when she married a man described as a severe alcoholic. Distressed by liquor's devastating effects in her home and marriage, she said, "I took this to God daily, feeling that He only could rescue." Her prayer: "Please show me something to do."

After her husband died, Carry married David Nation, a minister, editor, and attorney, in 1877. They moved to Medicine Lodge, Kansas, where Carry directed two Sunday schools, worked as a jail evangelist, and led a temperance group.

In 1890 Carry, with a Bible in her hand, stood outside a saloon, and with other women, sang hymns and prayed. Later, the ladies grew more aggressive in their efforts against the liquor traffic, throwing rocks through saloon windows and smashing liquor bottles. Carry was arrested thirty times in ten years for disturbing the peace.

While Carry Nation's methods of dealing with a problem were extreme, we admire her courage as she successfully called attention to a national problem.

The Bible alerts us to the dangers of alcohol; it dulls the senses, clouds a person's judgment, and should definitely not be used by persons in leadership (Proverbs 31:4).

If you are deceived by intoxicating beverages, take the wise advice of scripture: avoid strong drink and escape the pitfalls associated with alcohol.

Hulda Johnson Rees
Preacher, Evangelist
19th Century

> For the Spirit God gave us does not make us timid
> but gives us power, love and self-discipline.
> 2 TIMOTHY 1:7 NIV

When a revival swept through her Quaker community, sixteen-year-old Hulda Johnson was converted to Christ. Immediately she felt called to preach the gospel, but being "excessively timid," it was difficult for her to stand in front of a congregation.

Before preaching she would sit with her eyes closed to avoid seeing the people. On one occasion, when a large crowd came to hear her, she gave her text and in ten minutes sat down with no more to say. Humiliated, feeling "like a fool," Hulda earnestly sought God. In a dream, God assured her she could be as carefree and peaceful in her calling as a little child. While the dream didn't end all her fears, the "Pentecostal prophetess," as Hulda came to be known, gained confidence, and people who heard her said her preaching was "in the power of the Spirit."

Some fear is necessary in your life and keeps you from doing irrational things. However, too much can keep you from doing God's will. The Bible contains at least 365 verses that say, "Don't be afraid." That's one for every day of the year. These verses, coupled with Jesus' promise, "Never will I leave you" (Hebrews 13:5), will take you out of the realm of fear into Christ's peace and freedom.

Phillis Wheatley

African-American Poet
1753–1784

> In my Father's house are many mansions. . . . I go to prepare a place for you. . . . I will come again, and receive you unto myself.
> JOHN 14:2–3 KJV

In 1761 Phillis, an eight-year-old black girl, was brought to America on a slave ship. John Wheatley, a wealthy Boston merchant, bought her for his wife. The couple treated Phillis like a daughter and taught her to read and write. Later, she studied Latin, geography, and history.

Phillis, at age fourteen, began writing poetry. She was also an avid letter writer, and her letters to friends give insight into the heart of a deeply spiritual person.

Life in colonial America was uncertain; diseases and plagues often ravaged the countryside, cutting down the young and old. Phillis's letters, infused with Bible verses and admonitions, make numerous references to life after death. She wrote, "O may we all meet at length in that happy mansion." She said, "Till we meet in the regions of consummate blessedness. . .we shall die the death of the righteous." Because of her faith and knowledge of the Bible, Phillis had complete confidence she would go to heaven when her life ended.

Life today is no more certain than when Phillis Wheatley lived. Diseases and disasters continue to terrorize the human race. And Jesus' words are as true now as when He first spoke them. When you trust in Christ, at your death He promises to receive you into those glorious mansions. What a comforting promise!

Anna Letitia Barbauld

Author, Hymn Writer
1743–1825

> "Come to me, all you who are weary
> and burdened, and I will give you rest."
> MATTHEW 11:28 NIV

In 1773 Anna Barbauld published a book of poetry that became so popular it went through four printings. Twenty-one of the poems were set to music and became hymns of the church.

Together with her husband, a minister, Anna opened a school. But her husband was reported to have a violent temper and caused his wife many anxious moments. In one incident, he attacked her with a knife, and she was forced to commit him to an asylum. He managed to escape and eventually took his own life.

Anna no doubt depended on divine protection in more than one stressful situation, so it was not by accident she wrote a hymn that speaks of coming to Jesus for rest. The song, written about 1792, is entitled "The Gracious Call."

Come, said Jesus' sacred voice,
Come, and make My path your choice;
I will guide you to your home;
Weary pilgrim, hither come.

Hither come, for here is found
Balm that flows for every wound!
Peace that ever shall endure,
Rest eternal, sacred, sure.

There are no more beautiful words for a tired person to hear than the invitation to "come and rest." Draw near to Jesus today, leave your heavy load with Him, and trade your weariness for His peace and rest.

Hannah Whitall Smith

Author
1832–1911

> God has said, "I will never fail you. I will never abandon you."
> So we can say with confidence, "The Lord is my helper."
> HEBREWS 13:5–6 NLT

"Loneliness is not confined to unmarried people," Quaker Hannah Whitall Smith wrote to her single friend, Priscilla. "The loneliness thou speaks of I know all about."

During the course of her life, Hannah had experienced lonely times. When her husband of many years was unfaithful, her heart ached with rejection and loneliness. When she lost four children at various times, she repeatedly felt the loneliness of loss and separation.

"Thy loneliness is the loneliness of a heart made for God," Hannah explained to her friend. "Human love might for awhile satisfy thee, but it would not last." She added, "I am determined I will be satisfied with God alone. I said, 'Lord, Thou art enough for me, just You, not Your gifts or blessings, just Thyself.' "

Loneliness is an emotion common to all. Changes in location and circumstances will temporarily alleviate the symptoms. Friends die or reject us and we are lonely again.

When you face lonely hours or even years, use this emotion to drive you to the only One who can fill a life with meaning. Declare with Hannah, "God is enough! He is enough for time; God is enough for eternity."

Virginia Leftwich Bell

Missionary
1892–1974

He put a new song in my mouth, a hymn of praise to our God.
Many will see and fear the LORD and put their trust in him.
PSALM 40:3 NIV

What is the missionary's wife's priority on the mission field—her family or the work? This is the dilemma Virginia Leftwich, a nurse, faced when she married Dr. Nelson Bell, and they went as missionaries to China. The couple agreed Virginia's first consideration would be their children, Rosa and Ruth. When the girls reached school age, Virginia taught them. She also instructed the girls in music, sewing, and gardening. In the evenings, the family played games, and Virginia read aloud to them.

In 1925 the Bells were overjoyed with the arrival of a baby boy, Nelson Junior. The child thrived in the loving home. At ten months of age he became sick, and Virginia cared for him, expecting the illness to pass. But the child became increasingly ill and after eighteen days, he died.

Rosa and Ruth recall their parents' composure when they told them their brother had gone to be with Jesus. Although their hearts were broken, there was no sense of hopelessness. As the family left the cemetery, Virginia said, "I have a song in my heart, but it is hard to keep the tears from my eyes."

A song in loss! Believers will suffer loss, but they will never know despair. Because of Jesus' victory over death, you and I—people of faith—can sing even when our hearts are breaking.

Florence Soper Booth
Social Reformer, Author, Administrator
1861–1957

"Go out quickly into the streets and alleys of the town and bring in the poor, the crippled, the blind and the lame."
LUKE 14:21 NIV

When Florence Booth, a Salvation Army worker, first heard of young women being lured into prostitution, she thought the stories were exaggerated. But one morning a girl appeared at Florence's door. Promised a good job, she had come to London only to find the job was in a brothel. The girl managed to escape and found her way to the Salvation Army.

Florence and her husband, Bramwell, began an investigation and formed groups called Midnight Rescue Brigades. The workers went into alleys, cellars, and attics at night to find girls longing for another life. Florence provided a refuge for them.

Beginning with that one home, in the next thirty years, the Salvation Army opened 117 shelters for "fallen" women.

General William Booth said of the rescue effort, "It will constitute one of the most effective onslaughts on one of the blackest strongholds of the devil, and be a means of rescuing tens of thousands of the most despairing. . .victims of his fiendish designs."

When the man in Jesus' parable (Luke 14:16–24) sent out invitations to a banquet, the guests had excuses for refusing. The man then issued the invitation to unlikely guests. In the same way, Jesus' invitation to enter into His salvation is not for a select few. No matter how sordid your history, you are welcome to dine at the Savior's banquet—now!

Mattie M. Boteler
Sunday School Teacher, Author, Editor
1859–1929

> Be a good worker, one who does not need to be ashamed
> and who correctly explains the word of truth.
> 2 TIMOTHY 2:15 NLT

Mattie Boteler may have set a record when for fifty-four years, without interruption, she taught a Sunday school class. Through her excellent instruction, the class produced lay evangelists and church leaders ably equipped to explain the scriptures.

In her quest to better relay Bible truth, Mattie developed creative teaching methods such as short poems or sayings, called epigrams, to communicate spiritual truth. She also encouraged students to memorize Bible verses.

Mattie increased her sphere of influence when, from 1894 until 1911, she edited two publications, *Lookout* and *Christian Standard*. The magazines carried her epigrams as well as her articles and commentaries on scripture. A contemporary of Mattie said, "No preacher among us. . .is a safer expounder of scripture than was she."

Anyone can just get by, but it takes added effort to excel. Whether you teach the Bible as Mattie Boteler did, do housework and care for children, or have a nine-to-five job, strive for excellence. It will inspire those who observe your life, give you great satisfaction, and honor God whom you serve.

Katharine Bushnell
Social Reformer, Author, Evangelist
1855–1946

> The Word gave life to everything that was created, and his life brought light
> to everyone. The light shines in the darkness, and the darkness
> can never extinguish it.
> JOHN 1:4–5 NLT

Dr. Katharine Bushnell had been a medical missionary in China, but because of an injury, she returned to America and began working with the Women's Christian Temperance Union to restore "fallen" women.

Described as a person who reflected the light of Christ, Katharine established a shelter for prostitutes in Chicago. However, when she heard of the "white slave trade," she investigated and discovered women were being sent to Wisconsin lumber camps for sexual purposes. She managed to get into the camps and found women being held against their will. Katharine's investigation led the Wisconsin Senate to pass the "Kate Bushnell Bill," a law that protects unmarried women and mentally retarded women and girls from commercial prostitution.

In 1886, after learning of a British government memo stating that attractive and medically inspected prostitutes would be provided for British soldiers, Katharine traveled to Britain and India and interviewed prostitutes, medical personnel, and hospital patients. Not everyone was happy to have the injustices brought to light, and Katharine's life was often threatened.

It takes boldness to take a stand for right when others condone or willingly ignore evil. Nonetheless, let your godly beliefs be known in your home and community. The light will eventually prevail.

Katherine von Bora Luther
Wife of the Reformer
1499–1552

As Jesus and the disciples continued on their way to Jerusalem,
they came to a certain village where a woman named
Martha welcomed him into her home.
LUKE 10:38 NLT

Was it easy to be the wife of Martin Luther, the reformer? Perhaps
not. At times Katherine Luther may have wished herself back in
the convent, as bleak as that was. However, through strange circumstances, she had cast her lot with Luther.

As a nun cloistered in an order that forbade her to speak to
others, Katherine heard of Luther's reform activities. Twelve nuns
asked for his help to escape from the nunnery. He agreed to help
them—and free them he did. He promptly married off all but one
ex-nun, Katherine. At her suggestion, she and Luther married.

Luther, at age forty-one, was said to be set in his ways. Redheaded,
feisty, twenty-six-year-old Katherine proved up to the task. She
tended the gardens, managed the livestock, raised six children, cared
for her often depressed spouse, and welcomed the many guests who
came to confer with her famous husband. It can be said to her credit:
Katherine made a home for her family.

Whether you're a single mom, a career woman, or married with
children, you, too, can with effort, prayer, and a cheerful demeanor,
take the wood and cement of a house and make it a home where your
family feels safe and loved.

Sarah Osborn

Teacher
1714–1796

> Jesus saw the huge crowd as he stepped from the boat,
> and he had compassion on them and healed their sick.
> MATTHEW 14:14 NLT

Sarah Osborn never intended to teach the Bible to so many people in her Newport, Rhode Island community, but one thing led to another for this Christian woman. In 1767 she wrote a friend that during one week in January more than five hundred people had gathered in her parlor at various times to sing, read the Bible, and discuss spiritual topics.

After Sarah's husband died, she had opened a school to support herself and her child. Word of her teaching skills and compassionate heart spread in Newport, and a group of free blacks asked her to teach them the Bible. When a band of slaves wanted to learn more about the scriptures, Sarah opened her home for a Sunday evening class. White men, women, and children heard about the Bible studies and wanted to be included, too. Soon, her parlor was filled almost every night of the week.

What motivated Sarah to reach out to such diverse groups? No doubt she was an able teacher, but it was more than that: Sarah's heart was moved with compassion for those in Newport.

Are you concerned for neighbors who lack spiritual direction? Ask Jesus to touch your life with His compassion, and you will, in some way, reach out to the spiritually famished who live nearby.

Susan Carver
"Mother" of George Washington Carver
19th Century

Therefore, as God's chosen people. . .clothe yourselves
with compassion, kindness, humility, gentleness and patience.
Colossians 3:12 niv

Susan and Moses Carver had one slave on their small Missouri farm. When slave raiders snatched her and her baby away, Moses sent a neighbor in search of them. The slave was never found, but he brought back the infant, sick with whooping cough.

Susan nursed George, but the child remained frail. Perhaps that is why she kept him beside her while she cooked and cared for her garden. At a young age, the boy developed a passion for plants. And she rejoiced when one day eight-year-old George told her he had prayed in the old barn and asked Jesus into his heart.

When George told Susan he wanted to go to school, she told him the school was only for white children. Then she took out a primer and began to teach him the ABCs. Later, George set out for the town of Neosho in search of more schooling, and Susan, aware of lynchings of blacks, prayed for him daily. Later, when writing about his life, George said, "Mr. and Mrs. Carver were very kind to me."

Day after day, while nurturing a sickly child, Susan "put on" kindness. This "garment" paid big dividends in the life of George Washington Carver, who became one of the world's leading agriculturists. Today, before you venture into a world lacking in Christian virtues, choose to dress in the beautiful robes reflecting God's chosen people.

Emma Whittemore
Minister to Fallen Women
1850–1931

Therefore he [Jesus] is able to save completely those who come to
God through him, because he always lives to intercede for them.
HEBREWS 7:25 NIV

Imagine the hopelessness of a young woman in a city without family,
friends, or work. Where does she turn? Many have turned to the
oldest occupation for destitute women—prostitution.

After Emma Whittemore, a wealthy New York City socialite,
became a Christian, God directed her to reach out to women of
the street with Door of Hope homes. She began her first mission
in New York City in 1890. It was said of her, "She was used to save
more fallen women than any other person." At the time of her death,
nearly one hundred homes for fallen women were operating in the
United States and other countries.

In 1907, a book was written about the success of slum missions.
One example cited said, "Little Ella, who was sold as a prostitute for
five dollars, later became a Quaker and started preaching."

Have you stopped praying for a friend or relative because you
think the case is hopeless? No people are so hopeless, so lost, that
Jesus cannot find them, save them, and change their lives. Keep
praying. Jesus is also interceding for them, and in time He promises
to bring them to God and faith.

Hannah Hobbie
Christian Worker
1806–1831

The Spirit helps us in our weakness. We do not know what
we ought to pray for, but the Spirit himself intercedes for us.
ROMANS 8:26 NIV

Little is known of Hannah Hobbie other than what Reverend Robert
Armstrong wrote in the tract, "Memoir of Hannah Hobbie."

At age seventeen, Hannah became an invalid and remained
bedridden the remainder of her short life. Immobile, yet eager to do
some good, she became creative in her Christian service. She wrote
letters to her neighbors encouraging them to trust in Christ. Hannah
gathered Christian "sisters" around her bed, and together the women
sent up a concert of prayer. She gave money to missionary and tract
causes. And what about poor children in her neighborhood who did
not receive Bible instruction? Hannah's concern led her to begin a
Sunday school, and the boys and girls met beside her bed as she
taught them about Jesus. God saw Hannah's heart for service and
opened doors for her in spite of physical limitations.

What limits your service to God and others? You may face
barriers, yet none are so insurmountable but that the Holy Spirit can
help you overcome these. Even in weakness, you can reach out in
some way to touch others with Christ's kindness and love.

Gladys Aylward
Missionary
1902–1970

> "I looked for someone strong among them who would build up the wall and stand before me in the gap. . .but I found no one."
> EZEKIEL 22:30 NIV

Gladys Aylward was called to serve the Lord in China, but when she applied to a mission board, they said she wasn't qualified. She worked as a maid, saved her wages, and went on her own by rail through Europe and Russia to China in 1932. Working with an older missionary, Gladys learned the language and opened an inn for muleteers. After feeding the men, the women told them Bible stories. Gladys's first convert was a muleteer.

When the Japanese invaded China in 1940, she led one hundred children over a mountain range to safety. Later, she worked in an orphanage in Taiwan.

After many successful years in China, Gladys said, "I wasn't God's first choice for what I've done in China. . . . There was somebody else. . .I don't know who it was—God's first choice. It must have been a man—a wonderful man. . . . Perhaps he died. Perhaps he wasn't willing. . . . And God looked down. . .and saw Gladys Aylward."

God is looking for people to do His work. While you may feel unqualified for the job God has for you, don't worry about your qualifications. Whether you're called to stay at home and pray, raise a godly family, or go to a third world country, God always equips those He calls.

Bertha Smith
Missionary
1888–1988

> Great fear gripped the entire church and everyone else who heard what had happened. The apostles were performing many miraculous signs and wonders. . .more and more people believed and were brought to the Lord.
> Acts 5:11–12, 14 NLT

What happens when God sends revival to His church? Missionary Bertha Smith was witness of the Shantung Revival that began in China in 1927 and continued for nine years. She tells of the following happenings.

A former student came to Bertha one night. "Please don't turn the light on," the student said. "I can't look into your face." She confessed cheating on exams and surrendered her diploma to the missionary.

In another instance, a Chinese cook had accepted the Christian faith. When God moved on his heart in revival fire, he came to Bertha and confessed untrue and unkind words he had said about her. The cook also went to a missionary couple and admitted he had stolen money from them when he bought food at the market.

Two Chinese cooks were notorious in their hatred for each other. As the church became immersed in revival, the two men confessed their hatred, asked forgiveness of each other, and accepted Jesus into their hearts.

Unkind words, stealing, cheating, hatred: sin in any form is a serious matter. It should not be part of the church. If you are aware of sin in your life, confess it and abandon it. God works His wonders through a cleansed people.

Esther Bacon
Medical Missionary
1916–1972

> The weapons we fight with are not the weapons of the world.
> On the contrary, they have divine power to demolish strongholds.
> 2 CORINTHIANS 10:4 NIV

The hospital was built, the medical equipment in place when missionary Esther Bacon, a registered nurse, arrived at a jungle village in Liberia in 1941. Yet the native women did not come to the facility to have their babies. As a result, they and their infants died in astoundingly great numbers.

It was the power of the *zoes*—witch doctors and sorcerers. If the women sought help from western medicine, the zoes became angry.

Esther had been at the hospital a short while when she came up with a solution: If the women wouldn't come to her, she would go to them. Walking for hours in the steamy jungles was exhausting, but Esther did it. Later, a pastor gave her his horse to ride.

Slowly the power of the zoes was broken. The women allowed Esther to assist with their deliveries, and the infant mortality dropped from three deaths in every four births to one in five.

After only ten years in the country, Esther was honored by the Liberian government with an award usually given to a foreigner after a lifetime of service. Sadly, she contracted Lassa Fever and died in 1972.

Esther Bacon put to flight the demons of ignorance with love, patience, and prayer. These divine provisions are available to every believer. When you are faced with ungodly forces, counter with these powerful weapons.

Mary McLeod Bethune

Christian Educator
1875–1955

"Be strong and courageous. Do not be afraid or terrified because of them, for the LORD your God goes with you; he will never leave you nor forsake you."
DEUTERONOMY 31:6 NIV

Most black children living in the South in the early 1900s didn't have the same educational opportunities as white children did. Mary Bethune determined to change that.

With six students she opened a school in a shabby cottage in Daytona Beach, Florida. Because she had no money for operating costs, she held concerts to raise funds and went door to door begging for donations. Within a year, the school had one hundred students. Soon she added a dormitory for boarding students.

Mary's bold stand for black people voting in public elections evoked threats from the Ku Klux Klan. One night, eighty hooded men rode to her school, carrying torches and a fiery cross. "If you burn my buildings, I'll build them again," she cried out as she faced the men. "If you burn them a second time, I'll build them again." Then Mary and the students sang, "Be not dismayed what e'er betide, God will take care of you." The white hoods quietly slipped away.

Instead of being frightened of an angry mob, you may be cowering because of financial loss, a teenager on drugs, or a heartbreaking divorce. Fear is one of Satan's best weapons. Like Mary Bethune, stand firm. And, as she did, you may want to bolster your courage by singing a hymn of victory.

Anne Wager
Teacher in Colonial America
1732–1774

Jesus was praying in a certain place. When he finished,
one of his disciples said to him, "Lord, teach us to pray."
LUKE 11:1 NIV

Dr. Bray, a colonial educator, devised a plan to begin schools in Southern colonies to teach slave children to read the Bible and pray. The success of the Williamsburg, Virginia, school was said to be due to the superb teaching skills of Anne Wager.

Mrs. Wager, a widow, was hired as schoolmistress in 1761. The school opened with twenty-four pupils. The curriculum included the catechism, speaking, cleanliness, obedience, reading, writing, and prayer.

But there were problems. One was poor attendance. Most slave owners saw no benefit in educating slave children. Another dilemma Mrs. Wager faced was how long the children should stay in school. Most remained in the classroom only six months to two and a half years. Dr. Bray also was concerned about Anne Wager's age. He was afraid the job would soon be "too laborious for her."

No record remains of how many black children Mrs. Wager taught in the thirteen years she served, but no doubt much wisdom was imparted. Not the least was the knowledge that prayer is an open door to every person regardless of race, age, or station in life.

Seeing the effects of prayer in Jesus' life, the disciples asked Him to help them pray. How long since you've made this request?

Idelette Calvin
Wife of French Protestant Reformer
1499–1549

Rejoicing in hope; patient in tribulation; continuing instant in prayer.
ROMANS 12:12 KJV

John Calvin was said to be impatient and sometimes irritable. Idelette was patient and calm. When her first husband died in a plague, Idelette, who had been converted through Calvin's preaching, married the reformer. It seemed the two would balance each other's personalities, but outside forces arose that threatened the couple's happiness.

Their first home, a noisy boarding school where John taught, was not the ideal home for the newlyweds. Calvin's enemies, who despised him, spread rumors that Idelette was a bad woman whose two children had been born out of wedlock. The truth was that she and her first husband had been married in a church, not a civil ceremony, and in the eyes of the law, it was as if they had not married. The opposition also declared that because the Calvins had no children of their own, God was punishing them.

In this chaotic atmosphere, Idelette remained serene. Visitors sought counsel from her famous husband, who maintained a hectic schedule of preaching and writing. Yet Idelette went about her business unruffled, calmly caring for the needs of her family.

Idelette experienced troublesome times in her marriage, and so will you. Settle it now that you will use biblical principles to deal with every situation: patience, prayer, and a joy-filled soul.

Christiana Tsai
Christian Teacher
20th Century

> Live clean, innocent lives as children of God, shining like
> bright lights in a world full of crooked and perverse people.
> PHILIPPIANS 2:15 NLT

Christiana Tsai, a high-born Chinese, grew up in a family that worshiped ancestors. Her early education was by Buddhist teachers, but because she wanted to learn English, she attended a mission school. Christiana said, "God used my love for English to draw me to Himself." When she converted to Christianity, her family became hostile toward her.

Through Christiana's witness, her mother, an opium smoker, became a Christian and was delivered from the addiction. Relatives took notice and soon two of Christiana's brothers and their wives trusted in Christ. Because of her witness, fifty-five of her relatives eventually trusted in Jesus as their Savior.

Christiana took a teaching position in a government school, and through her efforts, seventy-two of the two hundred students became Christians. Outraged Buddhist parents complained to the dean, who confiscated the Bibles Christiana had given to students. Eventually, however, the dean also became a Christian.

Christiana didn't claim to be an evangelist or a missionary; she only shared with others what Jesus had done for her, and as a result, many embraced the Savior. Neither do you have to be a preacher to effectively witness for Christ. Keep connected to the Light, and your life will glow like a city on a hill!

Laura Smith Haviland

Relief Worker
1808–1898

> Therefore, as we have opportunity, let us do good to all people,
> especially to those who belong to the family of believers.
> GALATIANS 6:10 NIV

While Laura Haviland lived in Michigan before the Civil War, she became aware of slaves escaping the South through the Underground Railroad and, risking her life, she helped them travel from Cincinnati to Canada.

At the onset of the war, Laura received permission to go to Mississippi to help wounded soldiers and former slaves. Her efforts were said to greatly improve the conditions in military hospitals and the treatment of wounded men.

After the Civil War, Laura's compassion was put to the test as she aided black refugees pouring into Northern cities. She described the relief efforts in Kansas: "On July 12th and 13th two boat-loads more of refugees, numbering 400 persons, landed in lower Kansas City. I heard it again repeated, 'What shall we do? Here in Topeka are 200 poor people waiting to go somewhere to get work, and only $200 dollars in our treasury!' "

Eleven years after her death, a life-size statue of Laura was erected in Adrian, Michigan. Because of her courage and help to the people of the state, Haviland, Kansas, was named in her honor.

Doing good! Often it's easier to do nothing. However, the Bible encourages Christians to rally around those who have fallen on hard times. Give serious thought to your part in relieving a suffering world. Someday it may be you and your family who need help.

Maria Woodward-Etter

Evangelist, Author
Early 20th Century

> Now it is God who makes both us and you stand firm in Christ.
> He anointed us, set his seal of ownership on us, and put his
> Spirit in our hearts as a deposit, guaranteeing what is to come.
> 2 CORINTHIANS 1:21–22 NIV

Maria Woodward was saved as a teenager, and immediately she felt called to preach the gospel. But instead of pursuing a ministry, Maria married and had a family. After the deaths of two children, Maria began to "exhort" in Indiana churches. But there were hindrances. Her husband opposed her preaching, and Maria's health was poor. She said, "I promised God if he'd restore health, prepare me, show me the work, I'd do it." Immediately her health improved, and her husband joined her in ministry.

In 1902 Maria began preaching in camp meetings and revival services. Her largest meetings were held in 1912 and 1913, when it was reported twenty thousand people attended one service. When Maria came to a town, an anointing was said to come over the area. People working in fields had visions of heaven and hell. Housewives spoke of "seeing" Jesus on the cross.

Reverend Stanley Smith, a missionary to China, said, "Mrs. Etter is a woman who has had a ministry. . .unparalleled in the history of the church."

One benefit of belonging to Christ is His anointing—the presence of the Holy Spirit in the believer's life, helping, blessing, guiding. And that's just the down payment of all we will experience throughout eternity.

Josephine Butler
Author, Social Reformer
1828–1906

> "Then neither do I condemn you," Jesus declared.
> "Go now and leave your life of sin."
> JOHN 8:11 NIV

When Josephine Butler began visiting Liverpool's workhouses—places for prostitutes and unwed mothers—she received fierce criticism from friends and family.

Deeply religious and with a fiery hatred for injustice, Josephine befriended the fallen women and offered them refuge in her home. In 1867, she founded "House of Rest," a place for girls in danger of falling into prostitution.

At that time several British cities situated near military posts were attempting to legalize prostitution. Josephine, described as a woman of prayer, fought hard against these laws, which she said were a form of slavery. In pamphlets she informed the British people that by making prostitution legal, women were "no longer women, but only bits of numbered, inspected, and ticketed human flesh, flung by government into the public market."

Most people at that time viewed prostitutes as the "sewers of society." Instead of condemning them, Josephine understood that most girls were tricked into prostitution, ignorant of what they were getting into, or forced by circumstances to choose this lifestyle. She worked to restore the dignity of the women.

Jesus did not throw one stone of condemnation at the woman caught in an immoral act (John 8:3–11). Instead He told her to leave her old life. If you are condemned by any past sin, now is the time to forgive yourself and allow Jesus to restore your dignity.

Mary Slessor
Missionary
1848–1915

Pray in the Spirit at all times and on every occasion.
Stay alert and be persistent in your prayers for all believers everywhere.
EPHESIANS 6:18 NLT

Toward the end of her life, missionary Mary Slessor was asked to write her life story. "What have I ever done that should be put in a book?" she modestly asked. But when she was told her story would inspire others, she began to think of it as her duty, and Mary never shrank from duty.

While living in Africa's dark Calabar region, Mary lived in what many called the world's most dense spiritual darkness. She suffered from chronic malarial fever and was often depressed. But as a child growing up in Scotland, Mary had learned to pray, and for thirty-eight years, prayer sustained her.

Mary wrote in a letter, "My life is one long daily, hourly record of answered prayer. For physical health. . .for everything that goes to make up life and my poor service, I can testify with a full and often wonder-stricken awe that I believe God answers prayer."

Prayer is power surging from Almighty God to weak man. It is talking to God. Prayer is making requests, giving thanks, or quietly listening to God's voice. It is your lifeline, a link from earth to heaven. It's a good idea to do as Mary Slessor did: make your life one long, daily conversation with God.

Florence Steidel
Missionary
20th Century

> But the people that do know their God shall be strong, and do exploits.
> DANIEL 11:32 KJV

One day in 1924 while Florence Steidel prayed, in her mind she saw dark-skinned people crying out to her. "Why isn't something being done to help?" she wondered.

When Florence realized God was calling her to be a missionary, she said, "Not me! I'm timid and I've only got an eighth-grade education."

She went ahead to finish high school, nurses' training, and seminary, and, at age thirty-five, Florence went to Liberia. One day after she treated a leper, the man refused to leave.

"There's no place for you here," she told Jacob Freeman. He still didn't leave; instead, he put up a crude shelter, and in a few days other lepers came. This was the beginning of New Hope Town.

As the rainy season approached, Florence knew the lepers needed better shelter. Tribal chiefs gave 350 acres of thick jungle in an isolated area. Though many lepers were crippled, they helped clear the brush. Eventually more than eighty buildings were constructed, and by 1954 two missionary nurses and helpers were treating five hundred lepers a day at New Hope.

In 1957 V. S. Tubman, Liberia's president, conferred on Florence Steidel the decoration of Knight Official of the Humane Order of African Redemption, the first woman missionary to Liberia to receive the honor.

Although Florence Steidel felt unqualified to do the work, she was willing. That's all God asks of you. He will supply the strength and wisdom for you to do exploits.

Florence Crawford
Evangelist
20th Century

Count yourselves dead to sin but alive to God in Christ Jesus.
Therefore do not let sin reign in your mortal body.
ROMANS 6:11–12 NIV

God spoke to young Florence Crawford one day and said, "Daughter, give me your heart." Stirred by the message, she prayed and wept for three days. Later, she visited a friend who explained the plan of salvation to her, and Florence gave her life to Christ.

In 1906, she attended the Azusa Street revival and wrote of her experience. "I was baptized with the Holy Ghost and fire. Rivers of joy and love flooded my soul." At the same time Florence was miraculously healed of eye and lung ailments that had resulted from spinal meningitis. She testified, "The Christ of Calvary touched my body and made me whole."

Florence, described as a dynamic preacher, held evangelistic meetings in Oregon, Washington, Minnesota, and Canada. She later settled in Portland, Oregon, and founded the Apostolic Faith church and a city mission that seated three thousand people. One aspect of her powerful preaching included the message that born-again believers can live an overcoming life.

The enemy of our souls often seeks to convince us we cannot be victorious Christians. However, Jesus' death and resurrection make it possible for you and me to live not sinless, but above sin. And if we fall, cleansing and renewal is promised because of Jesus, our Savior (1 John 1:9).

Katherine von Bora Luther
Wife of the Reformer
1499–1552

> The Lord God said, "It is not good for the man to be alone.
> I will make a helper suitable for him."
> Genesis 2:18 NIV

When Katherine von Bora, an ex-nun, married reformer Martin Luther, she entered into a unique ministry as she helped define a role that had never before existed: pastor's wife.

Using her skills with herbs, poultices, and massage, Katherine ministered to her husband's numerous ailments and bouts of depressions. Their home, a forty-room monastery, was at times completely occupied with refugees, widows, students, and Luther's nieces and nephews.

As mistress of the household, Katherine managed the food preparation and lodging. None of this seemed to overwhelm Luther's ambitious wife. He said, "My lord Kate drives a team, farms, pastures and sells cows. . .and between times reads the Bible."

However, Katherine faced criticism. Luther's friends scorned the lowly nun for marrying the great reformer. Others accused her of breaking her vows to Christ, her bridegroom. None of this troubled Katherine or Luther. He humorously said of her, "I wouldn't trade Katie for France or Venice."

Katherine's role in marriage was the same as God intended for each wife since the time of Eve: she is to provide companionship for the man and be his helper. God's plans haven't changed. As a wife, your calling is great, the results fulfilling.

Rosalind Rinker
Author, Missionary
1907–2002

> "For where two or three gather in my name,
> there am I with them."
> MATTHEW 18:20 NIV

One wintry night in North Dakota, fifteen-year-old Rosalind Rinker had a decision to make. Should she go to a party at a friend's home or attend a house prayer meeting? Because she had recently become a Christian, she chose the prayer meeting. As the group knelt, first one prayed, then silence. Rosalind felt uncomfortable. An older German woman began to pray in broken English, her words mingled with tears. Suddenly Rosalind realized the lady was not speaking to those in the room, but to God. And He was there!

At age twenty, Rosalind went as a missionary to China. Again she observed how people prayed and over time, she concluded prayer is simply a conversation between two people who love and trust each other. She wrote a book about her discoveries called *Prayer: Conversing with God*. The book sold almost a million copies. Later, Rosalind conducted prayer workshops around the world.

When you gather with other Christians to pray, realize that Almighty God is there! And when God appears on the scene, faith is planted in hearts. What ordinarily seems impossible becomes possible when two or more of you agree in His name.

Almeda Pearce
Hymn Writer, Radio Broadcaster
1893–1966

> For the Lord himself will come down from heaven. . .and the dead in
> Christ will rise first. After that, we who are still alive and are left will
> be caught up together with them in the clouds to meet the Lord.
> 1 THESSALONIANS 4:16–17 NIV

Almeda Pearce's musical talents became apparent at a young age,
and, as her skills developed, she became good at sight-reading and
improvisation on the piano. For a brief time, she studied voice in
New York City. When she returned to her Pennsylvania home, she
joined a church quartet and married the bass member of the group.

In the 1930s, Almeda and her husband began a Christian radio
program in New Jersey called "Christian Voices." While suffering
and despair were all around because of the Great Depression, and
later World War II, every day for thirty-five years the couple gave
hope to listeners as Almeda sang and her husband preached. In these
critical times, she was inspired to write the hymn "When He Shall
Come."

When He shall come, resplendent in His glory,
To take His own from out this vale of night.
O may I know the joy of His appearing—
Only at morn to walk with Him in white!

Almeda's song reminds us of a joyous event yet to happen: the
return of Jesus. If your mind tends to dwell on the confusion of daily
life, project to another day—a joyous day when Christ will appear
and you will walk with Him wearing a white robe.

Harriet Atwood Newell

Missionary
1793–1812

> "And everyone who has left houses or brothers or sisters. . .or fields for my sake will receive a hundred times as much and will inherit eternal life."
> MATTHEW 19:29 NIV

Harriet Atwood wished to do good for Christ and be of service to the heathen, but in the early days of missions, the only way a woman could fulfill that call was as a missionary's wife. She arrived in Calcutta in 1812, the bride of Samuel Newell. Ten days after her stepping foot in India, the East India Company ordered all missionaries to leave, and Harriet and Samuel went to the Isle of France, where Harriet gave birth to a daughter. The infant lived five days. The grieving mother thrived for a time, then her health declined. At age nineteen Harriet died, the first American missionary to give her life on foreign soil.

Samuel later wrote *The Life and Writings of Mrs. Harriet Newell*. The book was translated into several languages and served to spur women to offer their lives to foreign fields.

Three decades later, a historian wrote of Harriet Newell, "Perhaps no early missionary, even by a long life of faithful labors, has accomplished more for the heathen than she accomplished by consecrating herself to their cause and dying for them before the mission had found a resting place."

Harriet's dedication to Christ led to an early death, yet her life inspired others to make the same dedication. Jesus assured His disciples that hundredfold rewards await the person who makes even the least sacrifice for His kingdom.

Ina Ogdon
Hymn Writer
1872–1964

Though the fig tree does not bud and there are no grapes on the vines. . .
yet I will rejoice in the LORD, I will be joyful in God my Savior.
HABAKKUK 3:17–18 NIV

Ina Ogdon, a gifted speaker, planned to lecture for the popular Chautauqua meetings—gatherings that combined Christian speaking, music, and fellowship. But the dream shattered when her father suffered a stroke, and instead of delivering speeches to an enrapt audience, Ina ended up caring for her sick father.

Day after day she prepared meals, did laundry, and fed and cared for the helpless man. In this setting Ina came to grips with her fate and expressed her feelings in the poem, "Brighten the Corner Where You Are." She sent the verses to Charles Gabriel, who wrote music for the words and gave the song to evangelist Billy Sunday. The melody became one of the most popular gospel songs in the early part of the twentieth century and was used by Theodore Roosevelt in his political rallies of 1916. Ina didn't lecture to hundreds; rather, she has brightened the lives of millions with her uplifting words.

Do not wait until some deed of greatness you may do,
Do not wait to shed your light afar,
To the many duties ever near you now be true,
Brighten the corner where you are.

When your plans dissolve and nothing makes sense, is it possible to accept life as it unfolds? Yes! If you will take your eyes off the situation and rejoice—in the Lord.

Henrietta Mears
Christian Educator
1890–1963

Always give yourselves fully to the work of the Lord,
because you know that your labor in the Lord is not in vain.
1 CORINTHIANS 15:58 NIV

In 1928, Henrietta Mears became the Christian Education Director at First Presbyterian Church in Hollywood, California. As she worked to build a better Sunday school program, she said, "The key is in one word—work. Webster spells it w-o-r-k, and it means just what he says it does. Wishful thinking will never take the place of hard work."

With untiring effort, Henrietta and her staff built a better and bigger Christian education department. Not satisfied with the literature available at the time, Henrietta wrote her own lessons, insisting every lesson honor Christ and teach the Bible as the inspired Word of God. Eventually she started Gospel Light Press, the first Sunday school publisher to provide Bible-based, Christ-centered, child-focused, and closely graded lessons.

Did Henrietta's hard work pay off? The Sunday school attendance at her church multiplied. She founded several camps and conference centers for Christian education. In 1961, she began Gospel Literature in National Tongues to send Sunday school literature throughout the world.

In your place of employment, do you work to the best of your ability? In Christian service, do you give yourself zealously to every task? To make a difference where you serve, remember Henrietta's "key"—hard work!

Marie Monson
Missionary
Early 20th Century

> Daniel answered, "May the King live forever! My God sent his angel, and he shut the mouths of the lions. They have not hurt me."
> DANIEL 6:21–22 NIV

Norwegian-born Marie Monson had much to overcome to realize her calling as a missionary. The ship on which she traveled to China was captured by bandits, and Marie was held captive for twenty-three days. She survived on chocolate pieces, a few dry biscuits, and apples.

On another occasion bandits surrounded Marie's mission station, which at that time sheltered hundreds of women and children refugees. Weak with malaria, Marie began to doubt God's ability to protect them. "What about all those promises you're trusting in?" the enemy whispered to her.

"Lord, I've been teaching young people all these years that Your promises are true," she prayed. "If they fail now, my mouth shall forever be closed."

All around the compound horrendous things happened, yet the bandits left the mission untouched. In the morning, the people of the city asked Marie, "Who were those four people, three sitting, and one standing on top of your house all night?" "No one," she said. They didn't believe her because they had seen the "people." Evidently God had dispatched angels to the scene, and they had frightened off the bandits.

If you're in a lions' den of difficulties, you're not without help. Call on God and don't be surprised if He sends angels to aid you.

Evelyn LeTourneau
Wife and Mother
1900–1987

> Her children arise and call her blessed;
> her husband also, and he praises her.
> PROVERBS 31:28 NIV

"I don't know how to cook for that many," Evelyn LeTourneau explained to her husband when he asked her to fix hot tamale pie for eight thousand people.

"Just take a recipe for eight and multiply the ingredients by a thousand," R. G. said. "Don't worry about a pan. I'll take care of that." He built a pan twenty feet long, and Evelyn made her husband's favorite dish. R. G. then baked it in a specially constructed oven.

Evelyn's life as the wife of R. G., inventor of large earth-moving equipment, was a succession of interesting projects. When her husband admitted thirty homeless boys into LeTourneau Technical Institute, she turned their three-story house into a home for them. During World War II, Evelyn opened her home to servicemen. It was no surprise she received the American National Mother of the Year award in 1969.

Evelyn's advice to wives: "You can't make your husband over, you can't make him good, but you can make him happy." This was her goal for fifty-two years of married life.

Jesus compares the husband-wife relationship to His union with the church (Ephesians 5:25) It is a sacred relationship, one to be guarded and respected. Perhaps your marriage is not ideal, but as you implement Bible principles and pray for your spouse, it will become a little bit of heaven on earth.

Marcella
Early Christian Woman
325–410

> "If you hold to my teaching, you are really my disciples. Then you will know the truth, and the truth will set you free."
> JOHN 8:31–32 NIV

Marcella was born into a noble and wealthy Roman family. Influenced by the lives of devout Christian men and women, she became a follower of Jesus. After a few years of marriage, her husband died, and Marcella made her home a center for women desiring to study the Bible.

Wealthy women of Rome at that time dressed in silks and jewels. They painted their faces, wore elaborate hairstyles, and were carried around on litters by slaves. After accepting Christ, Marcella—along with others in the study group—chose to wear plain brown gowns. They ate simply, walked or rode horses, and gave their wealth to good causes. One woman attending the Bible group founded Rome's first hospital.

Marcella eventually purchased a home outside the city where women devoted themselves to prayer, Bible study, singing psalms, and helping the poor. She also organized a society to distribute scripture portions.

Realizing the Bible is complete truth, Marcella gave top priority to studying and sharing the Word. Do you have questions with no apparent answers? Diligent and systematic study of the scriptures will eventually resolve those issues, allowing you freedom to be all God intended you to be.

Missionary, Author
1817–1854

> Let the godly strike me! It will be a kindness!
> If they correct me, it is soothing medicine. Don't let me refuse it.
> PSALM 141:5 NLT

At age eleven Emily Chubbuck went to work in a woolen factory for $1.25 a week. She said of that time, "My recollections are of noise, filth, bleeding hands, aching feet, and a very sad heart." Emily improved her education and became a teacher when she was fifteen. She had written a few poems, and by adulthood she was writing poetry of literary quality. For her first published book she received $51, but in four years she supported herself by writing.

Then Emily met missionary Adoniram Judson. He was fifty-eight, she was twenty-nine. Adoniram asked her to write a biography of his late wife. Their friendship blossomed into romance, and the couple soon married. But their union received much criticism. Her friends said by going to a primitive mission field she was throwing away a successful writing career. His friends criticized him for marrying so soon after his wife's death.

However, Emily's earlier life had prepared her for these thorny times. Undaunted by criticism, she went to Burma, learned the language, and finished Sarah Judson's biography.

How do you handle criticism? Constructive criticism can be helpful. Pray about the advice you receive, listen to your heart—and let God have the final word.

Mary Lathbury
Hymn Writer, Artist, Poet
1841–1913

> For the word of God is alive and active. Sharper than any double-edged sword, it penetrates even to dividing soul and spirit, joints and marrow; it judges the thoughts and attitudes of the heart.
>
> HEBREWS 4:12 NIV

The Chautauqua movement that existed in America from 1903 to 1930 was similar to a summer university. With attendees gathering under a tent in a scenic place, each meeting mixed Christian inspiration with culture, education, and entertainment.

One summer Mary Lathbury, a devout Christian who was labeled the "poet laureate" of Chautauqua, was asked to write a hymn for the meetings. Searching for inspiration one day, she sat reading her Bible by a lake in New York State. As she read of Jesus feeding five thousand people, she saw Him as actual bread—food for her soul. And she wrote the poem, "Break Thou the Bread of Life," intending the hymn to be used as a prayer before studying the Bible.

> *Break Thou the bread of life, Dear Lord to me,*
> *As Thou didst break the loaves Besides the sea;*
> *Beyond the sacred page I seek Thee, Lord;*
> *My spirit pants for Thee, O Living Word!*

The Bible is not a collection of dead words. It is alive! The Word demands that decisions be made and lives changed. Today, before you open the Bible, sincerely pray Mary's hymn. It will prepare your heart to receive, understand, and be changed by the Living Word—Jesus.

Elizabeth Hooten
Preacher
1598–1672

He [John] went into all the country around the Jordan,
preaching a baptism of repentance for the forgiveness of sins.
LUKE 3:3 NIV

Elizabeth Hooten, a middle-aged woman, heard George Fox, founder of the Quakers, speak when he came to her English town in 1647. She accepted his teaching of Christ as the Light in the heart of every believer. Three years after joining the Quakers she was put in prison. The charge? Exhorting people to repent.

When Elizabeth was nearly sixty, she heard that Quakers in the New World were being persecuted and, wanting to help, she sold her farm and sailed for Boston. Immediately upon her arrival she was arrested because the law said no Quaker could be entertained within the city. When Elizabeth stood trial before Governor John Endicott, he boasted he could easily hang more Quakers. "Your life is in the hands of God," she reminded him.

Elizabeth went from place to place on the Eastern seaboard preaching repentance. For this, she was thrown into dungeons, publicly beaten, and, on one occasion, abandoned in the woods. She survived and said, "The love I bear to the souls of men makes me willing to undergo whatsoever can be afflicted on me."

Repentance—Elizabeth's message—is not always a popular topic. For telling Herod to repent of acts of adultery, John the Baptist was beheaded. On the other side of the coin, when you and I repent of our sins and ask for forgiveness, the angels break into ecstatic praise (Luke 15:10)!

Amelia Taylor Broomhall

Missionary Supporter
1835–1918

Carry each other's burdens, and in this way you will fulfill the law of Christ.
GALATIANS 6:2 NIV

Amelia and her brother, Hudson Taylor, were close to each other during their childhood. When Hudson went to China as a missionary, he expected Amelia to follow. It was not to be. Instead, with her prayers and by her support, she became a long-distance partner with him.

While in China, Hudson wrote Amelia of Hunan, a Chinese province where foreigners were not welcome. He wanted to bring the gospel to the area. From her London home, Amelia set siege on the faraway place. She prayed and searched Hudson's letters for encouraging news, but none appeared. Amelia continued to pray and eventually the word came: Missionaries had entered Hunan.

Following a furlough, Hudson and his wife needed a home for their three young children when the parents returned to China. Although Amelia had ten children of her own, she opened her home to the Taylor children. Years later, when four of her children felt called to China, she gladly sent them to foreign soil. Amelia did not become a missionary, yet she helped her missionary brother by sharing his burdens.

Not everyone is called to foreign soil, but every Christian is called to help others. Do you know a fellow believer who needs a helping hand? Reach out to them. Your assistance is active fulfillment of the law of Christ, which is to *love*.

> "But store up for yourselves treasures in heaven, where moths and vermin do not destroy, and where thieves do not break in and steal."
> MATTHEW 6:20 NIV

While Sarah Dunn struggled with a decoration in her family's New York home, she heard an almost audible voice say, "What are you doing to decorate your heavenly home?" The message got her attention, but it didn't immediately change her life. She moved to Chicago and married George Clarke. Again God spoke to Sarah about the time she was giving to frivolous pursuits. She persuaded George to visit Chicago's skid row, but he was too busy making money to get involved. Then one day God impressed on George that people were more important than money, and he fell on his knees and made himself available to do God's work.

In 1877 Sarah and George set up wooden benches in a small building called Pacific Beer Garden. Later, the name was changed to Pacific Garden Mission. Over the next forty years, Sarah listened to the sad stories of the destitute men and women. She provided meals and beds for them and kept the drunken crowds in order while George preached.

Sarah Clarke discovered it is possible to work a lifetime and accomplish nothing of eternal consequence. It is also possible to widen the circle of your love and do works with eternal rewards. Today, assess your activities in the light of eternity. Will your efforts in some way increase heaven's population?

Margaret McKay
Writer, Hymn Writer
1802–1887

Then, when our dying bodies have been transformed into bodies that will never die, this Scripture will be fulfilled: "Death is swallowed up in victory."
1 CORINTHIANS 15:54 NLT

Margaret McKay enjoyed walks through the old cemeteries that dotted the English countryside near her home. One day she wandered through a succession of green lanes and came across a "marble orchard" in Devonshire. Walking under the trees in the soft grass, she pushed aside dead leaves to read the inscriptions and epitaphs on the headstones. The words on one stone caught her attention: SLEEP-ING IN JESUS. "That's all that's necessary," Margaret said. She knew the person, a Christian, was in heaven.

Margaret, moved by the thoughts that tumbled into her mind, quickly wrote the poem, "Asleep in Jesus." The hymn, published the same year, gave comfort to many in an age when people dealt with death almost daily from plagues and other diseases. It also comforted Margaret when her soldier-husband died in 1845, the year the couple would have celebrated their twenty-fifth wedding anniversary.

Because death seems to have the last word, the thought of it can be frightening. You need not be afraid. Christ has conquered this foe and will walk beside you through this final earthly experience.

Asleep in Jesus! Blessed sleep,
From which none ever wakes to weep:
A calm and undisturbed repose,
Unbroken by the last of foes.

Murilla B. Ingalls

Teacher, Overseer, Missionary
1830–1895

> Since you are eager for gifts of the Spirit,
> try to excel in those that build up the church.
> 1 Corinthians 14:12 NIV

In 1851 Murilla Baker Ingalls and her husband went as missionaries to Burma. Within two years Mr. Ingalls died. Grief stricken, Murilla went to America for a short time, but returned to Burma and founded one of the country's largest churches.

Possessing a calm spirit, good judgment, and an abundance of zeal, Murilla trained workers, taught theology and homiletics to pastors, and supervised the work at various preaching stations.

When she opened libraries with Christian books for employees of railroads, Burmese government officials and businesspeople took notice. She also had an effective ministry to Buddhist priests.

In an effort to reach various language groups with the gospel, Murilla printed and distributed gospel portions and tracts in French, English, and Burmese. No wonder the director of the mission board prayed for more workers like Murilla Ingalls!

Zeal goes a long way to getting a job done. And enthusiasm is contagious! While you may not have as much energy to expend as Murilla did, do God's work with fervor and this virtue will be reflected in those who labor alongside you.

Mehitable Simpkins
Missions Promoter
Early 19th Century

And everyone who was willing and whose heart moved them came and brought an offering to the LORD for the work on the tent of meeting.
EXODUS 35:21 NIV

In 1802, a Boston dinner party was in full swing when the conversation turned to the need for missionaries to go to the American frontier to evangelize the settlers. "But how would they be supported?" a guest asked. Someone suggested that if every family gave one penny a week—the cost of a glass of wine—all the missionaries' needs would be supplied.

Mehitable Simpkins, the hostess of the party, liked the idea. She spread the word on the Eastern seaboard, and soon maids, factory girls, and farmers' wives contributed their pennies to the "mite" society. Mehitable was deluged with money for the Massachusetts Missionary Society, of which her husband was treasurer. That same year the society sent the first missionaries to the frontier.

Mehitable's experience was similar to that of the Old Testament leader Moses. When he prepared to construct the tabernacle, he asked the Israelites to contribute. The people brought gold jewelry, fine linen, costly gems, and other materials until Moses finally had to say, "We have enough!" (Exodus 36:6 NLT).

Needs abound in your church, on missionary fields, and among the poor. You may not have a lot to give, but give your "mite" (Luke 21:2 KJV). Together with gifts from other willing hearts, it will be more than enough for these needs.

Lady Jane Grey

English Queen, Martyr
1537–1554

> Always be prepared to give an answer to everyone who asks you to give the reason for the hope that you have. But do this with gentleness and respect.
> 1 PETER 3:15 NIV

Lady Jane Grey's life was short, but her accomplishments were many, and her Christian testimony remained strong in the face of danger and death.

Under the tutorage of Mr. Aylmer, Lady Jane became skilled in Latin, Greek, French, and Italian. She also became a Christian with strong religious convictions; her testimony for Christ was bold.

Because King Edward VI did not want the throne to go to his sister, Mary, a Catholic, he gave Lady Jane the right to succeed him as ruler of England. When Edward died, Lady Jane was proclaimed the queen. She recognized Mary as the rightful heir to the throne, but being young, she had little to say in the decision. Nine days after being crowned, Mary's claim to rule was recognized and Lady Jane was charged with high treason.

At age seventeen, Lady Jane was imprisoned and condemned to die. Before her execution, she gave a brave testimony for Christ that moved onlookers to tears. To the end she remained courageous.

Your testimony is also a powerful tool the Holy Spirit can use to convince unbelieving people of the reality of Jesus. Be prepared to give an answer to those who inquire about your faith. No one can argue with a changed life.

Eliza Hewitt
Poet, Hymn Writer
1851–1920

> "You intended to harm me, but God intended it for good to accomplish what is now being done, the saving of many lives."
> GENESIS 50:20 NIV

Is it possible for good things to come from tragic situations? This is the question Eliza Hewitt asked as a teacher in Philadelphia when a student hit her with a slate and Eliza sustained a painful back injury. While she slowly recovered, Eliza discovered she had a talent for writing and she wrote programs for the children in her church.

Not daunted by one bad experience, when she regained strength Eliza worked as the superintendent of an orphanage. The pain reoccurred, and for therapy her doctor recommended walking. As Eliza ambled in Philadelphia's parks, she became aware of God in the sunshine, light, and stars—His creation—and wrote hymns such as "Sunshine in My Soul," "Stepping in the Light," and "Will There Be Any Stars in My Crown?"

With God's help, Eliza turned a bad situation around and, as a result, her life was a blessing to thousands. You, too, may have suffered a cruel blow to your body or spirit. This is not the end of the road. Look for the good in the circumstance and ask God, "What positive things do You want me to accomplish through this negative experience?"

Ellen Gates
Poet, Hymn Writer
1835–1920

"Please let me glean and gather among the sheaves behind the harvesters."
RUTH 2:7 NIV

"I don't need a snowstorm today," Ellen Gates said when it began to snow one winter day. "If I can't go out, I'll stay in." That was obvious, but it led Ellen to other thoughts. *If I can't cross the ocean, I'll stand on the shore and help launch the ships.* As one idea led to another, Ellen began to write. The result was the poem, "Your Mission." She dedicated the words to the Lord and sent copies to newspapers.

Philip Phillips, a musician, read Ellen's verses and saw potential for their use as a hymn. In 1865 when the United States Christian Commission met, President Abraham Lincoln was in the meeting. As Mr. Phillips sang Ellen Gates's song, the president scribbled a note to Secretary Seward which read, "Let us have 'Your Mission' repeated." This is one of the verses Phillips sang:

If you cannot in the conflict prove yourself a soldier true,
If, where the fire and smoke are thickest,
   there's no work for you to do,
When the battlefield is silent, you can go with careful tread,
You can bear away the wounded, you can cover up the dead.

Ellen's hymn highlights a biblical truth. Not every person is destined to do heroic deeds. Some are meant to plod on out-of-the-way paths. Perhaps you, like Ruth in the Bible, will glean unnoticed and unsung, yet faithful in gathering precious grain ignored by other harvesters.

Sarah Hale
Author, Editor, Hymn Writer
1788–1879

One of them, when he saw he was healed, came back, praising God in a loud
voice. He threw himself at Jesus' feet and thanked him.
LUKE 17:15–16 NIV

Sarah Hale was a woman ahead of her time. When other young
widows with children survived on their family's charity, Sarah
successfully earned her living as an editor of a woman's magazine—a
daring venture in 1822! Yet, when she attempted to organize a
women's missionary society in Philadelphia in 1851, her efforts met
with ridicule and defeat. "Doesn't she know only men are competent
to lead a missions program?" people said.

However, Sarah Hale's greatest contribution to her country took
an entirely different direction—making Thanksgiving a national
holiday. Thousands of handwritten letters poured from her desk
urging governors of the states and territories, presidents from
Buchanan to Lincoln, senators and other authorities, to establish and
support a national Thanksgiving Day.

On October 9, 1864, Sarah sent one last letter to the president
asking him to declare "a fixed Union Festival." When Abraham
Lincoln signed his name to the document, Sarah's long letter-writing
campaign ended successfully.

Why is it important to say thanks to God? A grateful attitude
honors God, expresses dependence upon Him, and opens your heart
to receive from Him. Every day, under all circumstances, give thanks.
This is God's will for you (1 Thessalonians 5:18).

Mabel Francis
Missionary
20th Century

Moses, when he grew up, refused to be called the son of
Pharaoh's daughter. He chose to share the oppression of
God's people instead of enjoying the fleeting pleasures of sin.
HEBREWS 11:24–25 NLT

When mission boards called missionaries home due to the Great
Depression of the 1930s, missionary Mabel Francis had a choice to
make. Would she comply with the board's request or stay in Japan?
Mabel chose to stay.

Money was scarce for Mabel during those years. She preferred
riding the bus to preaching points, but to save money, she chose
to pedal a bike over Japan's steep terrain. When the work became
difficult, she thought, *If only I'd married, things would be a lot different.*
At those times God reminded her, *"That wasn't My plan for you."*

As Japan became more militant in the 1930s, Mabel again had a
choice to make. Would she leave Japan? She stayed. When Japanese
planes bombed Pearl Harbor in 1941, Mabel was placed under
house arrest. Later, the government transferred her to a monastery,
where she gave a strong Christian witness to other detainees.

When faced with choices, Mabel Francis didn't take the easy
way out. What about your choices? Choose to share when you want
to keep things for yourself. Choose to go when you want to stay.
Choose to worship when you'd prefer to daydream. Like Mabel
Francis, choose the best, the highest; what truly honors God.

Faye Edgerton
Missionary
1889–1968

So Gideon, and the hundred men that were with him. . .blew the trumpets,
and brake the pitchers that were in their hands.
JUDGES 7:19 KJV

In 1950, Faye Edgerton wrote in her diary, "Gideon's pitchers had to
be broken before they gave out light. Let me be a broken pitcher; let
the light of Thy Word shine forth to the Navajos, at any cost." For
forty-four years, Faye was that broken pitcher.

When the train stopped in Navajo country in 1924, Faye—ill
after serving as a missionary in Korea—began working with the
native people of New Mexico and Arizona. She preached, counseled,
and prayed at the Ganado mission and area chapels. Yet it concerned
Faye that the Navajo people did not have the Bible in their language.

In 1942, workers from the Summer Institute of Linguistics
expressed a desire to begin a translation of the Bible into Navajo,
and Faye volunteered for the task. She first had to learn the difficult
language, then work with those who spoke the language to make an
accurate translation. The work took years of patient labor. At age
sixty-seven, a joyful, but weary, Faye Edgerton held in her hand the
Navajo New Testament.

God has other great works just waiting to be done. These jobs also
require uncompromising discipline and dedication. Make yourself
available. Pray Faye Edgerton's prayer: *Lord, let me be a broken pitcher!*

Ida Reed
Poet, Hymn Writer
1866–1951

> Now to the King eternal, immortal, invisible, the only God,
> be honor and glory for ever and ever. Amen.
> 1 TIMOTHY 1:17 NIV

In the late 1800s a diphtheria epidemic raged through the hills of West Virginia. Fifteen-year-old Ida Reed survived the disease, but her father succumbed to tuberculosis, leaving Ida and her mother to operate their small farm.

There was a bright spot in Ida's life: She received the magazine, *Christian Herald*. A serial in the periodical especially appealed to her. At one point in the story, the character remarked, "Oh, it's because I belong to the King!" The phrase stuck in Ida's mind.

While helping on the farm, Ida also tried her hand at teaching. She wrote poems for her students, and her brother pointed out that the poems were well written. When Ida submitted her work, editors published it.

During an illness, words from the magazine's story came back to Ida, and she wrote the following poem:

I belong to the King,
I'm a child of His love,
And He never forsaketh His own;
He will call me some day to His palace above,
I shall dwell by His glorified throne.

Ida's hymn deals with life's most weighty questions: who she belonged to, where she was going, and what the end would be. Does your future seem uncertain? You, too, can have confidence. Belonging to the King makes all the difference in the world!

Lydia Finney
Evangelist's Wife
1804–1847

> Give therefore thy servant an understanding heart.
> 1 Kings 3:9 KJV

When evangelist Charles Finney met Lydia Andrews, he couldn't get the beautiful lady out of his mind. Thoughts of her invaded his prayer time, and he eventually asked her to marry him. She was twenty, he was thirty-two. She was sunny, Charles was serious.

They married in 1824 and after a brief honeymoon, Charles received word of a revival in Perch River, New York. Would he come and preach? Leaving Lydia behind, he went. The meeting was scheduled for a few days, but God moved and Charles stayed. The awakening spread to a neighboring town, and the evangelist preached there also. Before he knew it, cold weather settled on the New York countryside, making travel impossible.

In the spring the bridegroom made his way to his bride. At one village his horse had to be reshod, and when the townspeople heard the famous evangelist was in town, they asked him to preach. Again Lydia waited as the Holy Spirit fell.

After being separated six months, the newlyweds were reunited. Did Lydia understand her husband's long delay? In his memoirs, Charles doesn't hint that she was upset. Apparently God had given Lydia an understanding heart.

You, too, may be dealing with an unusual situation in your home or workplace. Rather than pray for the circumstance to change, it may be wiser to ask God to give you special unction for the situation—that of an understanding heart.

Sarah Doremus
Missions Organizer
1802–1877

So whether you eat or drink or whatever you do, do it all for the glory of God. . .even as I try to please everyone in every way. For I am not seeking my own good but the good of many, so that they may be saved.
1 CORINTHIANS 10:31, 33 NIV

Whoever heard of women organizing a missionary society? was the outcry by some in the 1860s when Sarah Doremus, with other women, made plans to begin a missions organization. They eventually organized the Women's Union Missionary Society of America. Their purpose was to provide outfits for single women going to the mission field and offer hospitality to returning missionaries. For sixteen years, Sarah ably served as president of the society. Coworkers said of her, "She gave herself to the brain work while to others she gave the honor."

A woman of wealth and influence, Sarah organized the Women's Prison Association to assist released women prisoners. She provided relief for Greeks suppressed by the Turks. She served as manager of a tract society. During the Civil War she helped distribute supplies to hospitals. No wonder Sarah Doremus earned the title "Mother of Missions."

Workers are needed to tell about Jesus. Others are needed to support the efforts of those who tell. Where do you fit into this picture? As you, and every Christian, become involved in going, supporting those who go, or both, people who otherwise would never know, will hear the Good News.

Elizabeth Codner
Editor, Hymn Writer
1824–1919

Will you not revive us again, that your people may rejoice in you?
PSALM 85:6 NIV

When Elizabeth Codner's husband, a minister, died she moved to London to help in a busy church, where she edited a monthly magazine entitled *Woman's Work in the Great Harvest Field*. She also wrote books for women and taught a class of girls.

In 1861 news came of a great revival in Ireland. Girls from Elizabeth's class attended the meetings and returned excited about the spiritual refreshing people were experiencing. On one hand Elizabeth was happy for the revived Christians; yet, she was sad because she wasn't enjoying the same renewal. One day as she thought of the revival, feelings flowed from her heart to her pen, and she wrote the poem, "Lord, I Hear of Showers of Blessing."

Elizabeth showed the poem to friends, and eventually the verses came to the attention of evangelist D. L. Moody. William Bradbury wrote the music, and Elizabeth's poem became a popular hymn.

> *Lord, I hear of showers of blessing,*
> *Thou art scattering full and free,*
> *Showers the thirsty land refreshing;*
> *Let some drops descend on me—*
> *Even me.*

While your times with Jesus in the Word and prayer are fulfilling, you may long to sense His presence in greater ways. Pray Elizabeth's hymn, *Let some drops descend on me—even me.* Then see what spiritual depths and heights God will bring your way.

Helen "Nell" Sunday

Evangelist's Wife
1868–1957

> And let us consider how we may spur one another
> on toward love and good deeds. . .encouraging one
> another—and all the more as you see the Day approaching.
> HEBREWS 10:24–25 NIV

Helen Thompson met Billy Sunday, a new Christian and a Chicago White Stockings baseball player, at her church. When her boyfriend failed to show up for a Wednesday night service, Billy asked to walk her home. Thus began a relationship that endured for forty-seven years.

They married in 1888, and shortly after Billy Sunday began to preach evangelistic meetings, first assisting a seasoned preacher and later on his own. But he found it difficult to be separated from "his Nell." In spite of the responsibility of four children, Nell recognized that Billy needed her by his side. She eventually hired a nanny for the children and traveled with her husband doing administrative work, planning revivals, and supervising the staff. But most of all, Nell was there to encourage her husband. She once said, "Billy is my job." Without her encouraging presence, he might not have been the successful evangelist he was.

Speaking encouraging words is one of the most effective ways to help another person. In conversations with friends and family members, share a scripture verse or other appropriate cheerful words. It will help them keep their eyes on the goal—Jesus Christ and His appearing.

Maude Cary
Missionary
1878–1967

Fixing our eyes on Jesus, the pioneer and perfecter of faith.
For the joy set before him he endured the cross.
HEBREWS 12:2 NIV

At the beginning of her missionary career, Maude Cary had hoped to be both a missionary and a wife. It seemed she would achieve these goals when she went to Morocco in 1901 and met missionary George Reed. The two became engaged. But in 1914, after a long engagement, George called off their marriage. Maude said of the disappointment, "I am more of a weed than a tree. Oh, may some fragrance flow out of Jesus from this crushed weed!"

Maude worked in evangelism, taught children, and conducted Bible conferences. Then at age 73, she encountered another personal problem when her entire body became one open, painful sore. Fellow missionaries attempted to care for her, but the stench from the putrefying wounds was hard to bear. Doctors in Morocco treated her with little success. Maude was flown to America, where she was diagnosed with pemphigus.

Though the disease is fatal in most cases, much to her doctor's amazement, Maude made remarkable progress, and in 1952 she returned to Morocco. There she worked for three more years.

In the difficult times of life, we can pity ourselves and feel we don't deserve this trial. We can become angry. Or we can accept the challenges, as Maude Cary did, and with a hand in Jesus' hand, walk through them to the finish line.

Vestal Goodman
Gospel Singer
1929–2003

> Dear children, let us not love with words
> or speech but with actions and in truth.
> 1 John 3:18 NIV

Wearing a floor-length gown and waving a white handkerchief, Vestal Goodman was known as the "Queen of Gospel Music." Vestal, her husband Howard, and his brothers Sam and Rusty—known as "The Happy Goodmans"—won numerous Grammy and Dove awards and were inducted into the Gospel Music Hall of Fame in 1998.

In spite of awards and honors, Vestal's success in gospel music was secondary to the genuine love she showed to others. When Vestal met President Jimmy Carter during a performance at the White House, she hugged him and, while Secret Service men looked on, she prayed for the president. When a missionary couple needed $3,000 for their support, God spoke to Vestal, and she secretly gave a diamond watch to the cause. When the pastor announced the anonymous gift, the spirit of generosity touched the congregation, and the remainder of the money was easily raised.

In the 1980s, country singer Larry Gatlin was told he had dangerous nodules appearing on his vocal cords. Vestal visited him and said, "Don't worry about your throat; you're coming out of here fine." Soon Larry was singing again.

Ask Jesus to flood your heart with His love. As you visit those who need a supernatural touch, pray with them, and give to make up their lack; what a difference it makes!

Margaret Simpson
Wife of a Church Leader
1842–1924

"If you have faith as small as a mustard seed, you can say to this mulberry tree, 'Be uprooted and planted in the sea,' and it will obey you."
Luke 17:6 NIV

What will we live on? How will I feed my family? These questions plagued Margaret Simpson when she, her husband, A. B., and their five children moved from a comfortable pastorate to begin a faith work.

While pastoring in Kentucky, A. B. Simpson had received a vision of a Christless world, and he felt urged to go as an overseas missionary. When he related the vision to his wife, she said, "No! I'll remain at home, support and care for the children."

Writing about Margaret Simpson, A. W. Tozer said, "The wife of a prophet has no easy road to travel. . . . Mr. Simpson had heard the Voice. . . . His wife had heard nothing."

As Reverend Simpson prayed about the vision, God showed him he could labor for the heathen from home. However, their lives were never the same, and Margaret learned how to walk by faith as her husband followed the vision and began a mission society.

Has a secure lifestyle somehow slipped between your fingers, and you don't know how your needs will be met? For a believer, this is where faith steps in. Although your faith may be wobbly, place every concern in God's care. Then do it again and again until the problem is no longer yours. The God of abundance honors even mustard-seed-size faith.

Elizabeth Fry
Prison Reformer
1780–1845

"Leave her alone," said Jesus. "Why are you bothering her?
She has done a beautiful thing to me. . . . She did what she could."
MARK 14:6, 8 NIV

When Elizabeth Fry visited Newgate prison in London in 1814, she was sickened by the conditions under which the female prisoners existed. Women, whose crimes were often minor infractions, were crowded into filthy, cold cells with their children.

What could Elizabeth, a Quaker wife and mother, do to alleviate the appalling conditions? Women in the nineteenth century wielded little power, but that didn't stop Elizabeth. She brought the inmates warm clothes and read the Bible to them. And she did more. In 1817, she organized teams of ladies to regularly visit women prisoners, read the scriptures to them, and teach them to sew.

These simple changes radically changed prison life for the prisoners. Elizabeth's work caught the attention of businesspeople, and they began to support her reform efforts.

As she expanded her visiting groups, the British government became aware of the pitiful prison conditions. This led to the Prison Act of 1823, which drastically reformed British prisons. It all started when one woman did what she could.

Do you see a need? Is there some small thing you can do to bring about a change? As you pray about the problem, you will be prompted to reach out with Christ's love. Who knows what great things God will do when you do what you can?

Rosa Parks
Mother of the Civil Rights Movement
1913–2005

> Righteousness and justice are the foundation of your throne;
> love and faithfulness go before you.
> PSALM 89:14 NIV

Early in life, Rosa Parks noticed that white children rode a bus to school while she and other black children walked. She also became aware that the school she attended was a shack with no windows and few books.

One redeeming factor was Rosa's family. Before going into the cotton fields in the morning, she and her grandmother read the Bible. At an uncle's church, Rosa learned to trust God.

One day in 1955, Rosa needed to rest after standing all day at her job. On the city bus, she paid her fee, then exited and reentered by a back door. Rosa sat in the middle of the bus and when a white man needed the seat, Rosa refused to give hers up.

She said of that time, "I felt the presence of God on the bus and heard His quiet voice as I sat there waiting for the police. . . . I was lonely, but I was at peace."

As a result of her stand for justice, Rosa's life was threatened and she lost her job. She also helped overcome the injustices of segregation laws. In 1999 she received the Congressional Gold Medal, America's highest civilian honor.

We do not live in a fair world, but there is One who judges perfectly. As you and I make the choice to follow God's path of justice, we will show love without judgment of persons.

> Though one may be overpowered, two can defend themselves.
> A cord of three strands is not quickly broken.
> ECCLESIASTES 4:12 NIV

When Margaret Whitecross became the second wife of missionary Dr. John Paton in 1864, they immediately went to Aniwa, a small island in the New Hebrides. Fear of evil spirits ruled in the hearts of the natives. They practiced cannibalism and infanticide.

On one occasion, hostile natives surrounded the Paton home, intending to burn it and kill Margaret and John. The couple prayed all night and in the morning, to their surprise, the mob had left. Why weren't the threats carried out?

A year later, a chief who had participated in the hostilities became a Christian. John asked him what had happened that night. "Who were those men you had with you?" the chief asked. "Hundreds of big men in shining clothes with swords in their hands circled the house." The Patons knew God had answered their prayers in a supernatural manner.

Described as a woman of piety and strong character, Margaret, with her husband, was a powerful force in a spiritually dark place. Together they held services on the Lord's Day, trained native Christians in evangelism, translated the New Testament and a hymnbook into the language of the people. As a result, the entire island population turned to Christ!

Your home or workplace may be bereft of the light of the gospel. Pray with another Christian. Work as a team and together you, too, will see the glory of God.

Fanny Crosby
Hymn Writer
1820–1915

> We have different gifts, according to the grace given to each of us. . .
> if it is serving, then serve. . .if it is to encourage,
> then give encouragement. . .if it is to show mercy, do it cheerfully.
> ROMANS 12:6–8 NIV

When Fanny Crosby, the blind hymn writer, reached age sixty, she began spending several days a week ministering to prostitutes, homeless, and alcoholics in the Bowery district of New York City.

"You can't save a man by telling him of his sins," she said of those she counseled and prayed with. "Tell him there is pardon and love waiting for him. . .make him understand you believe in him."

In her nineties, Fanny, described as "extremely thin and bent over nearly double," continued to address large crowds. She said of her life in that era, "I'm so busy I hardly know my name." People who knew her then said, "As Fanny grew older her cheerfulness increased."

There is no retirement for a woman of God. Tasks may change, but God gave you talents and abilities to be used. Be aware as you serve that your attitude remains important. When God opens doors, do the job with all your might—cheerfully.

Lydia Sexton

Preacher, Prison Chaplain
1799–1873

He lifted me out of the slimy pit, out of the mud and mire;
he set my feet on a rock and gave me a firm place to stand.
PSALM 40:2 NIV

Tribulation seemed to lurk at every turn of the road for Lydia Sexton. When her father died, her mother gave young Lydia to relatives. As a young woman, Lydia married and had a son. Three years later, her husband died and, unable to support the child, Lydia gave him to a wealthy family to raise. Again she married, and within a year this husband also died.

Because of a difficult life, Lydia sought a stable base. She found it in Christ. Lydia became involved in a Bible study group, and eventually the door opened for her to preach. She became the first woman licensed to preach in the Methodist Church.

With her family, Lydia moved to Spring Hill, Kansas, where she held Bible studies for inmates at the state prison. In 1869, at age 70, she became the first woman prison chaplain in the history of Kansas.

After a "graveyard" past, Lydia found stability in Christ. Your life also may have followed a crooked path, but you need not be a victim. As a Christian, use your former experiences as a bridge to reach other hurting men and women.

Shanti Solomon
Founder of the Fellowship of the Least Coin
1920–1998

Pray for each other so that you may be healed. The earnest prayer of a righteous person has great power and produces wonderful results.
JAMES 5:16 NLT

The Korean War had recently ended and another conflict loomed in Vietnam when Shanti Solomon, a teacher in India, traveled with church women to South Korea. The purpose of their visit was to hold women's Bible studies in an attempt to end hostile feelings that existed between nations. Because of visa restrictions, Shanti was denied entry to South Korea. She remained in the Philippines, and during this time she tried to think of ways to unite women. In a flash the answer came: She would begin an organization where once a month each participant would donate the least coin in her currency. The coin would serve as a token of commitment to intercessory prayer for people of the world. Shanti's organization became known as the Fellowship of the Least Coin.

Philippine women adopted the proposal eagerly. Within ten years, the Fellowship had a worldwide membership. The money flowed in, designated to be used for world evangelism and relief work. To this day, many Christian women participate in the organization.

Shanti had a noble dream, and she made it a reality. Imagine the impact if every woman followed the Least Coin practice. Perhaps today would be a good time for you to place a coin in a jar and pray for a Christian sister or brother in another part of our world.

Anne Steele
Hymn Writer
1716–1778

> "I know that my redeemer lives,
> and that in the end he will stand on the earth."
> JOB 19:25 NIV

The wedding preparations were made. Guests were arriving, but the wedding never took place. The day before the ceremony, news came that Anne Steele's fiancé had drowned.

This was one more tragedy in a life already charged with hardships. Anne Steele's mother had died when Anne was three. She injured her hip while in her teens, which left her crippled. After her fiancé's death, Anne never married, but instead helped her father, a minister. The last nine years of her life, she was confined to bed.

In spite of her difficult life, Anne Steele's hymns ring with victorious messages. Her songs were so popular that when a Boston church published a hymnal, 59 of the 152 songs in the book were composed by Anne Steele. She became England's first woman hymn writer to have her works published in numerous hymnals.

As Anne lay dying, friends said she whispered, "I know that my Redeemer liveth." These words, spoken by Job, were also the theme of the following hymn that she wrote:

> *He lives! The great Redeemer lives!*
> *What joy the blest assurance gives!*
> *And now, before His Father, God*
> *Pleads the full merits of His blood.*

Because she knew the Redeemer, Ann Steele lived and died victoriously. You, too, can tap into this joy. Rejoice! Jesus is alive forevermore!

Anna Tomaseck
Missionary
20th Century

The Lord is my shepherd, I lack nothing.
He makes me lie down in green pastures.
PSALM 23:1–2 NIV

Anna Tomaseck sailed for India in 1926. During the first ten years, she used her nursing skills in hospitals and schools, yet she felt God had a specific ministry for her.

When three malnourished children came to her home on the Nepal-India border, Anna found her life's work: she was to care for India's unwanted children.

One Sunday the cribs were full and Anna, weary of the work, was resting on the porch when two men approached her. In their arms they carried a baby whose mother had died from a snakebite. Although there was no room, Anna took the child. After lunch another baby, this one covered with lice, appeared on the porch. Anna had no crib, but she pulled out a drawer for the child. Before the day was over, yet another child was left with her.

When a severe drought came to the area, Anna lacked milk for the babies. One day, she received a telegram that said, "Four barrels have arrived addressed to you. Contents look like powdered milk." Although the church in Chambersburg, Pennsylvania, did not know the need, they felt impressed to send the milk.

For forty years, Anna depended on God to supply the needs of her orphan children. All believers can tap into this abundant supply. Today, lean on a loving Shepherd who knows your needs even before you ask.

Mary Elizabeth Switzer
Promoter of Rights for the Disabled
1900–1971

And Mephibosheth lived in Jerusalem, because he always
ate at the king's table, he was lame in both feet.
2 SAMUEL 9:13 NIV

"Make the world a better place," an uncle encouraged young Mary
Switzer. In spite of losing her mother at a young age and being deserted
by her father, Mary took the uncle's advice. After college, she became
director of the Office of Vocational Rehabilitation in Washington
DC. Her goal was to see that mentally and physically challenged
persons received opportunities for training and employment.

Mary encouraged government officials and private organizations
to help *all* disabled persons find satisfactory work. It was said of
Mary, "She made light shine around her." No one in Congress ever
refused an appropriation request from her.

Mary Switzer's compassion for the disabled is much like that of
an Old Testament king. Most monarchs killed rival family members
when they came to the throne. Not David. He asked if any of Saul's
family remained alive and learned that Jonathan had a crippled
son, Mephibosheth. David restored land that rightfully belonged to
Mephibosheth, and for the rest of his life, Jonathan's son was cared
for by the king.

Physically and mentally handicapped persons deserve compassion. Can you think of someone in your church or community with
a physical or mental challenge? Befriend and help them. This is
pleasing to God.

Lady Selina Huntingdon
Benefactress, Revivalist
1707–1791

If you really keep the royal law found in Scripture, "Love your neighbor as yourself," you are doing right. But if you show favoritism, you sin and are convicted by the law as lawbreakers.
JAMES 2:8–9 NIV

England's society in the eighteenth century was strictly divided by class. For aristocrats to associate with people of less than noble birth was unthinkable. Vibrant, zealous for Christ, Lady Huntingdon befriended people regardless of their station. She frequently invited preacher John Wesley to her home to speak. Evangelist George Whitefield, a pub keeper's son, became her chaplain. When these and other preachers spoke in her home, Lady Huntingdon opened the kitchen doors to allow her servants to hear the gospel messages.

In an attempt to discourage his wife's lowly associations, Lady Huntingdon's husband asked a church bishop to speak to her. She argued convincingly that Christ's salvation had no favorites.

Lady Huntingdon's friends also disapproved of her associations. A duchess wrote, "It is monstrous to be told that you have a heart as sinful as the common wretches. . .this is highly offensive." Yet the woman attended the religious meetings held in the Huntingdon mansion.

God does not divide people by race, class, appearance, or financial or social status. The lowliest servant is as important to Him as a corporate president. Accept people as you find them. Your only debt to those around you is to love them.

Evelyn Roberts
Evangelist's Wife
1917–2005

Praise be to the God and Father of our Lord Jesus Christ, the Father of
compassion and the God of all comfort, who comforts us in all our troubles.

2 CORINTHIANS 1:3–4 NIV

Evelyn Lutman, a teacher, met Oral Roberts at a camp meeting.
Later, she wrote in her diary that she intended to marry him. Yet,
when they married in 1938, she didn't know she was marrying a man
destined to become a world-renowned evangelist.

Oral conducted evangelistic crusades while Evelyn stayed home
with the children and helped answer the letters that came from
hurting people. But it was not an easy life. In the 1940s, a crazed
man came into a meeting and shot at Oral, barely missing his head.
Neither did Evelyn know when she married what personal sorrow she
would suffer. Her oldest daughter, Rebecca, and her husband were
killed in a plane crash, leaving three young children. Son Ronald
became involved in drugs in Vietnam and, after many struggles, took
his own life. A grandson died in infancy.

As Evelyn tried to make sense of the deaths, she wrote *Coping
with Grief*. In the booklet, Evelyn told how she found a measure
of comfort by studying the Bible, reading Christian books, and
listening to worship music.

The grief you feel following a tragedy may never completely
disappear. However, as you look to the God of all comfort, His Holy
Spirit will give you strength for each day, courage to go on, and hope
for the future.

Daisy Smith
Pastor's Wife
Late 19th–Late 20th Century

Commit your actions to the LORD, and your plans will succeed.
PROVERBS 16:3 NLT

When a woman is called to preach the gospel and she marries an outstanding Bible preacher and teacher, does she continue her pulpit ministry or become content in a supportive role? This is the dilemma that faced Daisy Billings when she married Oswald J. Smith.

After Bible college and training as a deaconess, Daisy received opportunities to speak and discovered she had a natural gift for preaching. Her speaking abilities were further developed when, on one Sunday evening a month, Daisy's pastor asked her to fill his pulpit. Then the Toronto church hired an assistant, Oswald J. Smith. The deaconess and assistant fell in love and married. A family quickly followed.

Oswald's calling as pastor flourished, as did his ministry as a worldwide Bible teacher, author, promoter of missions, and hymn writer. Daisy stayed at home and raised the family. Her husband asked her to travel with him, yet she felt her place was with their children.

Because Daisy Smith remained in her famous husband's shadow, some would say she never attained her full potential for ministry. Did she regret her choice? History doesn't tell us. We only know she was faithful to the responsibilities that came across her pathway.

You, too, may feel you have not reached your full potential in various areas of ministry. God knows your willing heart. Faithfully perform the tasks before you and leave the rest to Him.

Mary Fletcher
Pastor's Wife
1739–1815

"I am carrying on a great project and cannot go down.
Why should the work stop while I leave it and go down to you?"
NEHEMIAH 6:3 NIV

When Mary Bosanquet, at age forty-five, married John Fletcher, a fifty-year-old pastor, he said, "When you marry me, you must marry my parish." She took the words seriously and eagerly worked in the Sunday school, did church visitation, and spoke regularly at preaching points in the large parish. After less than four years of marriage, John died. A grieving Mary wondered if her work was over.

Methodist leader John Wesley advised her to move to London, but she refused. When a new pastor came to the church, but lived outside the parish, Mary continued her ministry. She led the people in prayer and a short message before the three Sunday services. She also spoke as many as five times during the week, often to crowds in the thousands.

Mary said of her work, "I was never in any situation in which I had so much opportunity of doing good." Wesley affirmed Mary's pulpit ministry when he wrote, "You have an extraordinary call."

Life brings changes. However, one thing will never change: A Christian is called to work for the Lord. The death of a spouse may alter the ministry, retirement will modify your efforts, but the work waits. If you, like Mary Fletcher, find yourself at a crossroads, look to God and listen for new orders.

Elizabeth Newton
Mother of Hymn Writer John Newton
17th–Early 18th Century

Start children off on the way they should go,
and even when they are old they will not turn from it.
PROVERBS 22:6 NIV

Elizabeth Newton taught her young son John Bible verses, the catechism, poems, and hymns. Until her death when the boy was six, her time was occupied with his care and education. At age eleven, John went to sea with his father, a sea captain, and there he learned the wild ways of a sailor's life. By adulthood, he was steeped in sin and a confirmed infidel. He eventually became a slave trader and had little regard for his crew or the human cargo chained in the hold of his ship.

During narrow escapes with death, John remembered his mother's teachings and tried to reform. On Sundays, he read the Bible. But it took a violent storm at sea, when his life was almost lost, before he repented and sought a relationship with God. John Newton eventually became a pastor and wrote many hymns, the most famous being "Amazing Grace."

Mrs. Newton had only six years to train her child in godliness, yet it was enough. The Hebrew word for "train" means to dedicate. The end result of Christian training is that the child will dedicate himself to do the will of God. As a Christian parent, do your part; God has promised to do His.

Friederike Fliedner

Cofounder of the Protestant Nursing Sisters
1800–1842

Jesus was indignant. He reached out his hand
and touched the man. "I am willing," he said. "Be clean!"
MARK 1:41 NIV

Often a work that starts small eventually benefits thousands. This was the case in 1836 when Friederike Fliedner and her pastor-husband, Theodor, moved by the need of released female prisoners, opened a refuge for them in Kaiserswerth, Germany. Then, concerned because of the lack of care for poor sick people, they opened a small hospital.

Friederike, described as ambitious and energetic, trained women to care for the sick. The first year six women, called deaconesses, worked unpaid. Two years later the Fliedners took over a city hospital. Eventually their facility included an orphanage, a rehabilitation center for women prisoners, a kindergarten, a teacher training school, a girls' high school, a home for insane women, and a home for invalids.

Friederike had no idea when she took in a handful of women prisoners that within thirty years, Kaiserswerth would sponsor more than four hundred deaconesses at one hundred outstations. Young Florence Nightingale visited the facilities and observed the spirit in which the work was done. What she saw in Friederike and her deaconesses was later reflected in Florence's kind care to sick and wounded soldiers in the Crimean War.

Compassionate love is contagious. Allow human need to move you to deeds of love and watch those around you respond in similar ways.

Bertha Smith
Missionary
1888–1988

"Return home and tell how much God has done for you." So the man went away and told all over town how much Jesus had done for him.
LUKE 8:39 NIV

Bertha Smith retired after forty-one years of missionary service. Before she left China, God impressed upon her that she should go to the United States and "tell."

Haven't I told long enough? she thought. *Why not go home to rest?* But if she was to tell, what should she say? Bertha sensed that she was to tell of the great revival that had touched all of China and spurred the work in Taiwan.

In America, Bertha wrote the book, *Go Home and Tell.* The book became a best seller for the publisher. Pastors invited her to speak in their churches, and God used Bertha to tell for another thirty years. Her message: God revives His people.

From the Great Commission to the last chapter in the Bible, God exhorts His people to let others know what Jesus has done for them. Get creative in your telling—pass out tracts, write letters, give out religious magazines, teach a Bible class, sing in a choir, or feed the homeless. There is a "telling" job for every believer. Go! Until everyone in your home, neighborhood, city, and nation has heard of the redemption in Christ.

Maria Dyer Taylor

Missionary
1837–1870

> I have fought the good fight, I have finished the race,
> and I have remained faithful.
> 2 TIMOTHY 4:7 NLT

Maria Dyer was raised in China by missionary parents. When she married Hudson Taylor in 1858, her quiet life as a teacher changed forever as her husband determined to take the gospel to inland China.

Maria actively participated in founding the China Inland Mission. Proficient in the Ningpo dialect, she helped in Bible translation work and took charge of mission matters when her husband was away.

In 1866, after a furlough in England, Maria, Hudson, their four small children, and fifteen missionary recruits embarked on a four-month voyage to China. A short time out the passengers experienced seasickness. Then the new missionaries began to have what Hudson described as "a division among our party." This was followed by two typhoons, and Maria, with others, huddled in the hold of the ship singing hymns and praying while the sea grew boisterous and the crew threatened mutiny. One of the group later wrote, "Mrs. Taylor quieter, in some ways perhaps more mature, (has) such rare judgment; calm sweetness about her."

Maria faced her most difficult challenge in 1870 when the decision was made to send their three older children to England. The children never saw their mother again as the same year she died of cholera.

In spite of horrendous circumstances, Maria remained faithful to God. You, too, will one day discover that though the journey is often rough, the rewards at the end greatly outweigh the struggles.

Grace Payton Fuller
Radio Broadcaster
1889–1966

Put on salvation as your helmet, and take the
sword of the Spirit, which is the word of God.
EPHESIANS 6:17 NLT

When young Grace Payton returned from college, she met her mother's friend, Leonora Barnhill. Grace told Mrs. Barnhill she believed in God, but that Jesus was merely a good example. The older woman, a radiant Christian, quoted scriptures to prove Jesus was the Son of God, and Grace said later, "The scripture she quoted was the sword of the Spirit. . . . I believed that moment. . .and believing God's Word, I instantly became a new creature in Christ."

In 1911, Grace married Charles Fuller, her high school sweetheart. Soon after their marriage Charles became a pastor. Grace needed the comfort of the sword of the Spirit in the years ahead when she had a stillborn child and later contracted tuberculosis. She remained an invalid for three years.

In 1939, Charles began a radio broadcast, "The Old Fashioned Revival Hour." Soon the program was heard coast-to-coast. For almost thirty years, approximately twenty million people each week heard Grace's clear voice read letters from listeners who had also trusted Christ through believing God's Word, the sword of the Spirit.

God has given His armor to protect us from our enemy. When Satan attacks, we counter with our "sword"—a promise from the Bible. Ephesians 6:13–18 names other pieces of armor that protect believers: truth, righteousness, peace, faith, salvation, and prayer. Have you also put these on?

Anna Kröker
Christian Woman
1902–1999

Cast thy burden upon the LORD, and he shall sustain thee:
he shall never suffer the righteous to be moved.
PSALM 55:22 KJV

Life was dangerous in Russia during the 1930s, as the government closed churches and killed church leaders in its attempt to create an atheistic society.

In 1939 Anna Janzen married Abraham Kröker, a widower with nine children. He made her promise she would continue to care for his children if anything happened to him. And it did. Three years into their marriage, he was arrested and never heard from again.

Anna attempted to keep her word to Abraham, but it was difficult to provide even the basics for the large family. One day, in need of food, Anna picked up six sugar beets beside the road. For this "crime," she was arrested, accused of stealing from the commune, and sentenced to six years of hard labor.

As she lay in a cell waiting to be deported, she cried out in prayer. God appeared to her in a bright light and said, "*Anna, I love your children more than you do.*"

Miraculously, Anna and the children survived the separation. Later, they resettled in Germany, and friends told how Anna's face glowed as she recounted stories of God's provision during the years of hardship.

While physical suffering is not the fate of all Christians, God has made a special provision for all who suffer in this manner: Jesus said, "My grace is sufficient for you" (2 Corinthians 12:9 NIV).

Christina Georgina Rossetti
Hymn Writer, Poet
1830–1894

"For God so loved the world that he gave his one and only Son."
JOHN 3:16 NIV

Christina Rossetti was said to be a beautiful young woman, so beautiful that her brother and other English artists used her as a model for portraits of the mother of Jesus. Perhaps it was while posing as Mary that Christina received the inspiration to write the poem, "Love Came Down at Christmas." The verses, later set to music, use the word "love" twelve times.

Love came down at Christmas, love all lovely, love divine;
Love was born at Christmas, star and angels gave the sign.

Worship we the Godhead, love incarnate, love divine;
Worship we our Jesus: but wherewith for sacred sign?

Love shall be our token, love shall be yours and love be mine,
Love to God to all men, love for plea and gift and sign.

In her teens, Christina became seriously ill and suffered from depression her entire life. Twice she was engaged to be married, but both times she backed out for what she said were "religious reasons." Much of her life was lived in semi-seclusion, yet for a time she helped in a home for prostitutes. She spent her later years writing devotional material and children's poetry.

Christina's hymn reminds us that love requires expression. God expressed His love to the world by giving His Son, Jesus. And He did it in a beautiful way: a sweet, innocent baby. This one act tells us much about our God. He truly is love!

Phoebe Palmer

Evangelist, Author
1807–1874

> Work at living a holy life, for those who
> are not holy will not see the Lord.
> HEBREWS 12:14 NLT

At a revival meeting in 1832, Phoebe Palmer and her husband dedicated themselves to the pursuit of holiness. She said, "The Lord gave me such a view of my utter pollution. . .apart from the cleansing, energizing influences of the purifying blood of Jesus."

Phoebe felt called to preach, but because women in that era were not readily accepted in pulpits, instead she began a "Tuesday Meeting for the Promotion of Holiness." This informal women's prayer meeting was a success and inspired other women to begin such gatherings.

In the 1850s, with Phoebe as the "exhorter" and her husband the evangelist, the couple began a full-scale evangelistic ministry. Great crowds came to hear the eloquent woman preacher. At a meeting in Hamilton, Ontario, four hundred people were reported saved. She also created a sensation when she preached to packed auditoriums in England.

Phoebe Palmer was a major force in the holiness movement that swept across the country in the mid-1800s. She wrote the book, *The Way to Holiness,* and served as an inspiration for other women who felt called to preach.

The idea of holiness is as relevant today as when Phoebe promoted it. It is a worthy prayer for us to pray, "Holy Spirit, work in my heart daily to make me more like Jesus, the holy Son of God."

Hester Ann Rogers
Author
1756–1794

> They triumphed over him [the accuser] by the blood
> of the Lamb and by the word of their testimony.
> REVELATION 12:11 NIV

Overjoyed after receiving Christ, Hester Ann Rogers wanted to share her happiness with others, but she felt the constraints of her circumstances and the times in which she lived. Yet, she was not daunted. Hester wrote her spiritual experiences, published them in books, and had these distributed by her husband and other circuit preachers.

Especially appealing to readers were Hester's stories of her spiritual struggles. In her three books, *Memoirs*, *Life*, and *Letters*, she told of her efforts to become more Christlike. She said, "Shall I now ask small blessings only of my God? Lord, cried I, make this the moment of my full salvation." Using drama and pathos, Hester kept readers turning the pages as they followed her journey of faith. After one circuit trip, a preacher reported selling fourteen copies of her *Life* and seven of *Letters*.

Salvation is the unseen work in your heart. The testimony of what Christ means to you, what He has done for you, and answers to your prayers, are powerful evidences of that salvation. If you have resolved issues of faith, now is the time to share these with other struggling believers as Hester did. A few words of your testimony may be just what they need to make it over the next hurdle in their faith walk.

Eliza Shirley
Founder of the United States Salvation Army
Late 19th Century

Don't let anyone look down on you because you are young, but set an example for the believers in speech, in conduct, in love, in faith and in purity.
1 TIMOTHY 4:12 NIV

When Eliza Shirley's family made plans to emigrate to the United States, the seventeen-year-old was reluctant to abandon her work as an officer in England's Salvation Army. There was no army in America at this time, but General William Booth gave Eliza his blessing to begin a work.

In Philadelphia, Eliza and her mother rented a rundown chair factory. The women whitewashed the walls, put sawdust on the floor, built a platform, and hung kerosene lamps from the ceiling. They advertised as "Two Hallelujah Females" who sang and preached about Jesus.

Twelve people came to their first meeting. On a Saturday evening, Eliza held a street meeting near a tar-barrel fire. As a crowd gathered by the blazing flames, she sang and preached. Soon the mission had standing room only.

Later, General Booth officially "opened fire" on Philadelphia. But the work was actually begun a few years earlier by young Eliza, ablaze with zeal for Christ.

Age is never a handicap in working for God. However, it is important, regardless of your age, that you reflect attributes of God—love, faith, and purity. Lost, struggling people need a model for their lives. You can be an example of Jesus' redeeming love—whether you're young, old, or somewhere in between.

Velma Barfield
Convicted Murderer
1932–1984

> We are made right with God by placing our faith in Jesus Christ.
> And this is true for everyone who believes, no matter who we are.
> ROMANS 3:22 NLT

As a child, Velma was the target of her drunken father's abuse and to escape, she married at age seventeen. After an accident, she started taking tranquilizers and painkillers to deal with depression. When her husband began drinking, Velma worked two jobs, and as a result had a nervous breakdown.

Then her husband died in a house fire. While Velma lived with her mother, the older woman became ill with severe gastric complaints and died. Two elderly people Velma cared for developed the same symptoms and also died.

In 1978 Velma confessed to poisoning four people, including her mother. Five years later Velma was executed for the crimes. However, before her death, while a guard had his radio tuned to a Christian station, she heard a radio preacher urge listeners to surrender their lives to Christ, and Velma asked forgiveness for her sins.

During the five years of appeals, she attended a prison Bible study, prayed with other prisoners, and wrote her autobiography.

While murder has serious consequences, all sin cuts us off from a holy God and leads to eternal death. The Bible has wonderful news: The remedy for our sins—any sin—is the covering of Jesus' blood. How awesome is the mercy of God!

Adelaide A. Pollard
Hymn Writer
1862–1934

> So I went down to the potter's house, and I saw him working at the wheel.
> But the pot he was shaping from the clay was marred in his hands;
> so the potter formed it into another pot, shaping it as seemed best to him.
> JEREMIAH 18:3–4 NIV

"It doesn't matter what You bring into my life, Lord. Just have Your way with me," Adelaide Pollard heard someone pray in a prayer meeting she attended. Those words impacted her, and she felt prompted to make the same dedication.

Adelaide had desperately wanted to go to Africa as a missionary, but poor health and lack of finances prevented her. Struggles ensued. She felt frustrated with her life. When Adelaide finally released her future to the Lord, she expressed her submission in the hymn, "Have Thine Own Way, Lord."

When the potter shapes a lump of clay into a pot, defects may appear. He then reshapes the pot, perhaps changing its intended use. God, our potter, shapes our lives to conform to His purposes. While believers are not mindless in the process, they are willing lumps of clay on the potter's wheel.

Are you disappointed by twists of fate in your life? In the confusion do you wonder if there is a plan for you? Recognize these struggles as God's reshaping process and sincerely pray Adelaide's hymn:

Have Thine own way, Lord! Have Thine own way!
Thou art the Potter, I am the clay.
Mould me and make me after Thy will,
While I am waiting, yielded and still.

Lady Selina Huntingdon

Benefactress, Revivalist
1707–1791

> Each of you should give what you have decided in your heart to give, not reluctantly or under compulsion, for God loves a cheerful giver.
>
> 2 CORINTHIANS 9:7 NIV

When Lady Huntingdon, a wealthy English aristocrat, became a born-again believer, her generosity to the Methodist revival became legendary. John and Charles Wesley, George Whitefield, and other preachers of the Great Awakening were not always welcome to preach in England's established churches. Instead, people often assembled in fields to hear them. Around 1760, Lady Huntingdon began building chapels in which the men could preach. These chapels—sixty in all—were used mightily as places to evangelize the English people.

She also supported ministerial students attending Oxford University. But when the students were dismissed from the university for holding religious meetings, Lady Huntingdon provided funds to establish a theological college. Here the students were trained in the Bible and methods to further the revival begun by the Wesleys.

Lady Huntingdon supported the spiritual awakening in America and contributed to a college in Alabama, later named Huntingdon College in her honor.

Generous giving is a mark of a Christian believer. Jesus' disciples carried a pouch of money to share with the poor. The early church gave to famine-stricken Christians in Jerusalem. When you give generously and cheerfully, people's needs are met, and you are following the example of your heavenly Father. He gladly gave the world His very best—Jesus.

Kazue Miki
Christian Woman
20th Century

> Do not be surprised at the fiery ordeal that has come on you to test you,
> as though something strange were happening to you. . .if you suffer as a
> Christian, do not be ashamed, but praise God that you bear that name.
> 1 Peter 4:12, 16 NIV

When Kazue Miki, a Buddhist, attended a Bible class taught by missionary Irene Webster-Smith, Kazue accepted Christ. She testified to her Buddhist family, and they also became believers. Then, through strange circumstances, she was forced to live with her mother-in-law, who bitterly hated her daughter-in-law's faith. While Kazue's husband was at work, the mother-in-law abused Kazue and locked her in a cupboard. The young girl told no one of the cruel treatment.

While being abused, Kazue kept a diary that told how she repeatedly forgave her oppressor. After Kazue's death from tuberculosis, the writings were published as *Kazue's Diary*. The book was used to lead many Japanese to Christ. Her witness was also effective to her mother-in-law, who confessed at Kazue's funeral of her ill treatment of the young woman and repented of the sin.

Don't be surprised if persecution comes your way when you live a godly life. In the age-old battle between good and evil, a Christian's saintly life stands in stark contrast to those without Christ. However, good can come from persecution. Offer your sufferings to God with joyful expectation of how He will use them to impact others!

Ruth Siemens
Founder of Global Opportunities
1925–2005

> But if I say I'll never mention the LORD or speak in his name,
> his word burns in my heart like a fire. It's like a fire in my bones!
> JEREMIAH 20:9 NLT

Ruth Siemens had a burning desire to share Christ with peoples in other cultures and promised God she would serve Him overseas. Unfortunately, three surgeries left her with only one functioning lung. Knowing no mission board would send her to a third world country, she acquired a degree in English and education, learned good Bible study skills, and, in 1954, accepted a secular teaching job in Peru.

The first day on the job, Ruth met Marta, another teacher, who asked, "You probably know what is in the Bible. Would you teach me?" After a few sessions, Marta became a Christian. Soon other teachers participated. In time, almost all of Ruth's sixth grade class accepted Christ in a Sunday school class she taught.

"Christians. . .wanted to know how to get overseas jobs like mine," Ruth said, explaining why she later founded Global Opportunities, an organization that encourages Christian professionals to obtain secular jobs in foreign countries with the purpose to evangelize. Participants are called tentmakers, modeled after the apostle Paul, who financed his missionary efforts by making tents (Acts 18:3).

When the door to Ruth's original dream was shut, God opened a window of opportunity. Does your heart throb with a godly desire, but you've also run into a closed door? God made a way for Ruth Siemens, and He will do the same for anyone whose heart yearns to share Christ's love.

Paulina Foote
Missionary
Early 20th Century

> What shall we then say to these things?
> If God be for us, who can be against us?
> ROMANS 8:31 KJV

Before Paulina Foote left Oklahoma for missionary service in China in 1922, church elders planned to ordain her to the ministry. Secretly, Paulina had questions. What would it mean to be ordained? It was common knowledge that women in her denomination could preach to women and children but not to men. Would she stop preaching if a man came into a service? And what would be her duties in China?

The questions cleared up at Paulina's ordination service. As proof that women could preach the gospel, the elder who gave the message cited the example of Mary Magdalene, whom Christ commanded to carry the message of His resurrection to the disciples (John 20:17–18). Paulina said, "My problem about the ordination was solved. Later experiences proved that this was of the Lord."

When communist opposition arose in China in 1927, many missionaries left, but Paulina stayed. Dressed in Chinese garb, she went from village to village, preaching to those who gathered to hear. As a result, people were converted and churches established.

When Japanese and Chinese armies clashed during World War II, most foreigners were placed in detention camps. Yet Paulina evaded her captors and continued to travel and preach for nineteen more years.

Just as Paulina's questions weren't too difficult for God, neither is He overwhelmed by your problems today. He is on your side! In His time, the answer to your dilemmas will be made plain.

Index